# Diary of a Diva

## of a

# Behind the Lipstick

# Barbarella Fokos

*with commentary by David Fokos*

Reader

SAN DIEGO READER BOOKS

SAN DIEGO, CA

*Diary of a Diva: Behind the Lipstick*
ISBN 978-1-939938-24-4

Barbarella Fokos
Copyright © 2014, All Rights Reserved

Published by SAN DIEGO READER BOOKS
www.SDReaderBooks.com

San Diego *Reader*
2323 Broadway
San Diego, California 92102 U.S.A.

Cover Design by Terri Beth Mitchell
Inside Design by Jessica Wentzel
Publishing Services by Sellbox.com

# Contents

# Preface

 I'll let you know right now, I'm not a singer. Sure, I like to belt it out in the car, and at home when no one is around; occasionally I even manage to carry a tune. But I'm not that kind of Diva.

Another kind of Diva I'm not is the haughty, arrogant kind. I'm too neurotic to be arrogant. So why Diva?

In 2004, the publisher of the *San Diego Reader* contacted me after he happened upon my blog, Barbarella's Pillow Talk (the pillows being my ample bosom). After publishing a selection of my blogs as a cover feature, the *Reader* decided to take me on as a columnist, and I was asked to come up with a list of potential column titles. Diary of a Diva was the only one on the list that I didn't come up with myself. Other candidates included: Urban Chic, Barbarella Bared, Barbarella's Open

Book, Barbarella Unblogged, and Barbarella Uncensored. Diary of a Diva is credited to my sister Heather, who knows of my affinity for both alliteration and histrionics.

In my bio for the *Reader*, the word Diva is explained as "the best we could come up with for a dominant woman, control-freak, and socialite who loves to tell it like it is, even though we all know she's overcompensating for her inherent nerdiness."

If you've never read my column before, here are some things to know. I have a wacky family. I have voices in my head. (That's normal, right?) I enjoy being the weird-but-fun aunt for my six niephlings, but I don't want kids of my own. I tell people that if I ever settle down, I'll get a dog. I guess that makes me somewhat counterculture. I lead an alternative lifestyle in other ways, but those are stories for a different sort of book.

I'm married to my best friend, David, who is also my live-in cook, therapist, and partner-in-everything. Seriously. When I emcee an event,

David is on lipstick-watch, letting me
know when I need to reapply. When
I host a segment for NBC, David
films. When I write a column, David
edits. When I produce a television
show, David directs. When I go
grocery shopping, David pushes the
cart. I like to think this goes both
ways (e.g., When David is out taking
photographs, I hold his lenses), but the
truth is David does much more for me
than I do for him.

He even helped me write this book.
He grumbled at first, but I know that
David was glad to finally get to share
his thoughts in his own words. After
ten years of telling our stories, from
not wanting to get married to eloping,
from buying our first home to losing
our first home, from discovering new
countries to the death of a loved one:
all the joys, all the heartbreak, were all
told from my point of view. Until now.

In this collection, with David's help,
always with David's help, I have selected
50 of the more than 500 columns that
were published in the *Reader* over the
past decade. In addition to these stories

is our commentary — little insights and stories behind the stories as told by David and me. My commentary is marked with a quill, and David's — because he is an esteemed photographic artist — is marked with a camera. A lot of wine went into the making of this book. I'm talking cases. I hope you enjoy reading it as much as I (okay, we) enjoyed writing it.

 "Hi. I'm Mr. Barbarella." I have found this to be the most direct and efficient way of introducing myself. I like that, for the quizzical-eyed person shaking my hand, it not only provides context but also speaks to my relationship with Barbarella. When we travel to another city to attend a reception for an exhibition of my artwork, she is Mrs. Fokos, but in San Diego, I am definitely Mr. Barbarella.

Barbarella likes to use a term borrowed from the food service industry to describe our relationship — she says she is "front of the house" and I am "back of the house," meaning that she is the greeter, the talker, and the entertainer, while I whip things into shape in the kitchen and make sure that the plates are clean. We're a great team and we support each other in everything we do. She helps me with my projects and I help her with hers, which is how one day, not so long ago, I came to find myself sitting with her in a corner booth at a Belgian bistro, together with her book editor, Jane, as they discussed what was to become this book.

"You know," says Jane, "whenever I meet someone and they find out that I know Barbarella, the first thing they ask me is, 'What's David like?'"

"I've been trying to convince him to write a guest column for years," says Barb. "Hey! Maybe he can write his own commentary for the book!" offers my lovely wife.

"Yeah, and maybe someone will give me a beautiful house in the south of France," I respond, dipping another frite into the white wine, cream, and garlic sauce surrounding black mussels in the cast iron pot.

Well, okay, that's not exactly what I said. In actuality, as Barbarella and Jane carried on, I said nothing at all.

It's not that Barbarella takes me for granted; she doesn't. She knew I would be willing to write commentary because it just made sense. And I knew that she knew I'd agree, which is why I just sat there, quietly enjoying my frites. This is what happens when you live and work with someone 24/7 for 12 years.

People may wonder what I'm like, but when they meet me what they really want to know is if Barbarella is really as she seems. I am here to tell you: yes, she is.

One of the most remarkable things about my beautiful partner, and one that I admire greatly, is her willingness to be honest and vulnerable in front of hundreds of thousands of onlookers. Perhaps it's because when she's at home writing she doesn't see all those people. She just writes her column, emails it off, and that's it. I think it often surprises her to hear that someone has actually read what she wrote. Still, in the back of her mind she knows there are readers out there, yet that doesn't stop her from portraying herself in a brutally honest light, even when she knows the results will be unflattering.

As might be expected of two people who are rarely apart for more than a few hours, I appear in a fair number of Barbarella's stories. It has not always been my finest hour, and Barbarella and I usually have some "discussion" about whether or not she should write about it.

"C'monnnnnn, you know it's a great story. It's funny!" she'll say.

"NOOOOO!" I'll respond.

And then she writes the story.

For the most part, I'm ok with that. I feel that if you're going to be embarrassed by something you did, then you probably shouldn't have done it in the first place. So, whether I'm tearing a toilet paper holder from the wall in a drunken stupor, or nicking a bottle of champagne from my mother-in-law's house, I have come to accept having the details of my life broadcast to the world for your amusement.

You're welcome.

"What's in a Name" depicts my giddiness with my bright new future. It was one of my first columns, and I still had a lot to learn in life. Though I had high hopes and talked big in this fledgling story, the truth is I never imagined I'd have the good fortune to still be writing my column ten years later.

# What's in a Name

*"A sign of celebrity is often that their name is worth more than their services."*
— Daniel J. Boorstin

David's friend, the Man in the Hat (who prefers to remain anonymous), invited us to join him for dinner at the Four Seasons in Carlsbad, where the Hat was attending a three-day conference with *Wall Street Journal* and Web heavies. The last time I dined at a ritzy hotel, it was at the Beverly Hills Four Seasons with Mikhail Gorbachev. I'd like to tell you we were showing each other our birthmarks, but in truth, we were attending the same green-energy convention.

An interesting character, the Man in the Hat is a celebrity worshiper whose fascination began decades ago when he used to hang out with Bob Dylan and Andy Warhol. Now he's a big-time publisher in New York City and founder of an elite group of science intelligentsia. The Hat continues his legacy of having the *in* with the powers, the names, and the faces that be. He doesn't stand directly in the spotlight; he's content with secondhand luminescence.

He's helped make people, lending him a sense of accomplishment and something he can brag about later from a cool place in the shade. Hell, he has the right. After David's opening in a Manhattan gallery this year, the Hat threw a dinner party in my man's honor. Among the assembled prestige were a mysterious billionaire, a CBS news producer, and a columnist for *New York Magazine*. Most of them were pompous, but to each other, they were heavies, and I could smell the perfume of power emanating from them. Despite my feathers and all-around fabulousness, they did not detect their favorite fragrance on my skin, and I was ignored.

So when the Hat invites you to dinner, you go, even if it's way up in Carlsbad. We arrived early (one of my neuroses: I am never late). Before we entered the huge lobby, two men pulled up in a silver car. They leapt out screaming and tossed their keys at the valet. Why is it, the more privileged a person in youth, the bigger an asshole in adulthood? These guys — dressed in white button-downs, blue blazers, and red ties over khaki chinos — had to be in their late 30s, yet they acted like escapees from prep school. They ran by us, into the hotel, up and down the polished marble hallways, whooping and chasing each other until settling in the bar.

They must have spent the day on a yacht, drinking and snorting their energy in powder form. As we sat in the lobby, one or both would run by, jacket and tie flying, then sprint back to the bar, where they appeared to be hanging out with a fucked-up young woman and an old lady with white hair. We watched other folks pass, including one woman wearing all pink — top to toe — who dragged along a sulking man she forced to take her picture in front of paintings and flower displays as big as jacaranda trees.

Finally the Hat arrived, and we retreated to the outside patio. Before we sat down I said, "Here, a present," and tossed him the *Reader* featuring my mug amidst feathers on the cover. He was dazzled. I ordered Another Day in Paradise, a girly concoction; David had the chocolate-espresso Martini in Black. The Hat sipped a gin and tonic. While David and his friend caught up, I watched the two women from the bar make their way onto the patio. The young one looked weathered and impressively trashed for 7:00 p.m. The older one looked like Rose from *The Golden Girls*. Courtney Love-in-training wore a black dress with a plunging neckline; she held a martini in her right hand, an unlit cigarette in her left. Granny led her to a seat, oblivious to the girl's cries. "I just wanna CIGARETTE! Can't you smoke out here? Huh!?" People glanced, too well-mannered to gawk. I stared.

Young one's beautiful face was ruined by slipping lips and rolling eyes. This was not just alcohol — this girl had to be on heroin. She was more fucked-up than a crack-ho on a three-day bender. The old lady grabbed an elbow and led the inebriated chit back into the bar. Before they reached the door, the girl spilled her martini, drenching her chest and right leg. She didn't flinch. Drugged numb.

Once the sideshow ended, my attention returned to the conversation. The Hat was speaking at me: "I knew you had it in you. I know talent when I see it. This guy —" he waved his hand in David's direction, "He's small potatoes, but you. You're it."

Relieved that my mate doesn't require my level of adoration, I soaked in the accolade and assumed it was warranted. Drinks concluded, we reported to the California Bistro, where we traded cocktails for wine and a new view. Throughout dinner, the Hat dropped names the way Hansel and Gretel dropped breadcrumbs. Bill Gates, Steve Jobs, Harvey Weinstein, Shimon Peres, Michael Nesmith, and Michael Nesmith's mother (who invented Wite-Out). The rest were lost on me, but David, ever the intellectual, satisfied the Hat with knowing nods and smiles. I excused myself to the restroom — I did have to pee, but I'd also heard how fancy they were, and my curiosity needed a scratch.

Satisfied with my excursion, I returned to find the Hat talking into his cell phone. David held a finger up to his mouth. After I had stepped away, the Hat started making calls on my behalf. Someone in PR, someone in publishing. He'd done it a thousand times before — or so I'd been told; he has the names to prove it.

Our host treated us to a tasty meal and then walked us to the lobby, where he ran into his friend Yossi from the Israeli press, who was also there for the conference. "Yossi! This is Barbarella." He flashed my face on the *Reader* before pointing to me in person. "She's a big local celebrity. I've just been having dinner with her." Flattered that he was proud to know me, I stood silently as he explained who I was, what I do, and what I'm going to do. Big plans for a small-time San Diego Diva.

# Love and Marriage

Barbarella and I met in 2002 through online dating, which at the time still had an illicit, back-alley feel about it. We would have gotten fewer gasps of incredulity had we said that we met in chess club or at a meth lab.

Barbarella's online ad listed the five things she couldn't live without: family, friends, something to write with, something to write on, and red lipstick.

I'd never been with a woman who regularly wore lipstick. And Barbarella had never been with a guy for more than five months.

There were five other women B.B. (Before Barb). All of these relationships lasted longer than a year. One even lasted over ten years. I knew how to relationship. When it came to actual dating, however, I was still a bit naive.

I had grown up in a world that lacked safety belts, one that was rife with small, easily ingested toys. My world view was formed before elementary schools were ever "locked-down." As a 6-year-old I would walk a couple of miles to school each day, entirely on my own and without armed escort.

So, on our first actual date (after two weeks of hot chat) I had planned what I thought would be a lovely, romantic, pampering evening — one that said in no uncertain terms, this is a guy who knows how to treat a lady. My plan was to meet at the bar that Barbarella had selected, have one or two cocktails, and then head back to my loft where I would platonically (yes, platonically) pamper her with candlelight, soft music, a luxurious bubble bath, and a glass of champagne with fresh raspberries. To me, this seemed not at all date-rapey. But then, I was from another time, and Barbarella was from another family, whose patriarch would regularly regale his daughters with crimes committed against young women from the day's police blotter while they ate dinner. Understandably, things didn't go exactly as planned (Barb declined the bath), but despite my naïveté, everything seems to have worked out pretty well.

At first, I think that Barbarella, like a cat playing with a ball of string or a stunned mouse, thought of me as a temporary amusement. By way of warning, she announced that she had never kept a boyfriend for longer than five months. I chuckled softly at this and said, "Five months? I can do five *years* standing on my head." On the morning of our 5th anniversary, I woke up, rolled over, and said, "I told you so." Barbarella knew exactly what I meant.

 My father once told me it was better to be happy and alone than miserable with somebody else.

In my early twenties, I pined
for a partner. Every time I blew
out a candle on a birthday cake,
or tossed a coin in a fountain,
I wished for the same thing: to
love and be loved. But despite my
romantic yearning, on the few
occasions I was presented with a
potential opportunity to enter into
a boyfriend/girlfriend situation,
my dad's words resounded in my
mind, and I would admit to myself
that I wasn't really into the guy,
or, more painfully, vice versa. I
watched my female friends go from
boyfriend to boyfriend, sometimes
even overlapping relationships —
waiting until they had someone
lined up before dumping the
current guy. I pitied them their
apparent terror of solitude.

I reached the age of 26 without
ever referring to anyone as my
"boyfriend." I had become content
living alone and doing my own
thing. This didn't mean I'd given up
on the idea of finding that special
someone, just that it wasn't the

focus of my existence. I casually advertised my availability on matchmaking websites, and went on plenty of dates, but nothing ever came of them.

I had been doing the online thing for a few months and was about to throw in the towel when, a week before I turned 26, I received a message from David, and my life was forever changed.

# Mr. Unreal

*"I've been on so many blind dates,*
*I should get a free dog."*
— Wendy Liebman

As the leaves fail to fall in sunny San Diego, and the pages in my planner flip to September, I am reminded of my first date with David two years ago. I met David through an Internet dating service. Six years ago, I had tried my hand in online dating, but after a hat trick of failures, I concluded it was impossible to meet a person with social skills in the cyber world.

The first was an übernerd named Isaac, a momma's

boy who whined about his allergies to smoke when I lit up a cigarette, and who feared I was an alcoholic when I ordered a piña colada with my burger. The second, Steve, was an oversexed idiot. At the end of our second date, he said, "You wanna see my Woody?" As I struggled to process this offensive remark, he proceeded to pull through his zipper a small, Woody Woodpecker plush toy. I refused his invitation for a third date.

The last was Greek. I forget his name, because I always referred to him as Zorba. Our short romance ended when, on a double date with his friends, I failed to chat with the woman, preferring to share dirty jokes with the man. At this, Zorba realized I wasn't the kitchen type and ran away faster than the time he supposedly bolted through snow for ten miles on a military mission wearing only his shorts.

Isaac and Steve drove me to caller ID — I screened them for a month until I worked up the courage to say to each, "Uh, listen… don't call me any more, okay? Great. Thanks." After that, I refused to date. I went to clubs and parties, where I met men with whom I had sexual relations, but I had never had a boyfriend. Friends with privileges, one-night-stands with strangers, flirting with acquaintances — it can keep a girl busy. After a fun, five-month-long relationship with someone came to its end, I was ready for new blood. With no prospects at the office, and parties with the same friends, I hungered for the new and different. The romantic. The love. I'd never had the love, and I was almost 26 years old.

While surfing the net, I came across personal ads on *theonion.com*, a satirical news site. Reading through the clever entries inspired me to write one of my own. I entitled it, "Ruler of the Roost Seeking New Cocks." In it, I had written things like, "A smile is sexy; a smile and a growl is sexier," and "EVERYTHING can be laughed at. Even you." I had become so engrossed in the project of creating my ad, that I was surprised when my first response came through.

There were many messages in my box (it *was* a great ad), and I met a handful of men. One seemed promising — on the fourth date, I thought, *maybe this could work!* It was time to test him. I must know that a man can hold his own at a party, allowing me to mingle at will. But when I mixed this guy with my social crowd, things went awry. He didn't get their jokes, and they didn't get his. There were blank stares all around, as though they were members of the U.N., and there had been some colossal mix-up with the translators.

Despite this man's glaring failure to mesh with my friends, my desire for a match led me to go on more dates with him. After five weeks, I hadn't a clue as to whether or not he liked me. You know, in *that* way. I continued to correspond with other prospective suitors while trying to figure out the intentions of my number-one prospect. On my 26th birthday, as I was deciding not to invite Mr. Ambiguous to my gathering at Nunu's,

I received my first message from David.

The message was longer than others, thoughtful, and well-written. We exchanged titillating emails for eight days, at which point I gave him the URL to my blog (which, at the time, I'd been writing for two years), and set a date at my favorite bar. I expected that he might browse some entries and get a feel for the type of woman I was. We specified that he would wear leather and I would wear feathers, though the pictures we'd traded would aid our recognition. I've known most of the bartenders at Nunu's for years, so on the off-chance that David turned out to be a freak (and not the good kind), I would have backup.

On the day of the date, a Wednesday, David sent me a three-page email. In it, he summarized me, and his new perception of me, after reading my online diaries. His insight delved between my lines, and he had me pegged. I was nervous to meet him, more nervous than any previous man I'd met online — this one seemed to have his shit together, not just financially, but emotionally — this was uncharted territory.

I wore a mauve bustier under a black, sheer cardigan with a feather-lined neck, and made sure the one button on the outer shirt was expertly positioned to grant a peek of my abundant décolletage. Spritzed about me was Hypnotic Poison, a musky, spicy vanilla scent by Dior. After walking in the door of the dark little dive bar, I was surprised, considering my habitual earliness, to find David already there. His eyes were as blue as they appeared on my screen, his dimples as deep and adorable.

In David's email, he had described his understanding of my appreciation for nature, from the green leaves of summer to the rotting mulch beneath the snow of winter. Having lived in Alaska and New England, I grasped the concept and thought he was right on target. Here at the bar, he handed me a small wooden box, tied shut with a sky-blue bow and topped with a golden wax "B."

Ecstatic to receive a gift, I untied the bow and discovered inside a maple leaf, its two sides divided by complementary colors, one half a candy apple red, the other a rich, true green. He'd collected it on his recent trip to Martha's Vineyard. I recalled the words he'd written in his online ad: "I travel all over the place, and I'll take you with me; and when you can't come along, I'll bring colored autumn leaves back from New England for you."

After a few drinks (during which David kept freaking me out by knowing all of my stories — he had read ALL 500-something entries of my blog in one marathon sitting), he turned to me and said, "I like you. I think you're sexy, intelligent, beguiling, and I want to know you better. I'd like to take you back to my place, run you a bubble bath, give you a glass of champagne, and a tour of my toys." After five weeks with a man whom I couldn't read to save my life, my brows furrowed as I attempted to brace myself against this foreign directness.

I swallowed the rest of my drink, thought about his words, and said, "The bath's not going to happen. However, I could handle one drink, and I'd love to see your place. A drink and a tour, then I must get home." I followed him to his loft in Kensington; it was impressive, from the hardwood floors to the warm lighting. I took in the pleasant ambiance, stealing a glimpse out his wall-sized windows, as he hovered over the counter in the kitchen. When he handed me the glass of champagne, I gasped at what I saw — fresh raspberries dancing among bubbles!

I restrained myself from jumping him right there. No one had ever done such a thing! Who thought that the simple addition of fresh fruit to my drink, followed by brazen honesty, was all it would take to command my complete attention? The toys were impressive indeed, and after the drink and tour, David played DJ to his guest with music emanating from speakers he had designed himself (apparently, before becoming a world-famous photographer, he just happened to be a high-end audio design engineer).

With a soft kiss, I said goodnight and went home. For weeks in my diary, I referred to David as Mr. Unreal. Now I know that he's the realest thing I've ever had. Two months after our first date, he said, "I love you." It took me a full day to digest those words, to believe he could mean it, until 24 hours later I interrupted myself in a conversation to say, "I love you too." I've been rejoicing ever since.

# Love: It's What's for Dinner

*"There is always some madness in love.*
*But there is also always some reason in madness."*
— Friedrich Nietzsche

"Are you sure you don't need any help in there?" David asked when he heard me grunting.

"Nope! I got it!" I called back. He was not allowed in the kitchen tonight. I'd cooked for him only once before, and he often pokes fun at me for my belief that microwaving hot dogs is on par with baking a soufflé. As a special gift for the man I love, in honor of St. Valentine, I would dirty my hands to make a meal that would delight his taste buds and replace his memory of microwaved wieners. I'd only come up with the idea to cook for him a week before. Desperate to find the right dish in so short a time, I turned to my friend Renee, who offered a recipe she thought I could handle.

Now, alone and surrounded by foreign tools and ingredients, I worried that I might have bitten off more than I could cook as I chanted under my breath, *It's the thought that counts, it's the thought that counts.* Cooking for David is like dancing for Fred Astaire, and however it translates to the kitchen, I have two left feet. *This is crazy,* I thought, trying not to gag as I removed raw chicken from its packaging. *I must really love this guy.* Rather than imagining germs burrowing into my skin, I thought of how I'd spent this day in the past.

I lost my virginity on Valentine's Day. I was 19 and worked in a call center, supervising the night shift. He answered calls in a cubicle, ignorant of my right to a white wedding. Later that night, he tenderly brushed my hair. I hardly knew him — some tall, punk kid who lived with a bunch of guys in a house near San Diego State. The calendar date was not lost on me, and I imagined we were in love, that we cared for each other. The evening was magical, even if it was half fantasy.

One year I celebrated February 14 by purchasing new tires for my car. While the boys at Sears attached and aligned, I walked over to the mall and selected a sexy red-and-black bra, candles, and chocolates. That night, I danced around my apartment in my new lingerie by candlelight, pausing only to sip red wine or discover what was inside another nugget from the heart-shaped box. *People are really missing out,* I thought. *There's something to be said for geeking out in style.*

David and I had only been seeing each other for four months when we celebrated our first Valentine's Day together. He took me to a fancy restaurant, and I was nervous. Wearing a bright red bustier and uncomfortable shoes, I discovered French food for the first time. (I've yet to acquire a taste for it.)

I knew I'd enjoy this meal I was making, because the main ingredients were chicken and pasta. But despite my short shopping list, I'd spent an hour in the grocery store. Usually when I shop (once every few months), I know exactly what I'm getting — beverages, granola bars, frozen dinners, toiletries. This was different. I had to select vegetables, cheese, and meat — *fresh foods*. There are so many brands of cheese, so many kinds of meat! I found myself frozen in front of the zucchini. How can you tell which one is the *right* one? Are they supposed to be soft or firm? Do all those nicks in the skin matter?

I called my sister Heather, who learned to cook from her husband. I pushed my cart with one hand as I clutched my cell phone — my lifeline to the right products — with my other hand. I'm sure my awkward weaving annoyed everyone in the store (except perhaps for the guy who waltzed up and down the aisles and sang about love).

After I had everything I needed (David had confirmed our possession of butter, oil, salt, etc.), I lingered by the flowers. The roses were beautiful. In all the years I worked in an office, David was the only man who ever brought flowers for my desk. With our work and travel during the past several months, a long time had passed since fresh flowers gussied up our home.

I seized a bundle of variegated reds, tried not to choke on the price, and proceeded to the checkout lines. As I unloaded my cart, I recognized an alien sensation — I *wanted* people to see what I was buying. Purchases can reveal much about a person. Mine usually advertise that I can't (or am too lazy to) cook and that my tastes are limited to four varieties of Lean Cuisine. Summation: impatient, domestically challenged woman at whom we should furrow brows and shake heads in sympathy.

I hesitated as long as possible until an acceptable number of people queued behind me. I slowly placed fresh vegetables, chicken, cheese, herbs and such onto the conveyer belt. Summation: healthy, culinary genius of a woman, we wish she'd invite us over to sample that tasty meal, and look at those roses! He or she (this *is* Hillcrest) is a lucky person.

I was ecstatic to see my friends Mike and Damon hanging around when I pulled up outside my home. Two reasons existed for my ecstasy: Mike and Damon would help me carry my selections upstairs, and while so doing, they would also see what a wonderful woman I am. (Look at those roses! Are these *fresh* vegetables? Isn't she *wonderful?*)

"Turn around, don't look!" I called as my posse and I walked in the door. David put his hands up in the air and faced the wall in the front room, where he had been working on his photographs. I thanked the boys and reported to the kitchen. And stood there. For a while.

I managed to wash some dishes with an old sponge (again, struggling to ignore the bacteria infesting and probably entering my body). I read the recipe, searched for utensils, and began to cook. I pounded the chicken between wax paper, breaded it, put tomato-basil feta on each fillet, and folded over these fillets. When the chicken went in the oven, I set to work on a recipe Heather had given me for a side dish of orecchiette pasta, garlic, Parmesan, and sautéed zucchini.

I've heard the hardest part of preparing a meal is to orchestrate simultaneous completion, so that everything is served at the same time. Despite my inexperience, as if by divine intervention, the pasta and zucchini-Parmesan sauce were mixed together within two minutes of when the chicken was due from the oven. Voilà! Perfect, though unplanned, timing. David's trained nose followed the saliva-inducing smells, and he chose a white wine to go with dinner. I showed David his roses, and he fetched the tulips he'd gotten for my desk. We exchanged cards, each of them funny and flirtatious. Then he tasted my food, and the moment he looked at me and said, "Wow, this is delicious," I felt myself wanting to cook for him every night.

I left him alone for a moment while I prepared dessert — heart-shaped strawberries, blueberries, blackberries, and Häagen-Däzs ice cream on individual angel-food cakes. For this, David produced from the cupboard a raspberry wine we acquired on a trip to Vermont.

My father often tells people something he learned from his Church of What's Happening Now: "You are where you are right now because of a series of choices you have made in your life." This quote ran through my mind as I savored the sweets and the company of my Valentine and thought to myself, *You've chosen wisely.*

 A lot has changed since I wrote "Love: It's What's For Dinner." For example, I now like French food, and I shop for fresh groceries weekly. Then again, a lot hasn't changed — uncooked food and the idea of kitchen germs still skeeves me out. That meal of baked chicken and zucchini remains the only meal I have ever cooked for David. But it began our Valentine's Day tradition

— the Hallmark holiday is the one day I year I "cook" for my man. What actually happens, of course, is I help select the recipes, and David spends a full day preparing a more elaborate meal than usual while I supportively dance around the kitchen and sip rosé champagne, our official celebratory beverage.

# The Bald Truth

*"Oh, I know a lot of men are made uncomfortable by this monthly miracle. But not me. No, I embrace it. Embrace it the way some men embrace the weekend! Why, I anticipate it the way a child anticipates Christmas...for I have a good attitude towards MENSTRUATION!"*
— Dave Foley

"I'm breaking out," David complained, examining his scalp in the mirror. "Are you feeling emotional?" I didn't believe him the first time he told me, but after years of experience, I am now convinced that David's smooth, shaved head is a divining rod for menstruating women.

I learned of my partner's "early-warning system" the day after our second date, when I called to tell him I had had a great time.

"Me too!" he said. Then the conversation turned awkward. "This may sound weird," he added, "but are you by any chance about to get your period?"

*Uh, yeah, weird is a good word for it,* I thought. We'd only kissed once — where did this guy get off? My urge to keep my private parts just that was overwhelmed by my curiosity regarding how I'd let on that I was premenstrual.

"Yes, I am about to get my period," I snapped. "Why are you asking me that?"

"Well, you see, if I'm around a woman who is menstruating, the top of my head breaks out. I think it has something to do with female hormones," said David.

"Ha! You're trying to tell me that your head informed you of my impending monthly?"

"Yes." I strained to detect a hint of humor in his voice, waited a few seconds for him to tell me how he really knew, but nothing.

I have no idea how it is that David's body reacts in such a strong and obvious way to chemical changes in my body (or any woman's), but I have come to rely on his head's accuracy. It's to the point where I stopped keeping track of my period altogether. A few blemishes on his melon means I have about a week before my hormones begin to boil. And God help the poor pimply one when that happens.

I'd like to take a moment to congratulate any men who are still reading (even if morbid fascination is your motivating factor). David is the only man I've ever known who is sympathetic rather than dismissive when it comes to "the curse."

I grew up in a household of women. When his last daughter came of age, my father had to deal with not one but five unstable women every month. We were all hormonal at the same time, which is at least two weeks out of every four. For reasons not yet discovered by science (an industry dominated by men), cohabiting women end up with synchronized periods — those with submissive hormones naturally adjust their bodies to the "alpha" female, or she who could cause the biggest breakout on David's head.

By the time I "flowered" at 15, my father knew the difference between the words "ultra" and "long" and the significance of the word "unscented." He was regularly asked to stop by the commissary to pick up feminine products that were as individual and different as his wife and daughters. I couldn't tell you what kind of tampons I have under the bathroom sink today without checking, which is why I respect Dad's disciplined memory, dedicated to keeping his family from snapping his head off.

Every conceivable symptom that contributes to PMS was covered in our household. Heather's cramps were so bad she'd often have to stay home from school. Mom's lethargy was contagious. Jane became extra bitchy. Jenny, who was always a little psycho to begin with, was frighteningly unpredictable. And I was an emotional wreck.

I can't speak for my sisters, but I have noticed that with time, I have come to better understand my body's needs and wants. I now respond to my familiar symptoms with the speed and precision of an emergency medical technician. Even though I don't keep a calendar, I am always prepared, thanks to David's prophetic head. Unlike many women, whose bodies are regulated by some kind of birth control medication, mine is as consistent as a politician's version of the truth.

"How many do you have?" I asked David, my eyes meeting his in the mirror's reflection.

"Seven."

"Seven?"

"Yeah. It's going to be a bad one." Despite his history of female friends, a sister, and six prior relationships, David had never before encountered a woman with PMS as extreme as mine. He should be sainted for how he handles me during my tender time of the month.

As my body prepares to lose blood, my mood

alternates 60 times per hour between angry, ecstatic, miserable, amused, angry, and really, really angry. Have I mentioned I don't handle pain very well? At the first sign of a cramp, I'm practically sobbing in the cup of tea David has most likely brought to me, along with a hopeful dose of Pamprin.

My complaints about the tiny bump on my chin earn me two rolling eyes from David as he points emphatically to his seven signs of my fecundity. I crave meat and demand a quick trip to Adams Avenue Grill, home of my favorite burger in town.

The entire way there, I bitch about the drivers on the road and fret over how I look, even though an hour before I'd said I didn't feel like taking a shower or fixing my hair and moped about how I didn't want to bother with the task of grooming anymore. David, ever wise in times of trouble, refrains from bringing this up.

When we arrive home, I want to cry. But I have no good reason to cry, so I sift through the few tearjerkers we own until my eyes find my favorite movie of all time — *The Color Purple*. David runs downstairs to make popcorn and fetch me a glass of 20-year-old Fonseca Tawny Port.

Here is my theory on emotional cycles: The chemicals that make up my person, those glands that make me human, yearn to be exercised — crying is one such exercise, as the excessive joy and misery one perceives is a buildup of energy that must be purged. I have never cried without feeling cleansed and refreshed afterwards. The stronger the pull on my tears, the better it feels once I've shed them.

David returns with popcorn, port, and a welcome surprise — chocolate! Salt, sugar, Pamprin, and alcohol ensure balance. The title sequence theme music causes waves of emotion to course through me. I turn to David, who is sitting quietly in his black leather chair.

"Thank you," I say, but what I mean is, "Thank you for loving me, thank you for being so amazing and patient and, God, I don't deserve you, how do you put up with me, I'm so lucky to have you, so happy, so fucking grateful."

I look at David, urging him to read my mind, for I know if I utter one more word, I will become a blubbering mess.

"No worries," he says, taking note of the glistening sheen in my eyes. Then, with a long-overdue sigh, he lifts his hand to his scalp to gauge the damage and adds, "I figure we'll only have to go through this another 255 times... not that I'm counting."

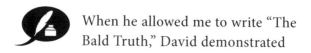 When he allowed me to write "The Bald Truth," David demonstrated

what I fondly refer to as his
"inhuman level of self-assuredness."
Around two years after this story
was first published, we were at a
wedding reception when a friend
of one of the grooms approached
to introduce herself as a fan of my
column. When I said, "And this is
David," the woman beamed and
blurted, "You're the one who gets zits
when Barbarella's on her period!"
I still laugh about that. David rolls
his eyes at the memory, but then he
follows the expression with a smile
and a shrug.

 It's absolutely true. For whatever
reason, I break out when I'm around
premenstrual women. I like to think that
this is somehow indicative of me being
more highly evolved. Otherwise I'm
just a guy who lost his hair but still gets
pimples, which seems hugely unfair.

From the moment we met, David was upfront about his never wanting to get married. "I like the idea that you can leave at any time," he'd say, as if buying a house with another person was any less complicated to get out of than a marriage certificate. But I agreed with him, or at least that's what I kept telling everyone. I even sat down to write a column about how stupid and pointless the idea of marriage really was. On deadline day, I had that column polished and ready to deliver. But on my final read-through, I broke down in tears. When David asked me what was wrong, I told him, "It's all a lie. This isn't how I feel." To this, he said, "Then write what you feel."

It took me just three hours to pour my heart out and turn in the replacement, which I called "Tiny Velvet Box." In this version, I admitted the truth — to David, to our friends and family, but most importantly, to myself.

# Tiny Velvet Box

*"Know thyself."*
— Socrates

As a girl, all I ever wanted in life was for my dream man to ride up on a horse or BMW, get on one knee, and profess his love for me while opening a tiny velvet box to reveal a ring so bright and shiny that every woman within a five-mile radius would sense the sparkling stones and swoon. I grew up believing, as many women do, that if a man did not propose by the time I reached a certain age, there was something wrong with me.

When David first told me he had no interest in marriage, I was crushed. Embarrassed. Rejected. "He's got one foot out the door," people whispered. "He'll come around," some said. But after the initial shock of learning that the man I fell in love with didn't want me in the way I'd always imagined he would, I came to understand that not wanting to get married does not equal not willing to commit. Now I find myself explaining the difference to close family members and distant acquaintances. The trouble is, I myself am only half convinced.

"What are the cons of marriage?" Heather asked, after I'd explained to her that I didn't want to get married and that one of the major reasons people marry is for social acceptance.

"Well, if you're not religious, one of the cons is that marriage is a religious institution," I replied. My sister Heather was married in a Catholic church. I call her almost every day to discuss books we read and share, and any other topics that bob above the water in our waves of conversation.

"What about civil ceremonies?" she asked. I had asked David the same question two weeks before.

"If civil ceremonies have no religious significance, then why can't gay people get married?" My response was an echo of David's answer to me.

"Barb, I still don't get it. There are atheists who get married civilly," Heather said.

I didn't have a response for that; I honestly hadn't thought much beyond the gay quip. So I tried another tactic. "David's got a philosophy about not getting married. It means a lot to him that I can walk out the door any time I'd like without any negative repercussions or penalties, and that I am with him for no other reason than that I want to be with him. He likes the idea of our love being string-free or something."

"But aren't you guys going to have a commitment ceremony? And didn't you tell me that you were having paperwork drawn up by a lawyer to give you the same rights as a married couple? If you're doing all that, why not just get married?"

"Yeah," I said. "But it's different."

"How? I mean, isn't it all just semantics at that point?"

I was stumped and felt the urge to defend myself, so I explained to Heather that I didn't like the word "wife" and that I bristled at traditional family values. My need for her approval blinded me to the fact that she was a married mother of two and that I was basically expecting her to denounce her own choices to praise mine. I told her that David and I didn't need to have a third party confirm our commitment. She pointed out how contradictory this sounded, considering our plans for a public commitment ceremony.

Finally, my mother beeped through on Heather's other line and we said we'd pick up the conversation later. I sat and thought about what I'd said. I remembered dozens of conversations in the last year in which I'd professed my disdain for marriage and stood behind David's opinions as if they were my own. Then it dawned on me — they weren't. I didn't believe a word of what I'd said. Not one word.

David bounded up the stairs when he heard my tortured sobs. He kneeled by my chair, put his arms around me, and asked what happened in a soft, soothing voice.

"I've been lying to myself," I said. He didn't have to ask about what.

"I know that you've listened to me when I've given

you my reasons for not wanting to get married, and that you've tried to understand them and make them your own. Perhaps, intellectually, you've been able to come to terms with that, but the truth is if I were to ask you to marry me right now, I think you'd be thrilled."

This terribly accurate insight voiced by the same person from whom I thought I had hidden it so well pierced my chest like a cold dagger, stealing my breath for a moment before I let it out again, hard and fast, through ragged gasps and renewed tears. David quickly fetched toilet paper to sop up the wetness leaking from my face.

"I... don't... believe what... I've... been saying," I said, my words punctuated by intakes of air. "I... don't... understand. I don't know that I ever will."

"You know I love you," David said.

"Yeah," I said, my voice taking on an edge of cynicism. "You love me. But how do I explain that to other people? Especially... when... you don't... even... want to... marry me?"

"I want to be with you," he said. "You already know how I feel. I don't care what other people think. I don't tell them how I think they should live their lives or how they should express their commitment to their partners and I don't like it when they try to tell me how I should do the same."

We'd been through this all before. The only difference was that in the past, I would nod and agree. But this time, I needed to be convinced more than anyone that the man

I loved did not, as they say, "have one foot out the door." Why did I feel this way? Am I that affected by what other people think? Am I that insecure about our relationship? I asked myself if marriage was a deal-breaker and felt a sure *no*. I want to be with David — tiny velvet box or no tiny velvet box.

As he wiped away more tears with the tissue, I guided myself through a mental checklist, the same way I did the first time he told me we would never be getting married. We just bought a home together, I reminded myself. We're with each other 24/7. We will have all of the same rights, through legal paperwork, that any other married couple has. He is *with* me. What more do I need? What more could I ask for than the love I'm receiving day in and day out? I shushed the inner voice that began chanting *tiny velvet box*, and looked my partner in the eyes for the first time since he'd rushed to my side.

"It doesn't matter to me," I said.

"I don't believe you," David said, his eyes wet, his mouth smiling. "But that's okay. I love you. I want to be with you."

"I know, beh beh. I know."

# Comfort Food

*"An easygoing husband is the one*
*indispensable comfort of life."*
— Marie Louise De La Ramee

"You know what sounds really good right now?"
David looked up from the magazine in his hands.
"Frozen ravioli with Hunt's tomato sauce," I said. I'm
not sure what I was expecting, but it wasn't for my beh
beh's face to sink the way it does when I say things such
as, "It's time to go to the gym." He looked... deflated.
"What? What's wrong?"

"I thought we'd made progress," said David. "I could
make you something that tastes a lot better than Hunt's
tomato sauce."

"Of course you could. I just had a craving, that's all.
What's up? You seem upset that I'm craving something."

"It's not that you're craving something," David said,
his eyes investigating my face. "It's that you're craving
comfort food, and if you're craving comfort food, it
means you're distressed."

"I don't feel distressed," I said, realizing it was
a lie once the words were out of my mouth. I'd been
feeling the pressure of unaccomplished tasks, the
creeping sensation of anxiety. That, compounded by
some extraordinary PMS symptoms, made me a wreck.

"I was just saying, it sounded good. Anyway, forget about it. Any good cartoons this week?" David held an interrogative gaze on me. Seemingly satisfied by my nonchalance, he opened the New Yorker and showed me a few select cartoons. Once we were in the throes of trying to interpret the meaning of one of the more ambiguous drawings, we'd both forgotten my hankering for Hunt's.

Two days later, David intercepted me as I was moping around the kitchen. With a firm but gentle hand on my elbow, he guided me to a chair by the window and brought me a glass of red wine. I was well into my second glass and under my love's watchful eye when the phone rang. I was staring out the window when David put the phone to his hip and said, "It's Josue. He's marinated some steaks and wants to share them with us."

"Tell him to come on up," I said listlessly. "But I don't want any. You guys go ahead and enjoy them, though. I'm sure I can find something else to eat." David had the phone back on his ear and was asking Josue to come on up when I stage-whispered, "Steak sounds gross."

A few minutes later our friend was at the door, proffering an unnecessary but courteous knock before entering. I gulped the last of the wine in my glass as Josue set a plastic container on the counter. "You're not going to have any steak?" he asked.

"It's okay, we have plenty of food here," David answered for me.

"We don't have frozen ravioli and Hunt's tomato sauce," I grumbled under my breath, apparently loud enough for both men to hear. David looked up from the shelves of the refrigerator; I felt bad as I realized he'd been searching for something to make for me. He closed the door and sighed. I held up my empty glass, and David indulged me before pouring a glass for Josue.

"Barb, we can wait to cook the steak if you want to go to the store right now," Josue suggested.

Swaying a bit, I looked to David beseechingly; again, he obliged. "Barb can't drive."

I held up my glass and smiled crookedly to prove the point and said, "It's okay, guys, there's plenty of stuff in the house." There was little conviction in my words, and I'm sure David sensed that I was secretly hoping for him to do exactly what he was about to do.

"You two stay here," David said. "I'll be right back." Just before David slipped through the front door, I made an additional plea for dark chocolate. Hearing me, he sighed again and disappeared. Josue shrugged his shoulders and sat in the chair across from me. We chatted and sipped our wine for 15 minutes, at which point David returned with a handful of grocery bags.

Josue and I stood and hovered around the granite island, doing what we could to help. David set a large pot of water on the stove to boil and then searched the cupboards for a good steak skillet. Josue took the lid off the plastic container, revealing the steaks as he detailed the composition of his marinade for David. I went straight to the bags and retrieved a small can of Hunt's tomato sauce, a packet of ravioli (not frozen, but that was cool), and a bundle of Trader Joe's dark chocolate. My spirits lifted upon seeing the comforting trinity.

I grabbed the plate David had set aside for me and exchanged it for a green bowl, an action I assumed was innocuous until David snapped, "What, you can't even use my plate?"

"What are you talking about? I just prefer to eat it out of a bowl," I said.

Enlisting Josue as mediator, David said, "She had that bowl before she met me. I guess she doesn't want to use one of mine."

"Whoa," I said, not to David, but to Josue. "This is just a good, sturdy bowl. It's not that I don't want to use *his* plate, I don't want to use *a* plate." Josue looked uncomfortable, so I tried to lighten the mood by saying, "David, I told you not to argue in front of the child." Josue laughed at this, but the scowl on David's face remained.

David turned back to the sizzling steak and the ravioli floating in water, the latter of which he poured into a strainer for me. "Whoa, what's that? There's all kinds of shit in here," I said, gesturing at chunks of orange and green clinging to the side of the colander.

"Those are tomatoes and basil," David said. "I thought you'd like the kind with stuff in it."

"Oh, well, yes, thank you, beh beh," I said. I scooped the ravioli into the green bowl with a spoon and lifted the can of Hunt's. "What the... this isn't the plain tomato sauce; it's flavored."

David looked contrite. "I'm sorry, I didn't notice. All the cans looked the same."

"No worries. It was nice of you to go out and get all this for me. It's perfect," I said. But in my head I was shrieking, *All wrong, this is all wrong!* I could never say anything, not after the trouble he went to, so I smiled, grabbed my bowl, and followed David to the couches. We sat down with our meals, the men with their steak and me with my bastardized version of nostalgia. David and Josue talked about how wrong it was to pour the sauce onto the ravioli straight from the can. "That's how we always ate it," I said.

A few hours later, after Josue had gone home and the plates (and bowl) had been loaded into the dishwasher, I confronted David about his weirdness over my craving. I asked him why it mattered to him whether or not I felt like eating sauce from a can.

"It bothers me to see you upset. I want your life to be all bluebirds and rainbows," he said.

"But it seems like you're more bothered by the kind of food I was craving than the reasons I was craving it," I argued.

"Well, it's just..." David looked frustrated for a moment, then put an arm around me and rested his chin on the top of my head. "When you get upset and the only thing that can comfort you is food from your childhood, it's like you fell and skinned your knee and then ran to your mom or dad instead of me."

"Oh," I said, because that's all I could think of to say. I squeezed him tighter and then took a step back so I could get a clear look at his face. I chuckled, unable to believe my luck in having someone who cares for me as much as David does. Before he could misinterpret my laughing, I said, "Don't you know that you're my rock? I mean, how the hell could I survive as such a spaz if I didn't have you to lean on? Come here." I pulled him close and embraced him with all my might, recognizing with both terror and relief that this anchor in my arms was the one thing keeping me on the pretty side of sanity.

 If you ask David whether or not he has any regrets in life, he will answer, "Only one — that I didn't save that list." He's referring of course to the to-do list I'd scrawled the morning of the day we eloped. That was back when I was in the habit of writing lists of tasks and chores every morning. At the end of each day, I'd crumple the paper and chuck it in the trash. It didn't occur to me to not toss the one on which I'd written, "Pick up dry cleaning, Get married, Go to Ralph's." (Ralph's is a local supermarket chain.)

It was a Wednesday in May. The specific date doesn't matter, because David and I celebrate our anniversary on September 25, the night we first met in person. We didn't tell anyone that we were going down to the county clerk's office to take care of what we viewed as more of a practical matter than anything else. Most of our friends learned of our nuptials much later, from reading my column.

This was three years after I wrote "Tiny Velvet Box." By then, I was accustomed to the idea of not getting married, and had even adopted David's perspective that marriage was not a necessary factor for a healthy

relationship. Our decision to head
down to the courthouse, shell over
a bit of cash, and sign some papers
was as logical and unromantic as Mr.
Spock. I'm a sentimental woman, so
I find it amusing that our wedding
ceremony was about as idyllic as a trip
to the DMV. But it was not without
its ironic charm, and I delighted in
horrifying our young officiant by
shaking my head and saying, "Nah, he
doesn't like this lip gloss," right after
she announced, "You may now kiss."
As if we'd never done that before. Later,
David and I had fun musing over
which one of us she thought was trying
to get citizenship.

I struggled with our families'
reaction to the news. It was as though
we'd never been a couple until the
moment we were married. David's
parents warmed to me in a way I hadn't
thought them capable before, and all
because of a piece of paper. It occurred
to me that, had we simply told them we
were married before, the outpouring of
acceptance and approval would have
happened much sooner. It's not like

anyone ever asked to see the certificate.
It bothered me that so many people
we love required the existence of that
form — a document, purchased from
the government, placed in a drawer,
which has, still to this day, not been seen
by any of them. But we are products of
our society, myself included, which is
probably why being married to David is
something I'd wanted all along.

# Lawfully Wedded

*"Marriage is a ghastly public confession*
*of a strictly private intention."*
— Ian Hay

"Hey, beh beh!" I called out, as I often do when I'm
comfy in my office and don't want to walk the 40
or so feet to where David sits in his. "Yeah?" he shouted
back, an indication that he, too, was serene in his seat.

"How does next Wednesday, around 10:30 a.m.,
work for you to get married?"

Asking was a polite formality — David doesn't keep
a calendar. Still, he paused as if it wasn't known by both
of us that he relies on me to administrate his schedule

before answering, "Next Wednesday sounds fine."

"Perfect!" I rose from my chair, walked over to his office, and said, "Get it? *WEDnesday?*" We shared a laugh at my pun, and then returned to our respective work.

I used to think that if David didn't want to marry me, it meant he didn't want to *be* with me. He would often explain, "I like the fact that you can easily walk out of this relationship. Every morning I wake up and find you next to me, I know you're here because you *want* to be here." Over the past few years, buying a home with me and rendering himself inseparable in many other ways, David has demonstrated that he is as committed to me as any husband to a wife and, in many cases, probably more so. I came to agree with him that getting married, in our case, would be pointless — we're not religious (only when our gay friends can be married will we consider marriage a nonreligious institution), we keep our finances separate, we don't want children, and neither one of us is into tradition for tradition's sake.

We did, however, want the rights accorded to one's *numero uno* — the "in case of emergency" stuff, like the right to make medical decisions should one of us become incapacitated. Domestic partnership would have been perfect — we could simply register without having to go through any hoopla. But in California, a couple has to be either over the age of 65 or homosexual in order to qualify. We consulted lawyers to see what it would take to compose the language that would grant us the rights we sought and found it would cost a few thousand dollars and several months of paper shuffling to reach our goal.

"How much does it cost to get married?" David asked as we lay in bed one evening.

"I dunno… a hundred bucks, maybe." We discussed the practicalities — one piece of paper obtainable in one day for $100 would do the same as several pieces of paper that cost thousands of dollars and took months to compile. We didn't want to get married, but, to use one of my dad's favorite phrases, we weren't about to cut off our nose to spite our face. David had always felt more strongly about his anti-institutional convictions than I had. So when he suggested marriage as an option, I said, "Are you sure this is something you're open to? You really want to get *married?*"

David looked at me like I'd asked the question in Farsi. "I married you a long time ago," he said. I'd heard him say this before, but this was the first time I fully understood what he meant: marriage doesn't make commitment, commitment makes marriage.

So it was, on a cloudy, cold Wednesday morning in May, that David and I gathered our identification papers and set out to complete our tasks for the day. "Get married" was scrawled between "pick up dry cleaning" and "Ralph's" on our to-do list. I wore black jeans and a long-sleeved v-neck. David wore jeans and a dark button-down shirt. David hadn't shaved.

My frizzy hair was twisted into a clip.

After collecting our cleaned, bamboo-green, silk duvet cover, we headed for Pacific Coast Highway. The middle of the week is a great time to visit the County Administration Building — nobody's there. We waited less than five minutes after signing in before our names were called. A few minutes later, we sat in a partitioned cubicle across from Michelle, who entered our information into the computer system. "Don't worry, babe," I said, taking out my checkbook when we were presented with the bill. "This one's on me."

The ceremony was forced upon us, something we *had* to do in order to get our certificate. Michelle donned a black robe to officiate. We had the option of two locales — the "beautiful county grounds," or the small room with a podium, lined with white plastic flowers. We chose the room because it was closer, quicker. We were made to repeat words that had been written by churchmen and refined by lawmakers to a representative of the court in front of our assigned witness, the girl from the adjoining cubicle. As I looked into David's eyes and uttered vows in short choppy fragments, I grew irritated that we had to suffer through this charade of declaring our love in an awkward, unnatural way, before strangers in some tacky little room. This attempt to regulate something as intricate and individual as a relationship between two people was bureaucracy at its best.

Feeling peckish, and wanting to relax and philosophize about what we'd just done, David and I headed to the Prado in Balboa Park for an early lunch. We were discussing the merits of keeping our marriage a secret from friends and family over a bowl of tortilla soup when our waiter, a tall blonde named Matt, stopped by our table. He asked if we were enjoying our soup, and we said yes. Then, in the naturally effervescent manner of servers working in restaurants frequented by tourists, he inquired, "Are you celebrating anything special today?"

David and I looked at each other, wondering telepathically what it was about our demeanor that might have suggested we weren't just grabbing lunch on a Wednesday. Matt sensed our hesitation and was about to back away when I squealed, "We just got *married!*"

"Oh, yeah? You mean the legal part, like getting the license?" he asked.

"No," I said. "The whole thing — license, ceremony, certificate, all of it in under an hour, about 20 minutes ago." Matt looked stunned. Before he had a chance to say anything, I added, "*And you're the only person who knows!* "

Matt looked from me to David and back again. I could see him processing the information, trying to decide if I was being serious. "You didn't have any witnesses?"

"Only the girls at the county office," I answered.

"Wow," Matt said, shaking his head as if to de-fog it.

"Well, congratulations!"

"Looks like you're the only guest at our wedding reception," I said. Smiling and offering more well wishes, Matt excused himself to check on other diners. When we were finished eating, he brought us a dessert we had not ordered, a flan, into which he'd placed two candles he'd melted together at the bottom.

"Are you bummed we didn't buy one of those 'Gregory J. Smith, County Assessor' memorial pens for five bucks?" I asked, slicing a bite of flan with my fork.

David laughed. "I think the bumper sticker was five and the pen was ten."

"So," I said, in a more sober tone. I waited for David to look at me before asking, "Do we tell anyone?"

David sipped his wine, considered my question, and finally replied, "We've been telling them for years."

 I am, of course, Barbarella's mother's favorite son-in-law, though it didn't start out that way.

See that? The way I joked about being Maria's favorite? That kind of joking is something I picked up from being around Barb's family for 12 years. My mother's sister Judith makes jokes like that — jokes that she stealthily launches with desiccating deadpan delivery — but neither of my parents do. Even as I was writing it I could hear Barb's mom's thick, Brooklyn accent in my head — *of co-ahss.* And though I joke about being Maria's favorite son-in-law, I wasn't kidding about her not liking me in the beginning.

We had been dating for a few months when Barb, who was working as a paralegal at the time, asked me how she should introduce me when we attended her work's holiday party. "Boyfriend," I said. As someone who'd already had five long-term relationships, this seemed obvious to me. But to Barb, who had never had a boyfriend, it was life-altering.

When Barb first told her family about me — that I was 16 years older than her, that I lived in a nice loft apartment with *uplighting* on my *plants* (which meant that I was probably gay), and that I'd had a vasectomy and said I never wanted to have kids — her mother said, "Dump him!" For Maria, it wasn't the fact that I was 60 percent older than Barb at the time, or even my flair for interior decorating; it was the not wanting to have children that was the deal-breaker.

But Barb was happy, and ambivalent about the kid thing. She was at a stage where, in the back of her mind, she expected to one day have kids because that's just what people do, even though she didn't have even a kindling desire to procreate. It was only years later, after watching her sister Heather give birth, that Barb firmly decided baby-making was not for her.

The primordial months of our relationship were not always easy. Barb and I had tearful discussions on a wide range of topics, from marriage to the afterlife. Whenever she was upset, or we'd have a disagreement, I made her talk about what she was feeling. This didn't come naturally to Barb, who only confided in her journal. Time after time, I'd doggedly wear her down and pry her feelings out of her until she realized that communication was a good thing.

After a while it became apparent that we were in it for the long haul. We proclaimed our undying love for one another and acknowledged that we were partners for life, which begged the question, "So, when are you getting married?" In Barb's family, like so many others, the math is simple: Love = Commitment, and Commitment = Marriage, therefore, Love = Marriage. QED. But my thinking was more nonlinear. I already considered us to be "married" in the commitment sense. Since we weren't religious and didn't want to have kids, I couldn't see a logical need for us to get the government's stamp of approval on our relationship. As you can imagine, this did not go over well with Barb's skeptical family.

My belief is that most people are generally good and decent. When I first meet people, my instinct is to give them the benefit of the doubt. Unless there's some huge red flag that suggests otherwise, I'll usually trust them until they betray that trust. Barb's family thinks I'm naïve and delusional, because "everyone is clearly out to fuck you over." Reality probably exists somewhere in between. So, when Barb tried to explain to her family that we were in a committed relationship, but that I didn't want to get married, their first comments were, "Why doesn't he want to marry you?" and "He's got one foot out the door." And Maria once again said, "Dump him!"

I feel that a relationship and commitment is between two partners, not between two partners and their God, or two partners and their government. There are logical, technical reasons for wanting to be married — shared children, property, inheritance, pull-the-plug rights, and so on — and that is what ultimately led Barb and me to get married, but needing to be married to somehow validate our relationship is not one of them.

Many people believe that tying the knot is what you do if you're serious about being partners for life. I totally respect that, but that's not what a marriage is to me. For those who say that getting married strengthens a relationship, I only need point to the 50-percent divorce rate as evidence that that is not necessarily true. And if you need marriage, or rather the fear of divorce, to keep you together during the rough patches, well then you probably shouldn't be married. That was the thing I really liked about not being married — every morning that I woke up with Barbarella lying next to me I knew she was there because she'd rather be there than anyplace else.

In the end, we did get married. Barb wanted to change her name, and we wanted medical rights. Getting married was the easiest way to accomplish that. Getting married was an interesting experience. I mean, how many times do you get married? (Put your hand down, Zsa Zsa.) Just as our to-do list commanded us, we first took care of our dry cleaning and then headed down to the County Administration Center to hook up nuptially, as it were. We hadn't thought to dress up, we were just there to sign some paperwork. We also hadn't thought to bring a witness along, so the clerk grabbed some office assistant who looked to be about 16 years old. Now that the wedding party had been assembled, we stepped into the County's sectarian wedding chapel, which felt like a cross between one of those get-hitched-quick places in Vegas and the post office. At the behest of the clerk, we promised to love, honor, and cherish, in sickness and in health, for better or for worse —things we'd promised each other every day for years. And that was that. All that remained was for us to decide if we wanted to purchase a San Diego County "Just Married" bumper sticker (no, thank you), a San Diego County commemorative pen (also tempting, but no), and where to have lunch. Getting married really works up an appetite.

Being married doesn't seem any different to me, but it made a surprisingly large difference to others, which strikes me as odd. We had been telling the people in our lives all along that we were a couple, but it seems they were reluctant to believe us. Why wouldn't they trust us?

Of course, I love being married to Barbarella, and I don't mean that in the *of co-ahss* sort of way. But I would have loved her just the same had we not gotten married.

# *Crazy* Kin

 Bat-shit crazy is usually how I describe my clan, but I wouldn't have it any other way. My parents were born and raised in Brooklyn, New York. Dad joined the Navy, so my sisters and I were born all over the country: Jane in New York, Heather in Texas, Jenny and me in California. We'd live in one place for a few years and then pick up and move, from San Diego, to the desolate islet of Adak, Alaska, 1500 miles out in the Aleutian Island chain, to Newport, Rhode Island, and back to San Diego. The majority of our upbringing (at least mine and Jenny's, as the youngest) was in San Diego.

I hadn't considered my family particularly quirky until I started sharing stories with friends and realized that their families weren't afflicted with the same level of dysfunction. I read somewhere that "the family of a writer is utterly doomed." In this regard, I think mine gets off pretty easy. I've never been out to hurt feelings, only to express mine. For the most part, I keep their business private. But if something happens that is at least as much my experience as theirs, then it's fair game.

I rarely mention the fact that my parents are separated. I can't remember why the divorce didn't happen, now that we're going on 20 years since my dad moved out of the house, but they may as well be divorced. They lead separate lives, at least in every regard save for family. Mom and Dad are both present at every holiday gathering, birthday celebration, and special event. But they don't speak to each other unless there's a family matter that needs resolving or they happen to be hanging out in the same backyard, watching their grandchildren play.

As she repeatedly reminds me, I don't write much about my mother. I think Mom has reluctantly come to accept that the reason I avoid writing about mother-daughter relationships is because ours was more rocky than Sylvester Stallone. Mom is strong in many ways, but I don't think she'd appreciate being under my literary microscope. Few people would. My sister Jane and my dad are the exceptions, and for this reason they, and their antics, feature prominently in many of my stories.

I also don't write as much about my sisters Jenny and Heather. At one point, years ago, Jenny told me to never write about her. But she's come around. I understand that as socially conservative citizens with high-profile jobs, they value privacy, and that to air some of our past disagreements — no matter how much those disputes may have affected me — would be relationship-ending. That's not a price I'm willing to pay for any story, though on a few occasions, I came close.

My family has put up with a lot, and I thank them for their support and patience, but even more than that, I thank them for the fodder. They helped me discover just how entertaining "a little fucked up" can be.

My mother always liked the finer things in life. Or at least, she liked the idea of liking the finer things. She was a teenager when she became a wife and mother, and the next 20 years were all about raising her four daughters. She never had the time or money to go to the spa or spend an afternoon at high tea.

I was super peeved when a copy editor at the *Reader* changed my column titled "Deep Cleansing" to "Deep Cleaning." This story is not just about getting a deep *cleansing* facial treatment with my mother, but also about a mother and daughter *cleansing* their souls of a turbid past. Deep *cleaning* made it sound like a goddamn dentist appointment. Yeah, I'm still pissed about it, but that's mostly because this story was so important to me. I wanted it to be perfect.

# Deep Cleansing

*"Yes, Mother. I can see you are flawed. You have not hidden it. That is your greatest gift to me."*
— Alice Walker

"You know how I can tell this is an elegant place?" I waited for her to enlighten me.

"It's because everything is round. You see this silver dish that holds the sugar packets? Round. In Denny's, it's square." Setting down the silver container, my mother looked around the restaurant, pausing to stare over my shoulder at the fountain in the courtyard behind me. She smiled and then, looking worried, said, "You really shouldn't have taken me here. We could have gone someplace cheaper."

"Haven't you been to a nice restaurant before?" I asked. She told me of the time she had dined at the Hotel del Coronado for a district fund-raiser. Mom had only gone because, as the assistant to the superintendent of the school district, she was given a free meal ticket.

Coincidentally, our chef today would be the same chef from the Del — Jesse Frost, brother to my sister Jane's husband Simon. When the new Estancia La Jolla Hotel and Spa opened four months ago, Jesse was taken on as executive chef; he left the Coronado landmark to create his own Spanish-influenced menu.

I'd tasted some of it already; two weeks before, I had organized a dinner party for 18 in the library — a private dining room — for David's birthday. Complete with a chef's tasting menu, endless wine (my credit card is still writhing in agony), good friends, and three servers, the night was a success, and I vowed to return. So for Christmas, my mother received a card informing her that she was to be my guest for a day of pampering at the spa, preceded by lunch at the hotel's restaurant.

My choice of gift was not entirely selfless — fabulous facial aside, I wanted to spend time with my mom, and I knew she would never go to the spa alone.

In the last few years, Mom and I have seen each other only at family gatherings, where she tends to be preoccupied with my sisters' kids. The two of us have had what one might call a rocky relationship. Of her four daughters, I was the one most likely to be harped on, for whatever reason. I never thought she could be proud of me, so I did everything in my power to manifest this perception — tattoos, piercings, drugs, and more. As a depressed teen, I wrote poetry about how much her words hurt me, and for a short time, I hated her. But after our fights, her words spoken and mine written, we came to a sort of understanding: we would get along better if we saw each other less.

After years of self-analysis, which included the dissection of my family's behavior, I came to understand her better. Mom is a giving person, used to putting everyone else before herself, and she has never let her daughters down. Being hard on me, wishing more for me by demanding I "make something of myself" was her way of ensuring I would not fall into a downward spiral of self-loathing — something she has been trying to overcome all her life. Only in the last few years has she come close to loving herself as much as we love her.

Still, I never felt as if we were friends. That was until today, when we planted the first seeds of a healthy mother/daughter relationship. I forgot how funny Mom could be. Sitting in the restaurant, she met my eyes in a serious way and said, "My pinky hurts."

"Why?" I inquired, thinking maybe she'd bumped it on something.

"Because I have to hold it up when I sip my coffee in a place like this," she said with a laugh.

After thoroughly offending the chef (I imagine) by demanding extra ketchup on our well-done Angus beef burgers, we headed over to the spa. The woman on the phone had suggested we arrive 30 minutes early, but when we did, Mom and I ended up waiting half an hour. Sure, we could have enjoyed the "eucalyptus sauna," but we aren't strip-down-to-sit-in-a-room-and-sweat type of women, and we'd sooner have our armpits tweezed than hang out in the buff with strangers. I halfheartedly tried to convince Mom to skinny-dip with me in the mostly private outdoor Jacuzzi, but she wouldn't have it.

With every nook and cranny of the locker room, showers, toilet stalls, and sauna examined, we decided to check out the Relaxation Room. "Let's wait in there," I said. "It's all part of the *experience.*" We sat in the quiet chamber, chairs at opposite walls, with two other women relaxing properly — one sprawled out on a chaise with a magazine, the other working a crossword puzzle. The silence was as oppressive as the steam that fogged my glasses during our fully clothed step into the sauna. Mom began to tap her hand rhythmically against her leg as I shifted uncomfortably in my chair. Finally, I motioned to her by wiggling my fingers and, with a nod of my head, pointed my thumb emphatically at the door.

Back in the locker room, we laughed, and I said, "We obviously don't know how to relax."

"I'm really nervous," Mom said.

"You don't have to be," I reassured.

"If I have a lot of blackheads will they charge us more?"

"No, Mom." I searched her face to see if she thought this might be a real possibility. She did.

So, I did what any loving, responsible, doting daughter would do — I decided to mess with her. "You have nothing to worry about," I said, and then continued, "It's all part of the process. You might experience a little pain, but you'll feel all the better for it later. When you bleed, they'll have ways to clean it up, and I promise you won't regret it when you see the results."

With that last sentence, Mom dropped her head in her hands and spoke in a muffled voice, "I can't do this. I can't!" I told her I was kidding about the whole "bleeding" thing but that some discomfort is possible with a deep-cleansing facial. She told me I was a horrible person but said it with a smile that let me know she was kidding. She began to giggle nervously. Then it was time.

We were led into separate rooms to experience an extensive facial. Mom looked frightened, and her last words to me were, "If I call your name out, can we leave right away?"

"You can wait for me in the Relaxation Room," I said. "I want to get my full treatment."

Almost two hours later, after overwhelming mixtures of natural herbs such as rose hips, apricot, and cucumber; after hot wax, hot towels, cool masks, and soft hands (and a sparkling conversation with my aesthetician Andrea), I stood up, nearly falling from lightheadedness, put my shirt back on, and made my way to the Relaxation Room. My mother had arrived before me. I found her with her head back, eyes closed, and a dreamy smile on her face. Spread out as she was (wearing the robe she had objected to earlier), she looked as though she had been dropped from a tall building onto the soft chair.

"What did you think?" I asked her.

"Oh, my God, it was *amazing.* It was *wonderful,* I could really get used to this," she said. She sounded as dreamy as she looked. Breathing deeply, she added, "The smells! Just when I thought I couldn't smell something new, another fruit or flower, one after another, they just kept coming and coming!" I knew what we needed, and it wasn't a cigarette — only chocolate could deliver the fix we craved.

I took Mom to Extraordinary Desserts, another first for her. As she sipped her vanilla-nut decaf and I made my way through a slice of Viking cake, we talked about things — *really* talked about things. Mom asked me if I was happy. I told her, "Yes. Very." And this seemed to brighten her already glowing post-facial visage.

I asked her if *she* was happy. Looking down at her cup, she said, "I'm starting to be." This honest, insightful answer grabbed my heart and held it tight. "You know," I said, "I'm really looking forward to our next facial."

# Tea High

*"Tea to the English is really a picnic indoors."*
— Alice Walker

Mom had been exercising her pinkie for three days. She told me the exhaustive sets of pinkie-extensions were in preparation for her first "high tea," an event to which I was taking her. Married with children before she turned 21 and soon the mother of four girls with a Navy husband often on deployment, Mom didn't have time to experience self-indulgent luxuries, those little extravagances to which at least one of her daughters has grown accustomed. She was well into her 30s before she got her first manicure, and she had never been to a spa (or received any spa treatments, like massages or facials) before I took her to Estancia in La Jolla three years ago. Prior to my invitation, Mom had never even heard of high tea — a traditionally English, late-afternoon meal composed of bite-sized savories, scones with clotted cream and jam, petit fours, and of course, tea.

Though her exposure to pampering is minimal, Mom has what seems to be a hereditary predisposition toward living the high life. Just as taking a kid to Disneyland might reawaken a parent's childlike wonder, lavishing my mother with deluxe services prompts me to appreciate how splendid is my average day. Because I wanted Mom's introduction to this historically aristocratic pastime to be relaxed and unpretentious, I researched high teas countywide and finally settled on Tea-Upon-Chatsworth in Point Loma.

Contrary to the English custom of taking tea in the afternoon, I figured we'd do more of a brunch thing and made reservations for the first seating at

11:30 a.m. Mom was giddy from the moment she arrived at my place; as I drove us to Point Loma, I wondered if some of her exuberance might be attributed to nervousness. We talked about manners, and Mom said, "When someone asks for a tissue, I throw the roll of Bounty at them. It's not like we sit down and I have linen napkins — we don't even do that at Thanksgiving." She refers to the notorious propriety of David's parents as "dainty manners" and added, "That's just not the way we were brought up."

Mom grew up in a three-story Brooklyn house with a family on each floor. The three families, all related, constituted 6 adults and 13 children; chaos was as much a member of the family as any of the 3 dogs also residing there. Mom is proud of her resultant ability to thrive in an environment in which many otherwise-competent people would surely falter. "You could put 90 people in my home right now, and I'd be absolutely comfortable with it," she said. "Just don't ask me to choose which fork goes with the salad."

In her own home here in San Diego, Mom carries on the traditions of Brooklyn — between her grandchildren, guests, and the television, the house resonates with a relentless din. Not in all of my childhood or teen memories can I single out any one moment I could define as "quiet." Lively is more like it. But regardless of how fun and exciting such a loud and bustling environment can be, it is my belief that the body and mind require some down time, lest one become unhinged. For someone like me, who is perpetually teetering on the edge between sanity and madness, it is important to balance the manic with the calm, just as a conscientious eater might follow a decadent evening of steak and cake with a night of tofu and broccoli.

We arrived at Tea-Upon-Chatsworth with ten minutes to spare. Because the door was locked, Mom and I wandered into the nearest open store, which happened to be a baby boutique. When the word "cute" became unbearable, we headed for the exit. On the way we spotted three women approaching the tea joint from across the street, so we casually picked up our pace to beat them to the locked door. Despite our principal entrance, tea patrons were led to their pre-assigned tables in some mystical predetermined order that left us as the last to take our seats.

The sound of chamber music inspired Mom and me to lower our voices. Over our table hung a wreath, affixed to which were real porcelain teacups. Mom acclimated to her surroundings, handling and commenting on every object within her reach. She marveled at the delicate linen and was astonished at the feathery weight of her fork and knife. When she'd finished with her side of the table, she surveyed mine. Clucking her tongue and looking around to make sure no one was paying attention, she leaned forward and said, "Your plate's not as pretty as mine."

I began to object, but after examining the illustration on my plate — a potted green plant above the word "DILL" — and then scanning the wispy pink flowers that adorned the edges of my mother's antique eggshell dish, I could only sigh and say, "Yeah, you're right. Yours is much prettier."

"I'll get you a prettier one, baby," said Mom, the protective nurturer in her roused by the fleeting look of disappointment she'd caught on her daughter's face.

"No, please, don't," I said, with a hint of panic.

Thinking my resistance was simply a matter of wanting to spare her the trouble, Mom insisted on hunting down a suitable dish for me. But when she finally realized doing so would not only cross some invisible line of etiquette but also cause me great embarrassment, she agreed to stay seated. Forgetting my unsightly plate for the moment, Mom's face lit up, and she said, "This is just like a tea party!"

"Right," I said, allowing sarcasm to seep into the pause before I continued, "because it is a tea party."

Mom laughed and said, "This is so much fun!"

An ornately painted teapot was set on the table, and our attendant, Carol, explained that it contained a freshly brewed white tea called *mutan*, which is the Chinese word for peony. I took a sip and commented on the delightful floral subtleties; Mom looked at the liquid in her cup and asked

Carol for Splenda. "Don't you even want to try it first?" I said. "Maybe take a few sips and see how the flavors open up on your tongue?"

Mom took a tiny sip and said, "It's a little bitter."

"Well, try taking another sip, and keep in mind that it will probably pair well with food."

Carol set a small dish on the table between us. Employing the silver tongs used for plucking sugar cubes, Mom selected one of the yellow packets. She dropped the packet into her other hand and laughed at her lark as she tore off the corner and shook a bit of the white powder into her cup. She sipped her adjusted brew, smiled with satisfaction, set the cup down, and then startled me by breaking into hysterical laughter. In answer to my baffled expression, Mom said, "My finger is stuck," and indeed it was, as she'd somehow gotten the tip of her index all the way through the narrow end of the handle.

When she'd finally wriggled free, Mom giggled her relief. "I don't know what's wrong with me," she said, her laughter tapering off and then regaining its momentum. "I think the tea is making me high. Ah! Get it? High tea? Tea high?"

A sucker for puns, I chuckled and added, "You better watch it, you could become a tea-head. Take it from me, you may be all tingly-scalped now, but the comedown sucks."

Mom's permagrin grew wider and she relaxed into

her chair. She cut a cucumber finger sandwich in half and used the fork to taste it. "What would these people think if they could see us eating at home? Because it's not like this," she said.

"Who cares?" I answered.

I refilled Mom's cup and then raised mine to her before taking a sip. A brief moment passed during which no words were spoken as we applied a dollop of fresh cream and rose-petal jam to our scones. "Oh my God, this is amazing," Mom said after taking a bite.

"Yeah, pretty tasty," I agreed.

"I really like this, Barb," said Mom.

"The scone? Yeah, great stuff, huh?"

"Is that what this is? I've never had one before. It's delicious. But no, I mean this. Being alone, just talking. Nobody yelling or arguing with each other. I really like this."

I set my cup down and dabbed at the corners of my mouth with the linen napkin. I swept the room with my eyes, taking in the English country decor, the curios displayed on shelves, and, returning my gaze to my mother's face, I said, "I had a feeling you would."

In David's words, my father is a
walking bundle of contradictions.
He grew up Irish Catholic but
has since embraced New Age,
self-help-style spirituality. He's a
conservative, straight white male
whose best friends are all liberal
gays. He works as a military war-
gamer and rides a Harley, but he
also meditates every morning,
and because he believes in the
"healing power of touch," he
studied for two years to earn a
certificate in massage. Dad prides
himself on penny-pinching, but is
generous with those around him.
He volunteers for Make-a-Wish
Foundation and half a dozen other
organizations, working closely with
handicapped people and minorities,
yet he consistently uses politically
incorrect terms to refer to the very
groups of people he spends most
of his time helping. And though
I cringe whenever he drops a
derogatory term, I know that, like
Archie Bunker, Dad's word-choices
are dictated by his culture and

generation, and his intentions are not malicious.

I see my father as a man just a beat or two behind the times, but certainly more hip to shit than anyone else I know in his peer group. Though I disagree with him on a handful of political and spiritual points, I am very much my father's daughter. Even if he is a little meshugenah.

In the family, Dad and I are the travelers, Dad even more so than me. He's a million-miler, and that's just on one airline. Though he clocks most of his miles while working on war games that take him to Korea and Japan, he also loves traveling for pleasure. I've lost track of how many European cruises he's been on.

Because we both live within five miles of the airport, we are each other's perennial rides, and the departures are always predawn. As we are both "pathologically punctual," as my dad would say, we can relax knowing that when one of us says, "Please pick me up at 5 a.m.," the other will be waiting outside in the car by 4:45. The San

Diego airport has been the hub for much of my connection with Dad over the years. My father likes the idea of traveling so much that even when he's home, he spends time at the airport helping others find their way.

# Lion King

*"You don't have to be a "person of influence" to be influential. In fact, the most influential people in my life are probably not even aware of the things they've taught me."*
— Scott Adams

It was 6:30 a.m. when I went downstairs, dragging my suitcase behind me. Dad was waiting in the parking lot, buzzing with energy. This was nothing for him — on any other day at this time, he'd just be returning home from a five-mile walk to have a bowl of Frosted Flakes, a banana, and a glass of orange juice before showering and dressing for work.

"I want to show you something I got that's really cool," Dad said, opening the passenger's side door for me. I sat down, taking note of the lion lying on its belly in front of me while my father walked around and got in the car.

"Watch this," he said, and then he faced the lion and asked, "Are you having a great morning?" The car began to shake forward and back, which startled me a bit but caused the lion to nod his head in answer to my dad.

"Do you want to see Barb leave?" To this, the car rocked from left to right — the lion's head shook back and forth in an obvious "No."

My father has security clearance that goes higher than top secret for the government, and he talks to a bobble-head lion that lives on his dashboard. David joined us in the car as the sky began to lighten, and we were off.

"I'm not a bobble-head kind of guy," Dad explained on the way to the airport. "But I was really impressed with this one. This lion doesn't bobble like other bobbles. He's got a *regal* bobble."

Dad shared that on his way back from one of his visits to the Tijuana orphanage, he haggled with a street vendor at the border for the lion now shaking its head at me. My frugal father told me, "The guy wanted seven bucks, but I talked him down to three if we bought four." He insisted that each person who was in the car go in on the purchase with him — those people being his fellow congregants of Midtown Church of Religious Science, or as Dad calls it, "The Church of What's Happenin' Now."

After explaining the bobble-head lion phenomenon to friends at a recent party, my friend Kip advised, "If the lion ever calls you on the phone, it's time to express concern." I laughed and continued to poke fun at my father's close friendship with the small, fuzzy car ornament, but not once did I judge him for his taste in companions. On the contrary, every time I sit in Dad's car I am taken with the lion, mesmerized by its bobbling head. It's quite probable that my own affinity for anthropomorphizing both animals and inanimate objects is a behavior I learned from you-know-who.

Because of how often we travel for both work and pleasure, Dad and I feel at home in the airport. As a volunteer Airport Ambassador, Dad hangs out at the airport once a week to assist travelers less savvy than himself. A new project has him out of town a lot lately, so in order for us to spend some time together this week, I accompanied him as he made his rounds at the airport.

In addition to OCD and germaphobia, my father and I share a passion for people-watching. Standing by the escalators to the sky bridge, we chatted while intermittently interrupting ourselves to point out a particularly interesting human specimen.

"Stephanie and I hung out the other day, it was nice — WHOA! Three-o'clock, get a load of those shoes. Ouch, how can she walk?" I'd say.

"Well, I'm happy you two were able to make some time to see each other, because — OH! Turn around! What a freak of nature. No, the other way, quick! See what I mean?"

Neither of us missed a beat, nor did we lose our place in our ongoing conversation about the people in our lives.

We both peripherally observed an elderly woman drop a dollar bill, begin to walk away, then find and retrieve her money.

"I'm bummed she saw it," I said in jest.

"I know," said Dad. "That hawkeyed bitch jumped at the bill before I could get over there." But both of us knew if he had gotten his hands on the buck, it would only be to chase after the woman until he could return it. Dad might be frugal, but he's also honest.

Our discussion turned to drugs as I mentioned those people I no longer hang out with.

"You know, Dad, I used to do a lot of drugs. I don't regret it; I had a great time, but my priorities have changed."

I was interrupted by a woman who had obviously read the back of my father's jacket, where "Ask Me" is written in large white letters, and he directed her where she needed to go to pick up her rental car. A plane had just landed, so Dad ventured forth to offer help to more travelers.

It wasn't until we were walking back to the car that we were able to pick up our conversation again. Dad had been telling me a familiar tale about how grateful he is to have so much joy in his life. I had been explaining a huge transition that took place around the time I met David.

"I find it so wonderful to know that all of my four daughters are in love," said Dad.

"It was after I met David that I started to turn around," I said. I waited until Dad was seated and seat-belted before continuing.

"I quit smoking, I stopped doing drugs... it's, like, when I fell in love with him, I really started to care about my health."

Dad faced me before starting the car. His eyes — which a moment ago had been sparkling with humor — took on a duller shade of guilt. He looked as if he was in pain. Not the kind of sharp, severe pain that a harsh weapon or word would inflict, but rather the agony of the good-intentioned realizing that his actions have caused only suffering.

"Did I not instill in you any self-love? Did I not teach you how important your health and happiness are in order to lead a good life?"

A thousand things floated by in my head, a thousand things I wanted to say to prove to my father just how much he has influenced me and my decisions in life. I wanted to list examples, to recite his positive, love-filled words that echo through my head every day, but I didn't want him to think I was merely attempting to assuage his guilt.

"Of course you did, Dad." When I said this, Dad stopped at a red light, and the lion's head went up and down, confirming everything I said... and everything I didn't.

# Divine Intervention

*"That's the thing with magic. You've got to know it's still here, all around us, or it just stays invisible for you."*
— Charles de Lint

"Two amazingly synchronistic things happened to me this morning, things that prove to me the power of my own intentions," Dad said, his voice effervescing with the sparkling tone of wonderment. "I'm all ears," I said into the phone.

"Well, you know how things have been a little up in the air for funding at work," he began.

"Yes, of course," I said. Rare is the topic not covered in my daily conversations with Dad.

"So, I'm pulling out of the garage this morning, and I was thinking that I shouldn't worry, everything always works out for the best, and I say to myself, 'Hey, take it easy.' And the *first* car I got behind at the stoplight had a bumper sticker that read, 'Hey!' and then underneath 'Hey!' was, 'Take it easy!'" Here he paused, his silence dismissing any considerations of coincidence.

"That is something," I agreed. I tend to be superstitious, often analyzing chance encounters for deeper meanings. Once, I began to dial my sister's number into the phone, but when I placed it to my ear, Heather was already on the line, having called me less

than a second before I'd tried to call her. To us, this was
nothing short of a miracle.

"What's the other thing?" I prodded, eager for more.

"Well, I was on my morning walk," Dad began,
referring to his daily five-mile peregrination from his
home in Mission Hills through Hillcrest to Balboa Park
and back, "and when I got to the park, I really had to
take a leak." Dad's walks are early, presunrise, before the
public restrooms are open. "There was no way I'd make
it — I was thinking I'd have to go in a bush. And then,
suddenly, where one had not been the day before, there
it was — a port-o-potty. I manifested a port-o-potty,
right in front of the Old Globe! Right when I needed it
most, in the most unlikely of places, there it was! And
it was unlocked!"

The bumper sticker thing I got. Toilet manifestation,
however, was a bit of a stretch for me. And yet, I could
understand how extreme relief in a seemingly dire
situation might lead one to suspect divine intervention,
even if our *deus ex machina* appears in the form of a
port-o-potty. I also knew that, as seen through my
father's eyes, that blue plastic bathroom wasn't just
*there*. It was there for *him*.

Dad was raised Catholic, one of the Big Three religions
that invokes God's divine wrath as a motivational tool. My
dad doesn't buy all the fire-and-brimstone, you'll-burn-in-
hell-unless-you-eat-your-vegetables stuff. But, as a deeply
spiritual person, Dad was not ready to give up on a higher

power entirely. From Ra to Zeus to Jesus, man has made God in his image, and imbued Him with mortal weaknesses like anger, love, jealousy, and fear. Thus, my father created the divinity that best suited his personal needs: a hodge-podge of only the positive, loving, all-embracing aspects of every religion he could find, with none of the bad shit.

"So, you hear about Dad's manifestation?" I asked my sister Jenny later that afternoon; she sometimes brings her laptop over between work and school, a few hours during which we are the best of office mates — professionally respecting each other's need for productivity while allowing intermittent interruptions for a bit of companionable gossip.

Jenny nodded at me and rolled her eyes for good measure. Of course she'd already heard about Dad's miraculous morning — she lived with him.

My cell phone screamed the loud aria I have programmed to sound when someone I know is calling. "Hey, Daddy! I've got Jenny over here; she's borrowing my dictator for some work project."

Before he could comment, Jenny called out, "Yo, Barb!" loud enough for my father to hear, "We've got 20 minutes to *manifest* some batteries for that thing before I have to leave."

Not missing a beat, my dad said into my ear, "Oh, she's so clever with that manifesting, eh?" The smile was evident in his voice. "Tell her she can manifest a fucking key to get in the house, 'cause I'm changing the locks!"

The next morning, I met up with Dad at Midtown Church; within the expansive embrace of Religious Science, he has found a place to worship his personal deity.

"Guess what? That port-o-potty? It was gone this morning," he said as he joined me by the entrance. "It was there yesterday, when I needed it, and now it's *gone*. Spooky, huh?" He made a shuddering noise, as if he'd just been poked on the back of the neck by the icy cold finger of a long-dead acquaintance. Like Kramer on *Seinfeld*, Dad often makes this noise whenever words fail him.

"Fuckin' crazy," I said, marveling at the mystery of it all.

As is usual when I join my father at his church, I found myself unable to repeat the words of the chant that preceded a minute of meditative silence. As the rest of the people in the room, eyes closed, did whatever they do when people meditate, I pondered my resistance to the words, "I am as God created me, in the light, in the love, in the glory." I stared at the candles flickering behind translucent orange and red glass before flowers on the altar.

*It's that word*, I thought. *I don't like the word "God." Maybe all those years of Catholic school have done to me what they did to Dad — too much negativity, too much guilt, too much bad shit.* I looked around at all the peaceful faces. *It's just semantics,* I continued in my head. *So if I take out that dreadful, overly wrought, meaning-laden word, I'm left with an underlying Popeye-esque sort of principle: I yam what I yam and that's all what I yam. Kind of self-help-y, but I'll take it over Bible-thump-y any day.*

The gentle tap of a cloth-covered stick against a glass bowl launched soft, sonorous ripples into the air that washed over the congregants, calling them back from a hundred individual reveries to focus their attention on the one speaker in front of the room.

After much listening, singing, smiling, and hand holding, we made our way to the community room. "There's such a great energy here, right?" Dad asked me.

"Yes, there is." Then, remembering my minute of meditation, I asked, "What do you think God is?" I'd always thought of religion as an elaborate fairy tale, filled with magical moments and superior beings with special powers, not unlike witches, warlocks, and leprechauns. When I was in Catholic school, the God of my imagination was a great sorcerer, casting spells to reward or punish on a whim. Now, the word seems an elusive idea for which every person has a different interpretation.

After taking a moment to think, Dad responded to my question: "There's one power in the universe. I call it 'God.' To me, it's that which makes my heart beat while I'm sleeping."

"And that which grants you port-o-potties while you're walking," I added.

"Very funny," said Dad. "You're going to hell for that, you know."

"Yeah. I know."

# Family Practice

*"As the lily among thorns,
so is my love among the daughters."*
— Solomon Ibn Gabirol

I waited in the lobby and watched through the window as the cold rain pelted the sidewalk. I nodded in appreciation of the weather's propriety like a maître d' tilting his head in approval of an elegantly dressed couple entering his high-end establishment. Now the dark cloud over my head would be tangible, the chill in my bones justified. On a conscious level, I knew trepidation was a waste of energy, that if I was to be of any help, I had to play the part of the supportive, upbeat daughter. But for all my efforts to remain positive, my inner pessimist prodded me toward pondering the worst-case scenario.

The day before, I had detected surprise and delight in my father's voice when I told him I wanted to accompany him to the hospital. His actual words were, "I'm just getting the stitches out, but okay."

"I thought you were supposed to get the results of your biopsy," I said. Dad told me he wasn't sure if the lab had already reported to his doctor. "Well, no matter," I said. "It'll be great to see you, and this way you won't have to pretend to read a magazine while hanging out in the waiting room."

"Good, then," he said. "I'll pick you up at 7:30." I could hear his smile through the phone.

When Dad's 16-year-old Camry pulled up, I hustled to make it to the car without getting soaked. We didn't have far to go. Balboa Hospital, the local nickname for the Naval Medical Center, is just over a mile from my place. As we pulled into the parking structure, I took a moment to consider the mysterious randomness of my having resided in Alaska, Rhode Island, and Los Angeles, but ending up living closer than ever to the facility in which I was born.

Once out of the car, we unfurled our umbrellas — Dad's was large and black; mine was red and white and barely covered my shoulders. "Are you going to need to share this one, since you brought that Barbie umbrella?" Dad asked with a teasing smile.

"I know, it's meager," I said. "I got it as a free gift when I bought lipstick. My legs are a lost cause, but at least my glasses should stay dry until we get over there." I darted across the small road and walkway as fast as the people holding their jackets over their heads. I hadn't realized how loud the water was until we reached the building, the overhang of which simultaneously sheltered us and shushed the rain.

I was reading my book in the waiting room when Jane (the family's medical expert by virtue of her job as a pharmaceutical saleswoman) arrived and took Dad's empty seat. "How is he?"

"Fine, I think. Been back there for, like, 20 minutes. He wants to go to Bread & Cie after this. You have time?" It was a silly question — we both knew Jane always makes time for her favorite cheese plate.

When Dad emerged, the golf-ball-sized bandage on his forehead was gone and in its place was a barely discernible cluster of butterfly stitches. He smiled when he saw us and greeted his eldest daughter with a hug and a kiss on each cheek. "Well?" I asked. "What'd he say?"

As the smile vanished from Dad's face, Jane's and mine also evaporated. "I'll explain when we get outside."

It was unlikely the outcome would be different from our expectations. The lab results were in, only to confirm a diagnosis about which the doctors had been fairly certain. Dad had survived melanoma, the malignant kind of skin cancer. At first, it was nothing more than a freckle, a dark spot just under his right eye that his daughters noticed and then monitored. Convinced the spot was growing larger and darker, we pestered Dad until he got it looked at, tested, and ultimately removed, along with a generous portion of flesh in the vicinity for good measure. That was years ago; aside from the thin white wisp of a scar, Dad was no worse for wear.

The cancer detected on Dad's forehead a few months ago was the milder squamous cell carcinoma. There was no need to worry, the doctors said, it was just a matter of removing the localized tumor. But then the pink splotch on his forehead began to hurt, which indicated the cancer had reached a nerve.

"The good news," Dad reported to Jane and me as we stood shivering in the outdoor walkway, "is that the tests don't show any evidence of cancer cells, which means they probably got it all. But," he let his breath out slowly and inhaled deeply before continuing. "They confirmed that it did, in fact, reach a nerve. So the doctor recommends radiation."

I bombarded him with questions. When would it begin? What were the side effects? How long would it last? Jane had only one: What was the next step?

"Well, first this has to heal, so nothing is happening before that, and it can take around six weeks," Dad said. He had an appointment for a month later to follow up with his doctor, who would then refer him to an oncologist, who would then decide when the radiation treatments would begin.

Jane, with all her hospital-insider knowledge, was determined to speed things up. "There's no reason you have to wait to speak with an oncologist," she said. I agreed. There had to be something we could do to hasten treatment — an appointment, a specialist's name... something. Dad was unable to get a word in edgewise as Jane and I hurled ideas as they popped into our heads and marched him back and forth to various departments, each of which was guarded by a receptionist who turned us away in the name of procedure.

We'd covered half the grounds when Jane, in a moment of awareness, turned to Dad and said, "This isn't helping, is it. We're not helping, we're just being annoying, aren't we."

Dad didn't speak, but his answer was in his smile, which burgeoned into a giggle that seemed to say, "Yes, but I don't mind." For the briefest of moments, the rambunctious energy that radiates from my father was muted. It must have been a lot to take on; before he'd had a chance to process the news and what it meant for the coming months, we'd been all over his shit with our ill-conceived scheme to accelerate the car before the key was even in the ignition.

The three of us left the laminated floors and medicinal odors of the hospital for the summery colors and comforting aroma of baked bread at our Hillcrest breakfast haunt. While Jane enjoyed her cheese plate, I my quiche and coffee, and Dad his demi-baguette and tea, we spoke of pleasant things. An hour later, we stepped outside to find that the rain had stopped, and the sidewalks glistened in the warm light of the sun.

# The Accident

*"Bad is never good until worse happens."*
— Danish proverb

"How's he doing, everything okay?" It was an empty question — I was sure of the answer. There was no room in my mind to consider any alternative to *fine*. Dad had still been in surgery when I'd called my sister Jane before going out to breakfast a few hours earlier. It was now around 10 a.m. on Tuesday where I was in Tokyo, 7 p.m. on Monday in San Diego. Jane had spent all day at the hospital: waiting, working on her laptop, and waiting some more. Last I spoke with her, she was leaving to chauffeur her kids to after-school activities; the nurse had promised she'd text Jane when it was time for her to come back.

I could hear the girls in the background, that high-pitched, ever-insistent drone of children. They must have been at the hospital — I recognized the tinny echo to their voices from the long, empty corridor outside the hospital waiting room.

"No, Barb, everything is *not* okay. Things are very not okay," Jane said.

Unprepared for the impossible, my body didn't register her words. I looked at David, who was checking email on his laptop; he was relaxed, untroubled. I still felt the way David looked. "Are you messing with me?"

"No, I am not." The edge in my sister's voice betrayed her exhaustion. I stared straight ahead, at the surreal view of Tokyo skyscrapers out the window of our room, and listened to Jane, her voice growing increasingly fretful, as she relayed what she'd been told: "Everything went fine on the left side, but when they flipped him over to do the right, the balloon they inflated tore the vena cava — that's a major artery — and he wouldn't stop bleeding, so they had to cut him open. He needed blood transfusions and they ended up taking out one of his kidneys. Dad went in thinking he was getting small bits removed to be biopsied and now he lost a whole *kidney*."

I heard the telltale gasp of a sob. Jane was always strong in front of her little girls; if she was crying, things were worse than I thought. I continued to stare out the window, not bothering to wipe the silent waterfall cascading down my cheeks. My voice was as even and calm as an air traffic controller when I said, "So what now?"

"They said they won't know for 24 to 48 hours if he'll *pull through*."

"Pull through? Jane, what does that mean? Pull through?"

I thought of the last time I'd spoken to Dad — 6:30 a.m. San Diego time, right before I was about to go to bed in Tokyo. He was getting all his things together and waiting for Jane to pick him up. I told him I wished I could be there. I chastised him for not waiting just a few more days. He reminded me that ever since he learned of the masses (inadvertently, during a CT scan to identify a small hernia at his belly button), he couldn't get them out soon enough. He hadn't planned for his surgery to coincide with my trip to Tokyo. And anyway, he said, he'd see me when I got home.

A dangerous thought flashed through my mind: *What if that was the last time I would ever get to speak to him?* Dad's biggest concern when we spoke was whether or not the small masses on each of his kidneys would prove cancerous. Even he didn't seem nervous about the procedure itself.

Because Dad didn't want people fussing over him, he'd asked Jane to contact friends and family only *after* he came out of surgery and everything was fine. There was nothing to do now but wait — Dad was in ICU, with a breathing tube jammed down his throat and machines monitoring every fluid and pulse through needles and pads. The doctors told Jane they wouldn't know anything, such as whether or not Dad's remaining kidney would "come online," until the following morning.

Jane was going to go home and get some sleep, then return first thing in the morning. By the time we got off the phone, I could tell from her clipped tone that she was short-tempered — she didn't have the answers I wanted, and this frustrated her, because she was after the same information. All we wanted was for someone to say, "It's all going to be okay." But all I could say to my sister before hanging up was, "I guess we'll see."

David watched me, patiently waiting for an update. "My dad almost died," I said. "And he still might."

David's sympathetic expression was my undoing. I put my head on his lap and howled, one hand clutching my stomach, as if that could somehow soothe the agony that was twisting within.

"The Accident" was part one of a two-part series. In the second column, I revealed that my father had indeed pulled through, although he was worse for wear. Instead of the planned itty-bitty robot incision, he had been sliced open 18 inches, from navel to back on one side. Upon arriving home from Japan, I went directly to the hospital, where Dad was released from ICU into my care. His recovery was slow, and what used to be a perpetually sunny disposition is now partly cloudy. While he was kept in a drug-induced coma after the surgery-gone-wrong, Dad suffered terrible nightmares that continued to haunt him for weeks. He was angry for a time, and I think part of him still is. It was strange for me to see my father — who has always insisted that we get to choose how we feel — struggle to find a silver lining. The best he could do was to avoid placing blame by referring to the whole fiasco as "the accident."

I went with Dad to meet with the surgeon a week after the accident. The doctor told us that everyone who was in the operating room that day was undergoing treatment for post-traumatic stress disorder. He said it was unlike anything he'd ever seen, that a "geyser of blood" just suddenly shot to the ceiling. My dad lost nearly as much blood as a body can hold. If it hadn't been for the team of military vascular trauma surgeons who happened to be on location for other reasons, the surgeon said, my father would have been beyond saving.

 My family had always assumed that David has been judging them. They insist that if David is sitting silently in a corner, it's because he must be busy actively hating everyone in the room. David says people are only worried about being judged when they know they're doing something wrong, and that my family is merely being neurotic when they grill him about what he's thinking about them.

I think the reason they're so concerned is that they see all their flaws reflected in his eyes (we are not an oblivious tribe). David comes across unnervingly confident and self-assured — the type of man who would be in his right to throw the first stone. "Rite of Passage" was one of the very few stories I had to work to convince David to let me write. He was embarrassed, but as he says, "I did it, so I have to own it."

 I was really hoping this next story would quietly fade into history. Thanks, Barb.

# Rite of Passage

*"Mistakes are part of the dues one pays for a full life."*
— Sophia Loren

To say I was "looking forward" to Thanksgiving would be a gross understatement. I was giddy with anticipation. This would be David's first time noshing the big bird with my clan, and I was just as eager to see my man become immersed in the pandemonium as I was to get caught up in the chaotic current myself. It was as if by participating in the one celebration he'd yet to experience with my people that David would finally become a bona fide member of my family.

David understood his role in the day's festivities. My DNA lacks the gene for domesticity. Save for my mother, who furnished the table by virtue of necessity while rearing four daughters, the women in my family do not cook. David had gleaned from my nostalgic narratives that before my brother-in-law Sean took over Mom's kitchen, our Thanksgiving dinners comprised overcooked turkey, potato flakes from a box, corn from a can, and Pillsbury crescent rolls, each of which was enjoyed with zeal, the level of which David couldn't possibly understand. My mother did her best for many years, for which we were grateful. But blood is blood — with the same conviction she employs when declaring her strengths, Mom conceded her weaknesses and was more than happy to step aside to make way for a master.

Aware that as a man married into the family he was expected to conjure culinary delights, David carefully considered his contributions before shopping and cooking in the days leading up to the grand feast.

The big day was mellower than any I could remember at Mom's. Jane and Jenny, who were also sharing Thanksgiving celebrations with their husbands' families, were only around for a few hours; Dad was away in Japan on business. After Jane left and before Jenny arrived, Heather, Mom, and I played Scrabble outside as my two nephews splashed around in the Jacuzzi. Inside, my friend Ollie entertained chefs David and Sean.

The dinner itself was subdued and short-lived. Heather's friend Molly and her mother Maggie dropped by in time for dessert. Finally, when they could eat and drink no more, Ollie, David, and Sean selected couches upon which they could each slip into a food coma. Eventually, when the women were finished talking, it came time to head home. While Heather was putting her boys to bed, I woke mine — Ollie and David. As I made my rounds kissing cheeks, David finished packing our empty Tupperware and ramekins back into the boxes we'd brought.

Once in my own bed, my belly distended and the rest of my body appropriately uncomfortable, I reflected on the day — it had been nice, but not as momentous as I'd expected. I couldn't put my finger on it, but something had been missing.

The following morning, David and I were seated outside Bread & Cie when I fished my ringing phone from my purse. It was my mother calling for the third time in as many minutes. After some pointless small talk, Mom finally asked, "Did you happen to see that bottle of champagne in the black box that Molly brought?"

"Yeah, it was on the counter when we left," I said.

"It wasn't there this morning, and we can't find it anywhere," said Mom.

"Well, it was there when we left, so I don't know what to tell you," I snapped. Before she could mention it again, and I could tell by her intake of breath that she was about to, I added, "I'm out to breakfast with David right now; I'll give you a call later." I dropped my phone back in my purse and looked at David. "I think my mom just stopped short of accusing me of taking the Moët Molly brought over last night," I said indignantly. "Can you believe that?"

David had an unsettling smile on his face, as if he were being tickled by a particularly intimidating clown. He leaned forward and, with a nervous giggle, said, "I snatched it."

"I'm sorry, you what?"

David, sheepish in response to my incredulous

glare, rushed to explain. "Your mom only drinks daiquiris. I struggled with whether or not to take it, but usually she asks us to take any leftover wine home with us anyway, and I had no idea that anyone had a plan for the bottle and—" While David gushed, I retrieved my iPhone, selected Mom's name, tapped her home number, and passed it to him. David looked horrified. "What am I supposed to — Hi, Maria! It's David. Yes, we had such a great time...um, look, about the champagne..."

I listened as David admitted he had the bottle and offered to return it that very morning. Before we could make it home, Heather was already calling to insist that we keep the bottle. She said she'd only looked for it because she and Molly had talked about popping it open but that it was really no big deal. "After all, you guys are always bringing great wines down here, you deserve it," she said. But I was adamant — the bottle would be returned. When I relayed the call to him, David was mortified.

Once home, David retrieved the black box and set it on the counter beside a bottle of Banfi Rosa Regale Brachetto. When I asked him what the Brachetto was for, he said, in a forlorn, beaten tone, "Restitution." Seeing him like that, so flustered and contrite, had a bizarre effect on me — I felt content.

On the drive down to Chula Vista, I analyzed the situation aloud. "You're all embarrassed and bummed and stuff, beh beh, but I have this uncanny sensation that your taking that bottle was a good thing, and not just because we get to eat those yummy leftovers for lunch." David looked at me as if I'd just declared my regret for not voting for the old guy and Caribou Barbie. "Trust me," I said.

Heather, Jane, and Mom greeted David with open arms. They fussed over the unnecessary gift of Brachetto and mentioned again that he should keep the champagne, that he would enjoy it most of all. There was an unmistakable and familiar enthusiasm in my mother's tone when she said, "If you ever want something, baby, you just take it, what's mine is yours, after all, you're family!" Heather was just as earnest when she consoled, "Don't worry, we all take stuff from here, especially when it's something you just know is going to go to waste."

As I sat and watched my mother and sisters, it occurred to me that I had never seen them so natural and relaxed around David. I had sensed this might happen. That before my family could ever truly embrace my man as one of their own, they would have to be convinced that he was just like them — flawed. I couldn't remember the last time I'd been so proud.

Barbarella's family loves scaring each other. I don't get it. I hate being scared. I don't go on amusement park rides. I don't watch horror films.

When I was a kid, every weekend my friends would go to the town movie theater to see cheesy B horror flicks. They loved it, but for the longest time I refused to go with them. Finally, I decided that there must be something to this that I was missing, so one weekend, despite my better judgment, I worked up the courage to go with them to see *Dracula Has Risen From His Grave*. Any aficionado of horror films will tell you that *Dracula Has Risen From His Grave* is a terrible movie, and not at all scary. I had nightmares for two weeks. I think there's something seriously wrong with Barb's family.

# Scare Tactics

*"A good scare is worth more to a man than good advice."*
— Edgar Watson Howe

Changing my position from right to left was a snap
decision, made in the half-second between the
second and third beeps that marked the elevator's
arrival on each floor. *Better to get her from behind*, I
thought. A fifth beep, a sixth, and *BING!* I held my
breath. I watched my sister Jenny as she exited the
lobby and turned right to head down the hallway
leading to my front door. With the stealthy silence
of a ninja, I tiptoed close behind her, then poked her
in the shoulder and shouted, "HEY!" Barely choking
back a scream, Jenny jerked around to face me, her
ponytail flipping around to the front of her face, her
nostrils flaring, the whites of her eyes bulging — like
a spooked mare.

"HA! Gotcha!" I said, and burst out in laughter.

Jenny exhaled and drew a measured breath to calm
her nerves and then smiled and said, "Man, it just
doesn't get any better than that. I feel so awake right
now!" She caught my contagious giggles and we walked
to my door, arm-in-arm, chortling.

"What's so funny?" David asked, eyeing us as we
cackled our way into the living room.

"I scared the shit out of Jenny," I said with pride. Jenny nodded confirmation.

"That's horrible," David said. "Why would you do such a sick thing?"

This took my sister and me by surprise. *Horrible? Sick?* More like *hilarious*, I thought — we were still suffering hiccups, the aftershocks from our earlier ground-shaking guffaws. Despite our attempts to convince him that scaring people was fun, for both the scarer and the scaree, an incredulous David announced his assessment: "You guys are deranged."

As we sat in my office considering David's words, Jenny told me she feels special when someone takes the time and energy to properly frighten her. Two people in my sister's life who go above and beyond when it comes to demonstrating their affection via terrorism are her boyfriend, Brad, and her roommate, Dad.

Earlier that week, Jenny was given a good fright while washing the dishes. Mounted to the wall above the sink at Dad's place is a framed print of Van Gogh's *Starry Night*. Because the picture itself is dark and the fluorescent lights of the kitchen are so bright, the glass that protects the print also functions as a mirror. Jenny had been focusing on the task at hand for several long minutes when she lifted her head to check her hair in the reflection, and glimpsed among the swirls of midnight-blue sky and golden stars the image of a beast hovering over her shoulder with hands like claws above her head, poised to attack. Jenny dropped a plate from her hands and let out a shriek.

"There's something wrong with you," she said when she turned to face the apparition, whose excessive laughter had left him in a fit of coughing.

Dad has always delighted in executing the perfect ambush. My mother was his ideal victim — she never suspected him, and her responses to his antics were worthy of Academy recognition. Some of his more famous coups featured the upstairs linen closet of our home in Chula Vista. "You coming up to bed?" he would ask. My mother would answer, "Yeah, in a minute." On occasion, it could take up to two hours for my mother to finally make her way up the stairs. As she rounded the corner, Dad would hop out of the linen closet, where, with the patience of a serial killer, he'd been waiting all that time, wedged between two shelves.

When we lived in Alaska, Dad invested in a giant gorilla glove. When my mother left to run one errand or another, he would inter himself beneath piles of shoes and thick hanging articles in the closet by the front door. Mom would return, remove her outermost layer, and open the closet to put it away, after which Dad would slowly extend the gorilla mitt from between two coats and wait for the payoff, which he always got.

Sometimes Mom would scream, other times she'd curse, and once, though she still denies it ever happened, she peed a little. After gasping, screaming, or cursing, she would flail her arms and say, "You're trying to kill me, I know it!"

As most children do, my sisters and I learned by watching our parents. We knew instinctively that Mom and Dad would not be amused if we attempted to startle them, so we focused our attention on each other.

We each had our favorite scare location. Mine was the bathroom. Exiting the only truly private room in the house, one is relieved and relaxed; one is also either distractingly confident or dejected, depending on how one has just interpreted the mirror's verdict: never is a person more vulnerable to being caught off guard.

But even a good spot can grow old; my sisters and I soon became wary of doors, especially the one to the bathroom. Once, smelling a setup, I lingered in the loo for a while to wear down the patience of my suspected attacker. With the water still running, I swung open the door and shouted. Jenny, frustrated and surprised that her plan to pounce on me had backfired, screamed and reflexively hit me in the arm.

To throw my sisters off, I graduated to more cunning plans — waiting down the hall instead of just beyond the door, crawling under a bed, or (the most thrilling, and well worth the wait) camping out in the backseat of a car. She who had the most patience received the greatest payoff.

In my family, setting out to terrorize someone for a laugh is akin to telling a joke, the goal for either of which is to extract an electric reaction. I am now beginning to see that, from the perspective of outsiders, my family's sense of humor might seem a tad on the demented side.

David's family's sense of humor, on the other hand, is as subtle as an unfrosted bundt cake. A perfect example of his family's inability to grasp my comic genius was the day I succeeded in convincing David to carry the bumper (which he had just removed from his father's jeep with the assistance of a small tree) into his parents' house. It didn't matter to me that I had only met David's parents two days before. The sidesplitting visual of him entering the living room with the giant bumper in his arms had me gasping for air. To overcome David's reluctance, I promised him there was no person *on earth* who wouldn't find this funny.

After we returned to the room in which David's parents had been quietly reading — David holding the bumper and me by his side — it took a good five minutes for me to notice that I was the only person laughing. Hard. Because I couldn't stop, I ran cackling like a hyena out of the house, and, accompanied only by the wildlife in the woods around me, let my fit of hysterics run its course.

 If our families were colors, David's would be green and mine would be red

— not only are these hues colorimetric opposites, but green is a subdued, calm color, while red is dramatic and attention grabbing. David's family is quiet to the point of passive, and mine is loud, in-your-face demanding. Our families have met only once, due in large part to the 2600 miles separating our homes. I can't help thinking this is probably a good thing.

 My parents are serious people, even when it comes to playing games. They play bridge at least three times a week. They travel to participate in bridge tournaments. They are closing in on having earned enough points to be Life Masters. Whenever they find themselves within proximity of two other bridge players, the cards come out.

I enjoy playing games — Scrabble, Rummikub, Cards Against Humanity — these are whimsical amusements intended for an evening with friends or some light pre-dinner entertainment.

But when it comes to bridge, I have neither the time nor the inclination to join the cult.

For years, Barbarella watched as I rebuffed my parents as they tried to persuade me to take up the game with the promise of lifelong pleasure and satisfaction. So they were understandably thrilled when, one night at the dinner table, Barb announced, "Did David tell you the news? He's taking bridge classes!" My parents' excitement quickly escalated.

"WHAT? Wait, when? REALLY? When?"

Barb's face burst into a painfully wide smile. The success of her prank had already exceeded her expectations.

"Huh? Wha? NO! I'm not taking bridge classes!" I cried.

This only made Barbarella laugh harder.

My mother was the first to catch on.

"Oh, you are *evil*," she said to Barb with a smirk.

But my father still didn't get the joke.

"How long have you been taking classes? What made you finally decide to learn?"

"No, Dad. I am NOT taking bridge lessons!"

It took several more adamant denials and Barb doubled-over in laughter for my father to finally realize that the story of my taking bridge lessons had been a hoax perpetrated by his demonic daughter-in-law.

And therein lies the fundamental difference between Barbarella's family and mine. Upon hearing Barb's "news," her family would have immediately assumed it to be apocryphal. Assuming everything is a joke or a prank, they laugh first and ask questions later. Conversely, my family takes what you say at face value, and assumes you are being earnest until notified otherwise.

It's not that my father doesn't enjoy a good joke; he actually has quite a good sense of humor. It just tends more toward the "A priest, a minister, and a rabbi walk into a bar" variety.

Both of my parents immigrated to this country from Hungary. They survived World War II — my father is a Holocaust survivor, and my mother's Lutheran and Catholic family had all their property taken from them. They survived the Hungarian Revolution, and with nothing to their name, they survived immigrating to a country whose language they didn't speak.

My opera-loving, art-film-watching, classical-music-listening mother descended from aristocracy on her mother's side. Her family has coats of arms, family trees, engraved silverware, ancient paintings of ancestors, and all the manners and breeding that one might expect. (Fun fact: I am a direct descendent of Anna von Frankenstein.) My mother's mother was a dry, humorless woman whom I believe was more likely to have had her children out of a sense of duty than desire. I liked her, though I'd never say that she was warm.

Conversely, my mother's father, who had no less sense of propriety, had an impish sense of humor. When tape recorders were first introduced to consumers, he purchased one, recorded his voice on it, and hid it behind the Christmas tree as a prank on his two young daughters.

Growing up, I would receive long letters from him imploring me to THINK, and to understand the importance of one's CHARACTER — words he emphasized by writing them in all caps. He was an Olympic fencer, an attorney, and an immaculately groomed gentleman, in the truest sense of the word. He wore sock garters, even with his shorts; his shirts were always pressed, and his nails buffed. He even died in the most tidy and gentlemanly way possible. He had been out that morning doing the grocery shopping. Upon returning home, he put away all the groceries, laid down on the sofa, set his hat on his chest, crossed his hands, and quietly expired. I'm sure he must have thought it ungentlemanly to shuffle off this mortal coil before stocking the pantry.

I only relate these stories to give you some sense of perspective when I say that Barbarella's family hit me like a tsunami.

"Blood is thicker than water"
would be an apt motto for them. They
are a tight, codependent clan who have
each other's back no matter what so
you better forget about fucking with
them right now. Barb speaks with her
father and her sister Jane every day,
and with the rest of the tribe almost
as frequently. Her mother, father,
three sisters, and their six kids, all live
nearby, and they gather en masse for
all birthdays and holidays. They move
like a school of fish.

Recently, for example, during one
of Barbarella's daily calls with her sister
Jane, they made a plan for the four
of us — Barbarella, me, Jane, and her
husband, Simon — to have dinner at a
restaurant down the street from where
we live. The day after making the
reservation, Jane called Barb to say that
she mentioned our dinner plan to their
sister, Heather, who remarked that it
sounded like fun. Motivated by guilt
— the nuclear force that binds their
family — Jane suggested that Heather
and her husband, Sean, should join
us. Now that three of the sisters were

going, Heather thought it would just
be wrong to not invite the fourth, at
which point their sister Jenny and her
husband, Brad, were added, increasing
the party to eight. Like a snowball
rolling down a hill, what had started
out as a little dinner get-together with
Jane and Simon rapidly expanded into
a Last Supper-esque to-do.

I love Barb's family, but they're
so different from the way I grew up
that, like a timid puppy, it took time
for me to relax around them. My first
impression was that they were LOUD.
That was also my second, third, fourth,
and all subsequent impressions. Barb's
parents come from Brooklyn — a loud
city. Her father is Irish, and her mother
is Italian — both stereotypically loud
cultures. Barb's father rides a loud
Harley. And with four girls who now
have six kids of their own, any family
gathering is guaranteed to be loud.

Having grown up in what I now
realize was an abnormally quiet home,
it's not surprising that, at the first
great gathering of Barbarella's family
I attended, I ended up sitting outside

feeling a bit shell-shocked. Barb noticed that I had gone missing and eventually tracked me to the far corner of her mother's back yard.

"Where have you been? Are you okay?" Barb asked.

"I needed a break. It's just too much," I replied.

I still occasionally steal away to the backyard for a quick respite, or linger just a bit longer than necessary in the bathroom.

At first, my parents didn't know what to make of Barbarella. It took years for them to finally come to appreciate her style and humor, which is why I was filled with more than a little trepidation when they began talking about coming to visit us in San Diego. Observing a single wolf in captivity is one thing, but to be standing in the middle of the entire pack in their native habitat is quite another. I wasn't concerned for myself, or even about what Barb's family might think of my folks. Rather, I was worried that my parents might suffer the same sort of PTSD I had experienced after my first meeting with Barb's family.

It's not just that each member

of the family is individually loud, but that they all talk *simultaneously*. Barbarella swears that they've learned how to both talk and listen at the same time, but to me it seems like each of them is more interested in the talking part than the listening part — not surprising, I suppose, for four sisters who grew up competing for everything, including attention.

Each of them has a rapid-fire, machine gun delivery, as though they feel they have to quickly get out whatever it is they want to say. I tend to talk a bit more slowly, with momentary pauses as I consider my words. During those interstitial lulls, Barbarella is often quick to jump in, leading to this common exchange:

"Hey! Let me finish! You're always interrupting me," I'll say.

"Oh. I thought you were done," Barb sheepishly replies.

"No, I was in the middle of a sentence."

"Okay, I'm sorry. Go ahead."

"I've forgotten what I was going to say."

# When Families Collide

*"People talk about 'dysfunctional' families;*
*I've never seen any other kind."*
— Sue Grafton

I don't know why I was so surprised. I mean, I'd been with him for four years — it was bound to happen sometime. But like getting your period for the first time, it's impossible to know how it will feel until it happens to you. Just as I accepted the fact that a week of discomfort each month would make me a woman, I embraced the idea that David's parents were going to leave their little island and come to San Diego to meet my family, a prospect that (like my first cramps) both excites and terrifies me. When David's mother, Ency, first mentioned her desire to meet my family, I took it as one of those things someone says to be nice but doesn't expect to be taken up on, like when the event planner David and I met at the Friar's Club in New York said, "Look me up if you're ever in New Orleans, and I'll take care of you!" But the subject came up again and again, and when she started throwing out calendar dates, it finally became clear that Ency meant business.

"I have only one request," said David's younger sister, Michelle, who makes her living as a glass artist in Seattle. "Please schedule the meeting so that I can

be there. This is something I don't want to miss."
Over the Thanksgiving holiday at David's parents'
house, the ladies (Ency, Michelle, Katie, and I) were
sipping wine and picking at leftover desserts in the
kitchen when Ency made a passing comment about
how she was looking forward to meeting my mother.

"If you really want to do this," I told her, "you should
be prepared."

"I know, I know," she said, in a rare post-entertaining
and alcohol-induced state of extreme relaxation. "I am
*zee boont.*"

Once, in an attempt to illustrate to his parents
the differences between his family and mine, David
referred to the movie, *My Big Fat Greek Wedding.*
"You see," he began, "Barb's family is like the Greeks,
partying and roasting a lamb on the front lawn,
and you're like the reserved, extra polite family that
brings the bundt cake." Ever since that explanation,
whenever Ency wants to apologize for her "bundty-
ness" (like when she freaks out over a ring of water
on her cherry wood cabinet or obsesses over what
to make for dinner), she'll say in her aristocratic
Hungarian accent, "I know, I know. I am *zee boont.*"

With wine and sugar fueling my tendency to
exaggerate, I tried to paint a picture of a typical family
gathering at my mother's house. "Imagine six people
all speaking really fast and really loud all at the same
time, okay? That's the ongoing din. When someone

really wants to be heard, they'll just speak *louder* than everyone else. You're smiling, but I'm serious here." Ency refilled her glass. "Yeah, you're gonna need a lot of that when you come over," I said with a laugh.

I continued, explaining that my mother's method of making people feel at home is to treat them like one of the family. The "welcome" a first-time guest receives is often delivered upon the doorstep as my mother, before saying hello, admonishes the new arrival for not having shown up sooner (whether or not the guest is actually late). If the house is not tidy, she will say in her thick Brooklyn brogue, "What's ah mattah wid you, comin' heah and makin' such a mess?" Warm greetings like these are meant to put guests at ease — to let them know that short of dropping their trousers to shit on the dining table, nothing they say or do is likely to offend my mother, and even a repulsive act such as that would most assuredly be forgiven.

Ency's husband, Robert, followed the laughter into the kitchen and asked what was so funny. I said I'd just been telling the girls about my family and then suggested that perhaps Ency might summarize for him. In her polite and euphemistic way, Ency said, "Barbarella says her family is... upfront." Robert watched for a moment as we broke into hysterics over Ency's polite synopsis and then, realizing he wasn't going to be let in on the joke, he dismissed us by pushing the air with his hands in an "okay, forget it" gesture and returned to the other room.

Whereas the information my mother dishes out is messy and raw, save for a liberal seasoning of salty expletives, Ency prefers to clean, cook, and garnish the facts until she deems them suitable for company. I have never heard anyone in David's bundt-cake family burp. In my Brooklyn-bred Irish/Italian, lamb-on-the-lawn clan, gaseous emissions win awards.

My family is more comfortable with playful, antagonistic teasing than with polite conversation. My mother is direct, demanding, and controlling, but in a palatably humorous way. For example, if someone places a foot on Mom's table and she decides in a rare moment of furniture awareness that she'd rather not have it there, she'll say, "What da Hell, were you born in a barn? Take your Goddamn foot offa my table!" This usually achieves the desired effect, which is a laugh, followed by the swift relocation of the suspect foot.

David's mother, who is perpetually mindful of her furniture, takes a more indirect approach. If a be-shoed foot verges too close to one of her clean white cushions, Ency will simply focus her gaze upon the trespassing appendage until its owner takes the hint.

As I imagine our parents' impending meeting, I see our fathers disappear into the TV room, where they loudly agree with a Fox News anchorperson. Robert regales my father with tales of life in Hungary under communism and Dad returns the favor by explaining to Robert the current state of the world in military terms. Meanwhile, over in the kitchen, my mother jokes to Ency that she should "make her own damn coffee." Realizing the miscommunication as Ency rushes to find a cup, Mom backtracks and says, "What da Hell are you doin'? Sit down, you're a guest, let me get it." They then retire to the living room, where they have a clear view of my nephews and niece running around the dining table and dragging a magic marker across the white carpet or the freshly painted wall.

Beneath their very different exteriors, however, Mom and Ency have a lot in common. They both strive, in their ways, to ensure the comfort of others; they love their children dearly and would do anything to see us happy; they were nervous and curious about meeting each other.

After I explained to my mother that Ency was a proper lady, one of good upbringing and acute attention to manners, she said, "So how do you want me to be? Phony-nice? Funny-entertaining?" It struck me that no matter how they behaved, our mothers' intentions were all good — they only wanted to make a positive impression for the sake of the family, because through David and me, they are family. Perhaps my worry was for nothing. After all, our parents are who they are, and we love them.

"You know what, Mom?" I said. "Don't be anything other than yourself, and we'll all have a great time."

# When Clans Converge

*"If I'd belched, I'd have cleared the table,*
*and some people would have passed out."*
— My father

It was decided months ago that if they wanted to jump into the deep end of the pool, David's family should meet mine for the first time on a holiday. The final head count for Easter dinner was 24, 19 of whom were related to me. When I passed along this information to David, he remarked, "I'm looking forward to seeing the bear on the unicycle and fez-wearing midgets riding by in a go-cart." Our families had been prepped. David's parents and sister were warned of bedlam and irreverence. I informed my brethren of their guests' perennial preference for propriety. "They don't curse," I'd explained to my perplexed parents. "They eat chicken legs with a fork and knife." I had to answer a series of questions regarding this fact before I could move on to the next. "Not one of their children has ever had a tattoo or exotic piercing. Conversations about bodily functions at the dinner table are right out."

David's parents stayed in a downtown hotel, while his sister, Michelle, camped on a futon in our living room. My cousin Jane from Staten Island, her husband, and their three children were staying at Mom's, or what I referred to as the "fun house."

"This might get confusing," I explained to David's family over breakfast at the Mission on Easter morning. "Today there will be two Janes, two Liams, and two Olivias. See, my *cousin* Jane has a Liam and Olivia. My *sister* Jane now has an Olivia, and my sister Heather has a Liam. It's easy, though, because with the kids, we say 'big or little Liam' or 'big or little Olivia' to indicate the older or younger ones; with the Janes, we just say 'cousin' Jane or 'sister' Jane, or we use their last names." Watching the looks of consternation grow on the faces surrounding me, I cheerily added, "You'll catch on."

Mom fretted over details. She'd had the house scrubbed, the yard relandscaped, the carpets cleaned, and the deck painted. She bought new towels for the bathrooms and made frequent trips to the grocery store. Michelle and David, however, seemed to be the most apprehensive. They struggled to prevent catastrophe by convincing their father not to wear his suit and desperately persuading me that applying red marker to the palms of my hands to simulate stigmata would *not* be as funny as I imagined.

Once through my Mom's door, we were presented with baskets of goodies. "The Easter bunny forgets no one," Mom said proudly. Thirty minutes after we'd arrived, David's mother, Ency, found me in the kitchen and said, "You overexaggerated, Barb; your family is so polite!"

"Just wait," I said, forebodingly. I hadn't told her they were "rude," but I *had* made it clear that my family's definition of the word was vastly different from hers. My mother also cornered me to complain about my misrepresentation. "Ency is *wonderful*," she said. "I was expecting her to be cold, but she's *warm*!"

"Mom, I told you she was 'proper' and 'elegant'; that doesn't mean 'tight-lipped' and 'cold,'" I replied.

David said that my family was the most "normal" he'd ever seen them, almost "too" normal. "I haven't heard anyone curse all day," he told me. "It's like *Invasion of the Body Snatchers*. It's creepy." He'd obviously missed my conversation with my cousin Jane in the back yard — in ten minutes, she'd dropped enough F-bombs to level Chicago.

While I was chatting with Ency and Michelle, my sister Jane appeared with little Olivia in her arms, and Michelle asked if she could hold her. As Jane transferred the pink-wrapped papoose into Michelle's arms, she said, "Don't worry, she shouldn't be too fussy. I just topped her off."

"You just what?" asked Ency.

"Did you give her one boob or two?" Mom shouted from across the counter.

"Two," Jane called back. Then, in answer to Ency's question, she said, "You know," pointing to her chest and then to the baby, "I topped her off. And she went to the bathroom, too. She's set for a while." Michelle and Ency raised their brows at each other and then turned their attention to the tiny, pacifier-sucking person between them.

Six of us bustled around the kitchen making last-minute preparations for the meal. Michelle helped Heather with the salad, Jenny and cousin Jane tended to different types of garlic bread, Mom kept an eye on the lasagna, and I sauced and cheesed dozens of chicken-parmesan cutlets. As the temperature in the room rose, so did the mingled scents of garlic, tomato, vinegar, and baked bread. Ency stood to the side, staring at us in awe. "I could never do this," she said. "I could never have this many people in my kitchen. It's amazing. I love watching the production."

As I had predicted they would, my dad and Robert, David's father, sequestered themselves in a corner of the living room and discussed politics with the enthusiasm of frat boys comparing notes on chicks and beer. I interrupted, telling them it was time to move to the table, where the chicken was already settled and losing heat. "What are you guys conspiring over here, anyway?" I asked my father.

"We're working on bringing you and David back to the fold," he said. Robert nodded emphatically.

"And what kind of fold might that be?"

"The right-thinking fold," Dad said.

"If this has to do with religion or politics, you can just forget it," I advised.

Dad directed his next words to Robert, who nodded along: "There are none so blind as those who will not see, none so deaf as those who will not hear."

"All right, all right, that's enough, you two," I said. *"Mangia."*

Robert, the archetypal patriarch, seemed startled by my tone. While in his castle, I do my best to pretend to be all the things I'm not — demure, submissive, secondary. At my mother's, the home that produced four strong, unyielding women, I can't help but hold my own. Robert half-teased my father, "What's this? First she runs the show with David, now she's telling you what to do?"

"That's right," Dad answered in kind. "I get no respect." Despite their Statler and Waldorf routine, the men obediently rose to their feet and walked to the table.

It would not have been practical to wait for every last person to settle into their seats before eating. Regardless, Ency and Robert waited patiently, as if for some kind of signal, to begin. Some were already eating. Finally, Ency asked no one in particular, "What should we do?" and I answered, "Eat," and took a bite of chicken to encourage her. Once she was convinced that enough people were chowing down, Ency allowed herself the first bite.

During the meal, Dad managed to slip in a suppository

joke. The chandelier above grew bright and dim, bright and dim, as Bella, on tiptoes, conducted scientific experiments on the rheostat. Like my sisters, I jumped in and out of conversations, keeping up with several of them at any given time. I intermittently glanced at Ency and Robert to see how they were holding up and often found them quiet, smiling, trying to take it all in.

When my sister Jane finished eating, she stood, grabbed her plate, and disappeared into the kitchen. Her husband, Simon, soon followed, then my cousin Jane, followed by her husband, Roger. Heather and Sean never even made it to the table; they had stayed in the kitchen, where they could see the dining room and still keep an eye on the children, who were parked in front of the blaring TV in the family room. "Where's everyone going?" Ency asked. In her house, people request permission to be excused before leaving the table. My family, accustomed to eating on TV trays or laps, sees no reason to regulate who stands or sits.

"They'll be back," my mother answered breezily.

Some wandered into the other room to check on the kids; a few returned to the table with their Easter baskets and nibbled on candy. Ency and Robert remained seated. Mom announced she was making coffee, and when Robert said he would like a cup, she asked, "Would you like regular or decaf?"

"Regular, please," answered Robert.

Mom guffawed, and said, "That's great because I don't even *have* decaf. I was going to *lie!*" She continued to laugh all the way into the kitchen, leaving the few people left at the table to stare after her in bemusement.

My family was scattered to the four corners of the house when Ency and Robert began to say their goodbyes. In her authoritative, no-is-not-a-word manner, Mom said, "So now you're going to do every holiday here, right? You're coming back for Thanksgiving, then Christmas, and then Easter again. Okay?" Before they had a chance to answer, Mom said, "Great, then it's settled." David and I caught each other's eyes, and agreed silently, *There's not enough wine in the world.*

 I'm fortunate to have suffered so few losses in life. When Grandmére, my father's mother and my favorite grandparent, died from emphysema, it all happened far away. The distance wasn't only physical — 2500 miles across the continent — but also emotional. I don't remember if it had to do with school, or money, or both, but attending the funeral wasn't an option for me. Because I grew up so far away from her, my grandmother's passing was not an emotional hit, but more of a cerebral shift, with no direct effect on my day-to-day life. I mourned her memory, and how special she'd made me feel as a child, but at the time I learned she'd succumbed to her illness, I honestly could not remember the last time I'd spoken to her.

Two of my brothers-in-law, Simon and Sean, have lost their mothers. I knew both women, two of the kindest souls I'd ever met, and I was heartbroken by their deaths, but heartbroken in a one-step-removed sort of way. Similar to losing Grandmére, it was a pain I felt more in the head than in the heart, particularly because I hadn't spent very much time with either of them.

The first death in the family to have a significant impact on me was that of my cousin, Jeffrey.

He was one of the first New York firefighters to arrive at the towers on 9/11. The event that shook the nation continues to send aftershocks of anguish throughout my family. "Never Forget" marked the tenth anniversary of Jeffrey's death.

# Never Forget

*"Firemen never die, they just burn forever in the hearts of the people whose lives they saved."*
— Susan Diane Murphree

Ten years, an even number, a milestone in time. We have this obsession with decades, and thinking they matter in some profound way. But it's not the anniversary that matters, it's the event, and the events on 9/11 were profound.

I couldn't tell you what I was doing last week. But I remember every detail of that day, the days that followed, that month ten years ago. Unlike the misty impressions of most things past, every emotion and tactile sensation I experienced on September 11, 2001 is well preserved, like a mosquito in amber, blood and wings intact.

I can remember the weight of the lined yellow paper in my hands, the one on which I'd scrawled the Prayer of St. Anthony, patron saint of all that is lost. My mother had asked her daughters to recite it every hour. It made us feel like we weren't so helpless being 3000 miles away, while all of the men in our family were there at Ground Zero, frantically searching through debris and body parts to find my cousin Jeffrey.

Four days later, I brought what was now a crinkly piece of yellow paper with me to Los Angeles, where I was hosting my birthday party. Jeffrey was still lost, and hope was fading, but my cousins, Jeffrey's brothers and brothers-in-law, were tireless in their search, despite the toxic dust, despite the horrific leftovers of life that they found.

I used my birthday as an excuse to escape. Jeffrey was older and way cooler than me, which was why I was always trying to impress him with my antics. During our last phone conversation months earlier, he had warned me about partying too hard. I can't remember his exact words — I'd blown off his concern, and the memory had receded into my mind, along with all of the others that didn't seem to matter at the time, the ones I wish I could get back.

As if rebelling could bring him round, I didn't heed my cousin's words. I remember every drug I took on that three-day bender, I recall each moment that I began to feel, to think again, which would motivate me to ingest more of this, or some of that, until the real world faded away and euphoria returned.

When the fog had finally lifted, when my body could take no more, I returned to San Diego. Hope of finding Jeffrey dwindled with each passing day. He was one of the first firefighters on the scene. His body was one of the last to be recovered.

Ten years. My dad is in New York right now, sitting beside his sister, my aunt, Jeffrey's mother. He was the youngest of her six children. Regardless of how many years have passed, when I see an image from that day, the amber is cracked, and my emotions, perfectly preserved, are released. That's why tomorrow, on what the news deems a significant benchmark in time, my television will remain off.

 As hard as Jeffrey's tragic death had been, it was the inevitable, expected passing of a man I'd never met in person that hit me the hardest. Love, connection… it sometimes appears where I least expect it.

# Guardian Angel

*"If Uncle Gerry can help you in any way,*
*you know the number."*
— Uncle Gerry

I think it's stupid to assign so much significance to last words, those final utterances of a dying man. As if his impending death adds an unprecedented depth to his sentiments. Stupid. And, yet, after I spoke into the phone — "Uncle Gerry? It's me. It's Barb" — and pressed the receiver so hard against my ear it hurt, my entire body ached with the need to hear one word, any word. I heard his voice as he half-gasped, half-moaned — *"Aaaaaahhh."* He made this sound twice. I almost said "I love you," but there wasn't time. Marcia was back on the phone. "I'll be up all night if you want to call later," she said. I removed the phone from my ear and glared at it as if it were somehow responsible for the sounds I'd just heard. I slid from my chair, onto my knees, and crawled from my desk to the drawers on the other side of the room. Silent, determined, I opened and searched the drawers, one by one, irritated by the steady stream of tears that blurred my vision. I finally found it between two folders, the 3- by 5-inch index card yellowed along the edges, creased down the middle from where it had once been folded. I held it in my hands, away from my face to protect it from getting wet, and began to read the handwritten words. Halfway through, when I reached the part that read, "I thought no one would ever cry over me," I made a tortured noise, not unlike the one I'd heard on the phone, and surrendered my body to convulsions, wails, and whimpers.

Uncle Gerry died in his sleep, eight hours after I tried to speak with him. For the rest of the day, I sat in my reading chair, my legs pulled in tight, my arms wrapped around my shoulders, rocking back and forth. My emotions vacillated between despair and puzzlement. When I wasn't sobbing, I wondered why I was taking it so hard — I never even met him in person.

My dad's cousin Gerry was drafted and sent off to Vietnam when he was still a teenager. While there, he was exposed to Agent Orange, an herbicide that was used to disintegrate the jungle — a toxic chemical substance that was later proven to cause a barrage of maladies in anyone unfortunate enough to have come into contact with it. People said it was the war that made him crazy. Could be. But I think it had more to do with what happened after he got back. Not the day he found his grandmother dead in the bathtub of her Brooklyn apartment and, with my grandfather's help, brought her body to the morgue. No, not that day; I am told he handled the situation like a man who'd grown used to carrying the dead. That was nothing compared to the bombshell dropped at the funeral. Gerry's dad, the man who was supposed to have died in the Korean War, which was the lie told to Gerry to spare him the truth — that he and his mother had been abandoned — materialized to pay his respects.

All of this happened before I was born. During my formative years, Uncle Gerry was just a guy who called once a week to talk to my dad or to check on my mother when my dad was temporarily stationed in some other Navy town. I was in high school the first time he called to speak with *me*. It was a few days after I'd hinted to my mom that something had happened to me, something involving a boy I knew, and, no, it wasn't "rape," I told her, "not really." She was hysterical for details, and I made her promise not to tell my father. She was quick to agree, probably because Dad had a lot on the line, a military job and a family to take care of, all of which would be lost if he did something stupid. Helpless and angry, Mom told Uncle Gerry, the family's protector-from-afar who had regularly insisted that should anything happen to her or any of her girls, she go to him instead of the police.

I didn't know why he was calling for me. We chatted about life, about school and stuff. Uncle Gerry was funny, he appreciated my irreverence, and that first day, we spoke for almost an hour. An underlying hint of a smile was evident in his tone and his laugh — a surprising gravelly giggle in contrast to his sonorous voice — was infectious. At the end of the conversation, his motives became clear. "Give me a name, Barb." I pretended not to know what he was talking about. "Come on, honey. I don't even need a full name. Just a first name, a nickname even. Where he hangs out. That will do." I pleaded ignorance and ended the phone call.

A few days later, Uncle Gerry called again. This time, he chatted with Mom for a few minutes before asking for me. Again, we spoke at length about life in general, mostly about how lucky I was to have my dad for a father — Dad represented everything Uncle Gerry had ever wanted to be. "Listen, honey," Uncle Gerry coaxed me, "I'm not looking to whack the kid, just to smack him, you know, send him to a hospital for a few weeks. He won't even know what hit him. Come on, now. Give me his name."

I never did.

The knowledge that I could, with a word, punish someone who had wronged me gave me a sense of empowerment. After a year, Uncle Gerry stopped asking me for a name. Instead, at the end of each of our talks, he'd say, "Anyone giving you a hard time? Hmm? You tell Uncle Gerry if anybody fucks with you, and I'll take care of it."

Uncle Gerry was a tough guy. He was known in New York as "Do Daly," the bouncer at many clubs, the guy who did the dirty work to collect money owed to the Hells Angels. He was big, over six feet tall and muscle thick. He had his mother's liquid-blue eyes and jet-black hair, which he wore to his shoulders. He was a champion of women, in a misogynist-meets-Don Quixote way. Uncle Gerry didn't think before he punched, especially if a woman's honor was at stake. Nearly every one of his arrest stories begins with, "This guy was harassing a lady in a bar." He had broken every bone in his hands countless times beating men unconscious. Once he was arrested for assaulting a police officer in a bar. Uncle Gerry had the man up against the wall by the throat and shoulder when the guy choked out the words, "I'm a cop!" My uncle's defense to the judge was, "Your honor, this man was being very rude to the young lady." When the judge asked Uncle Gerry what he should do with him, Uncle Gerry responded, "Your honor, I believe a severe verbal reprimand is in order." And that's all he got. Uncle Gerry was also a charmer.

Since that first phone call over a decade ago, my Uncle Gerry and I spoke regularly. We sent each other cards, pictures; sometimes he'd send me money. He told me how wonderful my father was, had always been. He confessed to me his fear that he would not be forgiven for his sins, to which I'd say, "I don't believe in Hell." At some point during every conversation, he would tell me how much he loved me. How much fun he had talking to me.

In recent years, Uncle Gerry's tiny Latina wife, Marcia, nursed her giant husband as his body deteriorated like the foliage in that jungle 40 years ago. When she spoke with my father a few hours after Uncle Gerry was no more, Marcia said, "Who will protect me now?" As if she hadn't realized he'd become an invalid.

Uncle Gerry was my glass box to break in case of emergency. Just knowing he existed made me feel safe. The offer stood — if I wanted someone, anyone, out of my life, all I had to do was make one phone call, no questions asked. I like to think that, in a fatherly way, Uncle Gerry was proud of me for never having taken him up on it.

 Jane is the eldest of the four girls in my family. As a kid, I barely saw her — I was in elementary school when she was in high school. But as grown-ups, she and I have grown tight. Partly because of our flexible work schedules, and partly because of our similar sensibilities (i.e., our appreciation for spa days and our affinity for overanalyzing every little goddamn thing that happens in the day). For a handful of years, Jane was over at my place at least three days a week, sharing my home office and assisting me in taking David on a long, slow road-trip to Crazy Town.

Jane remains my favorite real-life character to write about. She's unapologetic about her hilarious, adorable insanity, and although she sometimes balks, she still allows me to share the screwball situations she gets herself into. In "My Ask of Jane" and "Potty Princess," you can see how easy she makes it for David and me to mock her, and how well she takes it when we do.

 Jane. Oh, Jane. Jane, Jane, Jane, Jane, Jane. Many are the mornings that I roll over in bed to be greeted by her sunny smile. As my eyes work hard to adjust to the light and my brain floods my system with cortisol, there's Jane. "What's today's drama," I mumble. Lying next to me, Barbarella, with her arm extended holding her phone aloft, ignores my rhetorical question and pokes at Jane's face to accept her call.

Without even pausing to say hello, Jane launches into the crisis du jour. Perhaps Jane's annoyed that her daughter's coach is making a fuss because her kid, who didn't want to go to cheer class, faked a seizure. Maybe she's on the freeway and wants Barb to look up driving directions for her because she

didn't think to look them up *before* she
began driving toward her destination.
Or, perhaps today, she's convinced that
she's contracted mad cow disease from
the scalpel that she accidentally poked
herself with while dissecting a cow's eye
in her daughter's science class. Another
possibility is that she's at a loss because
she wants to get her nails done *and* have
the car washed, but doesn't know which
to do first. Or maybe she just wants to
know how to hard-boil an egg, or find
out if she's a bad person for buying those
new shoes. This early in the morning, it's
more likely a job-related crisis. Should
she send more cookies to this person
or that person? Is it weird to include
pictures of her family in a card to a
coworker?

I both love Jane and like her. She
is funny and entertaining, though not
always deliberately. She often seems a
bit ditzy, but I think she's just distracted.
The two main driving forces in her life
are her job with a major pharmaceutical
company and her family. She is so
ambitious and hardworking that she can
hardly think of much else other than her

job and how to help her two daughters become famous. And she worries. About everything. In fact, her worrying is on par with Barbarella, and that's saying a lot. Nearly every day, Barbarella talks her sister down from some absurd ledge that Jane has manifested in her mind. Jane is perpetually on the brink of crisis. Consequently, whenever we see or talk with Jane, her head is someplace else. It's entertaining for us, but I'm sure it must really leave Jane knackered.

# My Ask of Jane

*"People use jargon because they want to sound smart and credible when in fact they sound profoundly dim-witted and typically can't be understood, which defeats the purpose of speaking in the first place."*
— Karen Friedman

I am usually able to tune out my sister when she's yapping away on her phone in the office we sometimes share — her words burble behind me as I type and click about my own business. But every so often there is a distinct phrase that breaks through the sound bubble and jerks me to attention.

I was toggling between Twitter and Facebook the other day when one such cluster of sounds formed a jagged rock that hit me in the back of the head, causing me to turn around and stare in disbelief at the woman who threw it. "Really?" I said in a loud whisper, not wanting to disrupt Jane's business discussion, but unable to stifle my irritation. Eyes wide, I mouthed the offending phrase with exaggerated enunciation so my sister would know the source of my sudden ire.

"*MY ASK OF YOU?*"

Jane suppressed a giggle, made some spastic movement between shrugging and waving me off, and returned her full attention to the guy on the other end of the line. But she knew I wouldn't let it go. I never do.

As soon as I heard the telltale sound of Jane's conversation coming to a close — a drop in the energy of her voice — I turned around and stared at her until she put down her phone. "What?" she said in an overly defensive way that told me she knew exactly what.

"What the freak is 'My ask of you' supposed to mean?"

"It's, like, when you're requesting something from someone," Jane said.

"It sounds moronic."

"I didn't make it up — everyone says it," Jane countered.

"Well, then everyone's a moron. If you have a request of someone, why not simply say, 'Would you?' Please, Jane, promise me you won't ever say that again. I can't have a sister going around saying stupid shit like that."

"You think that's bad, you should hear the new one that's going around — I almost texted you from my meeting yesterday," Jane said. I braced myself and waited. Jane dragged out the silence for maximum effect. When she saw she was losing me, Jane finally said, "Servant leadership." I raised my brows. "I know," she said, "I didn't understand it. They kept saying it throughout the meeting; it was even highlighted on the board. It means, like, you have to lead by serving, so 'servant leadership.'"

David, who'd been down the hallway sorting laundry, poked his head through the door and said, "That makes absolutely no sense."

"It's what people say," Jane argued.

"People in middle management make up terms for things they want to say, but it would be so much better if they would just *say* what they want to say. Corporate-speak drives me crazy. You'll never hear an executive bloviating bullshit like that. They're too busy making decisions and getting shit done. That's why you're so successful in everything you do," I said to my sister. "You don't pirouette around a point in some awkward toe-step — you pin it down with a spike heel."

From what I witness and hear (not only from Jane, but also from friends who work for major corporations or smaller hifalutin' offices) I'm positive I couldn't survive in the corporate world. I had a friend in middle management at a major IT company. When I learned he insisted on having daily progress meetings with his staff, I was baffled. "Isn't that a waste of time?" I asked. "To take an hour out of each day to micromanage what everyone did the day before?"

He insisted it was helpful and necessary, but I couldn't help wondering if that was how he justified his position. On his conference calls, he used terms like "skin in the game" and "bubble it up." In emails to both his team and upper management that he asked me to help edit, I flinched at the words "synergy" and "incentivize," and phrases such as, "circle back" and "mission critical."

The term "stakeholder management" came up enough times that I went to look it up online and found this: "The art of acquiring enough opinions from people, groups, or leaders within a company to deflect blame if a project doesn't meet expectations and/or outright fails."

When I'm helping a friend in the corporate world write an email or prepare for a presentation (something I am often called upon to do), I don't have much patience for all the buzzwords and jargon. All those expressions with distorted verbs and made-up nouns make for an uncrackable code. But perhaps that's the point. How better to appear smart and seem like you know shit than to baffle your coworkers with verbiage that they are embarrassed to admit they don't understand for fear that they will come off looking unknowledgeable?

I'll look to the muddled gibberish on the screen, then turn to my friend and ask, "What is it you want to say?" Then I spend half an hour trying to convince him that the clear, concise explanation he just gave to me verbally is way better than the imbroglio he created in an email containing all those empty phrases.

I'm not immune to business jargon — some words leak out of tall buildings and onto the street, where they get picked up and carried into coffee shops and tattoo parlors. I've heard myself say things such as "touch base" and "reach out" when what I really meant was, "contact." But I see this as a minor infringement on straight-talk.

The next time I overhear my sister saying something asinine along the lines of "matrix partners," I am going to bring her to the table, where I can demonstrate my best practices and showcase my centers of excellence so that she'll realize how critical is the path she's on and recognize her core competencies so that going forward she can reassess her metrics and monetize her minutes. In other words, I'll tell her to knock it off.

# Potty Princess

*"The most important thing that parents can teach*
*their children is how to get along without them."*
— Frank A. Clark

The phone was ringing again. "Your turn," I said to David. He dropped the sheet he'd been folding onto the closet floor and hurried through our bedroom to reach the phone on the bathroom counter. As he ran, I could hear him mutter, "Jesus, leave us alone," under his breath and then an annoyed, "Hello?" Up until now, the calls had been from telemarketers (despite the dozens of lists we've been "removed from"). "Hang on, Jane, here she is." When I heard my sister's name, I set the towel I'd just folded on the pile before me and took the receiver from David, who quickly disappeared back inside our closet. I put the phone to my ear and heard screaming.

"Jane? What's going on?"

"Barb, I need your help." Her voice was raspy, barely there. The screaming continued in the background, making it even more difficult for me to understand Jane as she tried to explain. "We're potty-training Bella. Simon's out with his employees and he's not answering his cell phone, and Dad's out of town and Jenny's still in school or else I wouldn't have called you. I've been trying to get it off myself but I just can't do it alone, and I know how busy you are on Mondays but I just, I just, I just..."

"Hey, it's all right," I said. "I'm fine. We're just cleaning. What do you need?" Silence for a moment, Bella even paused in her screaming as though aware of the importance of her mother's next words.

"Bella has a toilet seat stuck on her head." Before I could laugh, the screaming returned full force and I said, "I'm on my way, Jane. Don't do anything else until I get there."

I answered David's expectant look with, "I've gotta run. Bella's got a toilet seat on her head and Jane can't get it off."

"Don't forget your camera," David called when I was halfway down the stairs.

"I'm on it!" I yelled back before the door closed behind me.

On the way there, I called my father, who punctuated his giggle with, "It's only funny if she's not hurt." I also called Jane to further assess the situation. Things seemed to have calmed down, or at least there was no more screaming.

"She's fine. I gave her a popsicle," said Jane. "She's not hurt, but I just need someone to hold her arms so I can get it off." Jane had been trying for 45 minutes to extricate her two-year-old daughter's head from the miniature seat, and the toddler was, understandably, fed up with the whole fiasco.

When I pulled up, Jane was standing in her doorway. As I approached, she began explaining again. "I couldn't take her to the hospital. Most of the doctors know me." Jane's a pharmaceutical rep. "I couldn't ask my neighbors. What would they think?" I nodded as she spoke and then stepped into the house.

There she was, that tiny body sitting on the edge of the brown leather chaise, with Bert, Ernie, Cookie Monster, and Big Bird all smiling up blankly from the oval around her neck. Her curly blond hair was tied up in a little bun with one silky tendril hanging down the left side of her face, half of which was sticky and orange. She was laughing at the characters dancing on the television screen. I took out my camera and shot a few pictures.

Then I turned back to Jane, who looked like she'd been wrestling with a bear. The thick, dark curls that frame Jane's delicate face had become an unruly mane, a frizzy fire burning up and out in every direction. On her petite frame, she wore striped flannel pajama bottoms and a cropped black V-necked tee. She looked exasperated. Exhausted. Embarrassed. She looked adorable. Who was the little girl I had come to help rescue? It certainly wasn't the teensy blond queen sitting confidently on her throne with a crown around her neck.

"Maybe you can put her on your lap and then grab her arms, like a straitjacket, and then I'll get it off her head," said Jane.

"Right. Let's not scare her, though. There's no need to do some kind of sneak attack." I didn't know that she had already tried to plead, bribe, and threaten Bella.

Distraction and action was the last resort of a frazzled woman. Jane had tied up Bella's hair because she couldn't see her ears, the real culprits in this situation, for the toilet seat kept getting caught on them. Poor Bella.

The plan worked. I lifted Bella like a watermelon and sat her on my lap. Jane crept toward us from the left and when she said, "Now!" I held my niece's arms firmly in mine, and Jane went to town on the toilet seat. Bella screamed. There was a moment of doubt as Jane and I searched her head for signs of wounds. Her little ears had suffered some — they were red, and one of them boasted a minuscule scrape no longer than my pinky nail.

I consoled the crying child while Jane ran to fetch her another Popsicle.

"Do you want a cup of tea?" she asked from the other side of the knee-high gate at the kitchen's entrance.

"Sure." After Jane disappeared around the corner, I watched as Bella, sporting a mischievous smile, applied the orange Popsicle to the brown leather in broad strokes.

"Uh, Jane? You might want to take a peek in here, Little Miss O'Keefe is creating a masterpiece on your furniture."

"Bella, NOOOO!" I probably could have stopped her myself, but in order for me to maintain my role as the favorite aunt, it is crucial that I never involve myself with anything relating to discipline. Jane, a stack of paper towels in hand, rushed in for damage control. Bella smiled as she watched her mother wipe the cushion and the floor.

"I just need to sit for a minute," croaked Jane. Her

voice was almost gone now, something she attributed to the previous day spent at a nut farm (a place up north where pumpkins and nuts were being sold, though if you had drawn other conclusions, I'd be the last to blame you). Nearly the whole family went to the nut farm — Heather and Sean, their two boys, Jenny, Mom, and Jane and Bella. I forget what I was doing that day, but I'm sure it was *very* important.

I added Splenda to my gingerbread herbal tea, and Jane sat across from me at the dining table. "Thank you so much. I know you're busy and I didn't want to bother you, but I really appreciate... what are you writing?" A note of hysteria entered Jane's voice.

"Nothing," I assured her. "If anything like this ever happens again, Jane, I don't mind coming to help. I don't live that far from you, so feel free to call me first."

"What do you mean, 'if anything like this happens again?' Nothing *like this* is going to happen again." Her eyes were darting back and forth between my notebook and her daughter.

"I'm just saying. *If.* I'm just a phone call away. All right, it's time for us to get some sleep." As is our custom, Jane and I kissed each other on each cheek and hugged. I held out my arms and Bella trotted toward me. As I squeezed my niece in an embrace, I whispered in her scraped ear, "Keep up the good work, Bella Boo."

# The Voices in  My Head

It wasn't long after we began dating that David noticed some quirks in my behavior. What neither he nor I had realized, was that these idiosyncrasies were merely symptoms of an underlying psychological issue (okay, probably more than one issue) that would take a few more years to come to a head.

In the beginning, it was all fun and games, mostly for David. He would conduct experiments, without my knowledge, to discover how deep my dysfunction ran. One such experiment involved my obsession with symmetry. We'd be at a restaurant with friends, and, unbeknownst to me, David would give them a heads-up and tell them what to be watching for. Then he would nudge a glass of ice water toward me until it grazed one of my wrists, which, in turn would trigger me to automatically adjust my arms and bump my other wrist against the cold glass to even out the sensation. It was only when everyone else at the table erupted in laughter that I became conscious of what I'd done. After a few, "you got me" type laughs, I got fed up with David's tests, and since then he has been kind enough to stop treating me like a lab rat.

I insisted, and still do, that my actions, which David maintains is proof of OCD, were merely "Minor Preferences."

 I find Barb's OCD to be very endearing. It's harmless and endlessly entertaining. I tease her about it, and occasionally amuse myself at her expense, but it's part of what makes Barbarella who she is, and I would miss it if it were gone. Her story, "Minor Preferences," is one of my favorites.

# Minor Preferences

*"But society has now fairly got the better of individuality; and the danger which threatens human nature is not the excess, but the deficiency, of personal impulses and preferences."*
— John Stuart Mill

"Careful, the plate is hot," she warned, before placing my dinner on the table, obviously unaware of the real danger of putting anything of extreme temperature (hot or cold) within my grasp. Reaching for the fork, my left thumb knuckle inadvertently brushed against the searing ceramic. As the sting of the burn ebbed, I intentionally brushed my right thumb against the plate. Still feeling uneven, working on compulsion, I deliberately touched each thumb to the plate again, applying equal amounts of pressure. I took a deep breath, steeling myself for the familiar urge that would direct every other finger to take its turn with the hot plate, but it never came. I sighed with relief, picked up my fork, and did my best to ignore David's knowing smile.

Early in our relationship, when I explained my symmetrical requirements, David was quick to turn my "issues" into a form of amusement. He still does. Just the other night, I was lying comfortably in bed, on the edge of sleep, when I felt it — a short puff of air that finished with a subtle pressure on the back of my left hand. I tried not to move. I knew that if I opened my eyes, I would see him watching me, waiting for me to "perform." I don't *have* to do it, I told myself. As if he read my mind, David said, "Yes you do." I don't *have* to... but I *want* to. Convinced of my self-control, I turned away from him (hoping he would think I was simply changing positions to enhance my comfort) and casually exhaled, fast and hard, as quietly as possible, on the back of my *right* hand. Missing nothing, David giggled, earning himself a healthy slap; this only made him laugh harder.

I've never been, nor will I ever be, "diagnosed" with Obsessive Compulsive Disorder (OCD). I'm not debilitated by my urges and impulses, as was Jack Nicholson's character in *As Good As it Gets*. I find it odd that more people haven't discovered the peace of mind that comes with maintaining a sense of order, however arbitrary and insignificant it may seem. I've heard it said that "victims" of OCD are subconsciously seeking to bring an element of control to their lives, which may otherwise be lacking. But despite being an avowed control freak, I don't believe that the specific things I do are manifestations of a perceived lack of control. I don't think of OCD (or at least my diluted version of it) as a "problem." As one might choose yellow over orange, I *choose* to do these "crazy" things.

One time, David and I were out for a stroll in our Kensington neighborhood. As we walked, chatting about our day, he paused in the conversation to ask, "What are you doing?"

"What are you talking about?" was my deft reply.

"I'm not sure, it's something in your step... did you just go out of your way to avoid walking on that line?" Playing dumb seemed ineffective, so I chose to fess up. I explained to my baffled lover that I wasn't exactly "avoiding" the lines, as much as I was ensuring that my feet passed over them sequentially. He looked befuddled, so I spelled it out for him: "I am adjusting my step so that my feet fall over these lines alternately. Right, left, right, left, without the same foot passing over the lines twice in a row. Okay?"

David smiled at me. A moment later, three syllables escaped from behind his Cheshire cat grin — "O. C. D." Determined to make him understand that my choices are not the result of a "disorder," I returned his grin with a smirk and spoke for the first time the words that would become my mantra of rationalization. "Minor Preferences, beh beh. I don't *need* my feet to step alternately over these cracks. I *prefer* to walk this way. So you see, I don't have OCD, I have *minor preferences*, like everyone else. Like the way you *prefer* one radio station over another, it's as simple as that." This may have made him laugh, but he had no argument, and I considered the battle won. But the war waged on.

Months later, I would again unsheathe my mantra in self-defense. Ascending the stairs at home, I muttered complaints to myself regarding the number of steps — 15, an odd number. David said he had never noticed how many stairs there were. Then, narrowing his eyes, he asked me why it mattered. I confessed that it bothers me when I can't climb a set of stairs beginning with my right foot and ending with my left. It's not as important for me to start with my right as it is for me to end with my left, so when encountering a staircase, I can tell at a glance whether or not it's "safe" to begin with my right foot. He actually pointed at me as he cried, "OCD!" I remained calm. "No, darling, what I meant was, I *prefer* to end with my left foot. It's not the end of the world if I can't — certainly I'd be able to get on with my day."

It's true, I can suppress the urges when situations require conformity, but not without some distress. When David wants to toy with me outside of the bedroom, he'll give me a sloppy kiss on one of my cheeks and refuse to kiss the other. This game has become familiar: I struggle to get his head into a position that allows me to press my unkissed cheek against his whisker-framed lips — he strains to deny me the sensation I crave, laughing, always laughing, until either I succeed, or he gives in. I admit I have fun with these games, partly because I know that my so-called strange urge will be sated. But not every situation is as preferable as I would like.

A creature of habit, it makes me happy to take a lunch break and go to my local *Subway* on El Cajon Blvd. Carlos, *El Jefe del Emparedado*, knows exactly what I like, because my order never changes (with the exception of the recent, and very bold, additions of pickles and olives to my turkey creation). The same bag of chips — Miss Vickie's Jalapeno flavor — is the perfect match. So perfect, that if the restaurant is out of them, I skip the sandwich altogether. My system of selecting and rationing chips is so complex, even I don't completely understand it. It was during a typical visit to *Subway* that David discovered yet another one of my minor preferences.

He always knew there was something odd in the way I consumed my lunch — a subtle, mystical pattern operating below the surface of our midday repast. This day he was eyeing my hands closely, trying to break the code. Aware of his attention, I feared for my chips. I don't mind if he takes one when I've just opened the bag, because I can adjust the soft/crunch, spicy/mild ratios to compensate for the loss. However, once past the Sandwich Failsafe Point (when I can count the remaining chips at a glance), losing one spells dining disaster. David's hand moved toward my pile of Miss Vickie's best, scooping up a chip. Instinctively, my hand shot out and clutched his wrist as I commanded him to release his tasty prey. When I realized what I had done, I felt guilty, humiliated, exposed as a greedy miser of crispy goodness — how could I not share my last bite with the man I love? I beseeched him with puppy dog eyes to understand my plight as my mouth told him to "back off, Buster, I've got plans for those."

His look of shock and hurt quickly gave way to a visage of queer understanding. He released the chip, even as I begged him to take it, the recognition of my inappropriate behavior overriding any sense of taste preference I had just moments before. "No, babe, it's okay, I don't need it," David said. "I know it's just one of your OCD things, and I don't want to disturb whatever formula you have going on there."

Intent on explaining my selfishness, I told him about my ratios; how particular combinations maximize the pleasure I derive from my simple lunch. Then I said, "NOT OCD. Minor preferences."

He smiled that knowing smile, and nodded his head. "Sure, babe. Whatever you say."

Everybody has a threshold for dealing with shit before they reach a point where they can no longer cope. In "Bad Santa," I wrote about reaching mine. At the time, it was confusing and frustrating, mostly because I didn't understand what was happening to me. It wasn't until after this event, and writing about it, that I realized I'd been documenting my first panic attack.

# Bad Santa

*"Love looks forward hate looks back,*
*anxiety has eyes all over its head."*
— Mignon McLaughlin

Everything had been going so well. The Seattle sky was uncommonly clear for December. The overall atmosphere was festive and convivial. With a cup of Bailey's-spiked coffee in hand, I pranced around the gallery answering questions and volunteering information about David, the star of the show. For most of the evening, I was *on* — speaking energetically about David's work, explaining his process and adding my own flourish ("When he took this one, I stayed in the car so I could avoid mosquitoes and play Scrabble on my phone"; "He had to brave 11-degree weather in the middle of February in New England to get these two shots"; and "David's modest about his success, but I'm not — his work is sold in galleries from L.A. to New York and from Zurich to Tokyo." Gallery employees made their rounds, greeting visitors and keeping people from accidentally backing into the artwork by regularly announcing, "You scratch it, you own it." Two hours passed like minutes; the lights were dimmed to signify the end of the show, and the crowd was asked to leave, save for the chosen guests who would retire upstairs for the private reception party. I was looking forward to getting off of my feet, relaxing with a glass of wine, and chatting with new and old friends over the meal that had been prepared by the gallery's owner. I was on my way to do just that when a flash of red caught my eye. It was the shimmer of a Santa hat, shaped stiff and tall like a dunce cap, covered in red glitter and perched atop the head of a tall, wiry man. He was older, his silver hair and beard trimmed close, his gray suit tailored, his Converse sneakers red to round out his festive attire. At a glance, he appeared to be a distinguished gentleman with a playful pinch of panache.

My first inclination that something was wrong came just after the man did a little hop-skip-and-a-jump and then stepped back as if to bow to the lady before him. From where I stood, nothing seemed amiss. But then Nina, a gallery employee, darted over and led the unconstrained man away from the pictures he had come close to "owning." My body tensed in apprehension as the sloshed Santa made his way to the private event, and my eyes widened in horror as, watching him greet people along the way, I realized that he had been *invited*.

I don't see anything wrong with getting tipsy, especially in the winter season of eggnog and brandy, but it was 8 p.m. on a Thursday, and this guy was already more plastered than the gallery walls. A friend handed me a glass of champagne, and I turned to take stock of the hors d'oeuvres that were on a table. The hairs stood on my neck when the sparkling red cone popped into view. My stomach turned as I watched the soused Santa lean over and plant his face just millimeters away from the platters of food as he sniffed and examined each offering. I decided I could hold out until dinner.

I didn't have to wait long. An announcement was made for the 20 or so guests to go back downstairs and help themselves to the buffet. I was standing to the side, speaking with Nina, when I felt an elbow at my back and stepped forward. When a second offending nudge followed, I interrupted Nina and said, "We need to move, I can't have someone pushing on me like this." As if on cue, the man in the festive dunce cap, who turned out to be the source of the back jabs, came around to face me. Unsteady on his feet, he leaned in too close and blathered, "You know these are called temples," then lunged for my red-and-black frames.

"Hey! How about you don't touch me?" I snapped, taking a step back. He continued to ramble about temples and eyewear, to which I said, "Great, sounds good, whatever it is you're saying. I'm going over there." I rolled my eyes at Nina and put some space between myself and the inebriate.

From a few feet away, I watched the disaster unfold as the guy tried to negotiate the buffet table. First, he knocked all of the plastic knives onto the floor. Then he grabbed the long serrated bread knife and stabbed at a loaf. I couldn't keep myself from intervening, "Hey, you — the last person in here who should be holding a knife — there's a big basket of bread already sliced right in front of you." After missing a few times, the man finally seized onto a slice and slurred a thank you. I grimaced as he confronted the butter and then watched him stumble to a seat, after which I quickly collected my food and hustled to the opposite end of the building where I parked myself on a couch with David's sister Michelle. David sat on a chair across from us, and everyone began to eat.

I thought the worst was over. I thought that once I was away from that guy everything would be fine. I took a bite of my food, but it turned to dirt in my mouth and I spit it into a napkin. A woman sat in the chair next to Michelle and struck up a conversation with the siblings. I winced as a stabbing pain began to shred my abdomen, and pasted a blank smile on my face as I bit the inside of my cheeks to distract myself from the agony in my belly. I dropped my plate on the table and sat back. At one point, Michelle turned to me with a conspiratorial smile on her face, her lips moving. I mimicked her smile, sensing her intention to share an inside joke, but I hadn't heard what she'd said. In fact, I realized, as my heart began to beat faster, I hadn't heard anything — the room was full of moving mouths, but my ears were inundated with a resounding silence, interrupted only by the voice in my head, which sounded strangely like my own, saying, "I need to get out of here. I need to get out of here," over and over and over.

"Are you okay?" It was David. I hadn't heard the words, but the question was written all over his face. I shook my head, left to right.

I heard Michelle as if we were underwater, "I've never seen you look so flushed before, Barb. Your face is beet red. Are you hot?" My eyes widened, my jaw remained clenched. Without saying a word, I stood and walked through the dining room, down the back stairs, and into the gallery storeroom, where I could be alone with my thoughts, the first of which was, *What the hell is wrong with you?* I wondered if I was having some kind of allergic reaction to the food and then remembered I hadn't swallowed my first bite. My body seemed to be under attack, but if that were the case, where was my attacker? I'd heard of "panic attacks," but I always thought that was when someone freaked out over some irrational fear. My evening had been wonderful, full of great conversation and incredible compliments to my man — what was there to be *afraid* of?

I breathed deeply, savoring the solitude. Once I relaxed, I decided to go back upstairs, but then the mere thought of rejoining the party caused me to double over in pain as my insides twisted in protest, and I felt the blood rushing back to my face. Suddenly, the image of the man in the Santa hat popped into my head. I noted that his appearance at the gathering had coincided with the onset of my discomfort. But *why?* Why would some drunk guy upset me to the point of needing to hide in a storeroom in order to breathe? Neither of my parents was an alcoholic. As I thought about it more, I realized it wasn't the alcohol on his breath that had disturbed me — it was his behavior, his sloppiness, his apparent inability to control himself.

Maybe I had been afraid of something after all. Maybe seeing that man reminded my nerves of the one dread I have above all others — the one that causes me to alternate my feet over the cracks in the sidewalk, that requires me to methodically burn the tips of my other nine fingers should the tenth have foolishly brushed against something hot, and that compels me to arrive two hours early for a movie so that I can be assured of sitting in "my" seat — my fear of losing control.

 "What are you thinking about?" Barbarella asks.

"Nothing," I reply.

"C'mon, you're thinking about something. What is it?"

"No, really." I insist, "Nothing. I was just sitting here enjoying the sun and the air and my mind was completely blank."

This is impossible for Barbarella to comprehend. Her mind is never blank, not for an instant, not ever. In fact, it is about as far from blank as one can be while still functioning more or less normally. Her head is a very noisy and crowded place filled with many voices competing for her attention. All the time. She's usually thinking (or perhaps fretting would be a better word) about six or eight different things simultaneously.

It's like a multitrack recording in her brain, except that instead of instruments and voices blending harmoniously, one track is a panicked voice telling her there is no time to get her work done, another is a bully telling her she is ugly and worthless, a third wonders if she's crazy, a fourth is feeling guilty for not going to her two-year-old nephew's birthday party, a fifth worries that people won't like her. There's a voice worrying about food in the fridge that has passed its expiration date, a voice that really wants to watch that new pay-per-view movie, a voice feeling bad that she hasn't stopped by her friend's restaurant in a long time, a voice petitioning her to book a trip, a voice that urges her to lure

that hummingbird outside the window
into the house, a voice wondering what
to write about next, a voice trying to
persuade her that I probably won't mind
if she brings home a sugar glider, a voice
worried that a spider will crawl into her
ear and lay eggs while she sleeps, and
so on. And they never stop. It must be
exhausting. It exhausts me just thinking
about it.

We might be sitting on the outside
patio of a restaurant; it's a beautiful day
and I am feeling relaxed. I'm enjoying
my food, sipping my wine and, in the
back of my head, I am vaguely aware of
my surroundings. I know there's music
playing, but I'm not necessarily paying
attention to what song it is. I see that
there are other patrons around me, but
I don't pay them much attention either.

Not only does Barbarella know what
the people around us are talking about,
she's analyzing their accents, their body
language, their clothing, and what they
are saying so she can fully understand
the relationship between each person.
She watches how the patrons interact
with the waitstaff, and she scrutinizes the

microexpressions on our server's face
when she stops by our table — Barb is
worried that our server is having a tough
day, or perhaps she doesn't like us. Barb
knows what song is playing. She worries
about the potential for our server to be
inconvenienced by the patron next to us
who decided to scoot his chair around to
the side of his table. She eyes the take-out
container I placed on the concrete wall
next to me, fearing bugs may crawl into it.
And she is concerned that after she finishes
her glass of wine she might want to order a
Spritz, but that by then the air temperature
may have dropped, so she's not sure if a
Spritz would be too cold for her. Barbarella
sees, hears, and analyzes *everything*. She is
like Neo in *The Matrix*, if Neo were played
by Woody Allen.

I patiently reassure Barb that that
our server is a pro and if she needs that
person to move his chair back she'll
let him know, and I am sure that that
she doesn't hate us, and no, bugs can't
get into our take-out container, and so
on. I spend a fair bit of time each day
Ghostbusting Barb's demons.

I have tried to offer you a fleeting

glimpse of what daily life with Barbarella might be like. However, as I read over my words, I realize how massively inadequate they are. To try to understand the immense complexity of Barbarella and her thoughts from what I have written here is like trying to comprehend the vastness of the U.S. Mint by holding a roll of quarters in your hand.

# Matters of the Heart

*"When I look at my hands and in my heart,*
*I see stress as Lady Macbeth saw blood."*
— Berri Clove

I was going to tell him after we'd ordered our entrées, but I had not yet finished questioning my motives. Was I seeking attention? I knew he'd probably worry if I told him, and worry is a form of attention. If not for attention, could it be that I was soliciting some kind of pity? Or maybe I was just looking for an excuse for my erratic behavior. While David sipped his wine, my inner voices suggested possibilities, each louder than the one before, until the noise was so deafening I had to ask him to repeat what he'd said. A comment about the

Grenache, how nice it went with his soup. Here I was, undergoing a self-inflicted mental Spanish Inquisition, and his only concern was how well the wine was paired? Enough was enough.

"My heart has been skipping all day," I blurted, wishing I hadn't.

"What do you mean?"

I had to think about that one. What did I mean? After a moment of silence, I answered, "It's probably nothing, but, well... like, it's been skipping beats, and sometimes beating really fast, and sometimes, when it skips, I have to cough to catch my breath."

David — my partner, my lover, my constant companion — looked horrified. "I think that's called arrhythmia." He whipped out his iPhone and commenced googling.

"I'm the epitome of health," I said. It occurred to me that what I'd wanted was for him to say it was no big deal, that I was being dumb to even mention it. I wanted him to reassure me that my little skips should draw no more alarm than a mild case of hiccups.

"You could die of arrhythmia," David said, dashing my hopes for a quick end to the discussion. "It says right here that arrhythmia can be caused by smoking—"

"I haven't smoked in over five years," I countered.

"And excessive drinking—"

"I'd hardly call the wine I occasionally drink with dinner 'excessive,'" I reasoned.

"Stress." David paused in expectation of being interrupted, but this time my mouth remained shut. "And caffeine," he concluded. "How many coffees do you drink a day? That's it, no more caffeine." He may as well have said, "Hey, watch while I torture and kill this kitten."

"There has to be another way," I whispered. How would I survive without my mind-clearing fixes of hazelnut coffee, shots of espresso, and Diet Coke?

The topic was tabled when our entrées were set before us. I steered the conversation toward our plans for the week ahead and refrained from mentioning the intermittent cough-inducing palpitations I experienced throughout the meal. During the natural lulls that come with chewing and sipping, I contemplated the erratic beating of my heart. The amount of caffeine I consume is ridiculous, and it's true I've been a little Britney lately, what with a few random panic attacks and unwarranted freak-outs. But why the stress?

"Hey, you have your elevens, what's up?" David asked, indicating the two lines that appear between my brows whenever I'm distressed.

"I'm trying to figure out what it is that stresses me out," I said.

"Everything," David offered. In response to my bewildered expression, he elaborated: "Every day you have a hundred worries — you worry whether someone is going to be on 'your' elliptical at the gym; you worry you might catch a disease from the crosswalk button; you worry there might be cilantro hidden in your food; every time we're in the car you worry that your engine might be on fire; and you're terrified of public restrooms. I could go on and on and on. And you wonder what might be causing you stress?" He sounded exasperated. I could do nothing but hang my head in defeat. David was right. There are few things in life that don't cause me stress.

As soon as I walked through our door, having already promised David I would restrict my caffeine intake, I set about researching ways to reduce stress. Most of the websites I visited advised their high-strung readers to "eat right" and "exercise." But I already work out at least four days a week, and my diet is healthy and varied (aside from the unrestrained consumption of caffeine, of course, but I'd already resolved to adjust that). As I continued reading, I kept coming across the same method being touted by experts as the panacea for all anxiety-related woes: yoga.

The majority of people I know have tried yoga at least once, and a significant number of them swear by it. Even my dad is a fan. "It's very good for your chakras," Dad once told me. "You want to keep those things open and get them flowing. My favorite poses are the corpse, the warrior, and the downward-facing dog — that one looks really simple, but it's a bitch for me." He could have been speaking Urdu for all I understood. To me, yoga has always been like Scientology — a mysterious cult with a flair for fostering starry-eyed devotees. Still, hoping that it might help alleviate the pressure on my pumper, I decided to suppress my judgment of the unknown and give it a try.

I looked to like-minded friends for advice — people who practiced yoga, but didn't buy into the cosmic hoopla. Amy sent me information on the studio she attends. After I expressed my reluctance to attempt my first pretzel poses in public, Ronaldo suggested I try *yogatoday.com*, a site that offered free instructional videos I could follow in private.

I went to the site and launched a video for beginners. A blonde woman seated on a grassy knoll appeared. Between inhales and exhales that seemed to go on FOR-EV-ER, she introduced her two companions. The introductions took three minutes. My frustration grew, as, like the scenic brook behind her, she continued babbling about her heart and the earth and the rivers in her body. "Enough with the heavy breathing! Just tell me where to put my freakin' foot, for Christ's sake!" I snapped at the screen. "Jesus, like I want to sit here all day listening to some hippie on Quaaludes wax poetic about ashanti-majumbo-shakira?"

"What's going on?" David had followed the sound of shouting into my office.

"She won't shut up about her rivers and chakras

and stop her heavy breathing long enough to teach me a pose," I complained. "And she talks so *slooowww*. Jane was right," I continued, invoking my eldest sister. "If I want to relax, I should just get a massage." Jane had also said that she found yoga to be more stressful and annoying than relaxing.

David was laughing. I slapped at the keyboard until the woman was silenced and turned to find him holding his stomach, presumably from the pain of laughing so hard. "And what, may I ask, is so funny?"

David's eyes were welling up with tears of hilarity. Between gasps for air, he said, "That's the whole point!" and then fell back into a fit of laughter that eventually tapered to giggles, allowing him to explain himself while basking in the heat of my glare. "Yoga is all about breathing," he chuckled. "It's supposed to be slow and relaxing. You're like an alcoholic complaining that there's no open bar at the AA meetings." David grinned with amusement.

"She sounds like she smoked a big spliff," I muttered. "I don't have patience for people who talk that slow. I just want to learn the poses without having to listen to some new-age hippie bimbo trying to speak Hindi."

"Look," David said, with a note of compassion. "Maybe yoga isn't for you."

"But all the websites said—"

"*Shh*," he interrupted. "All they said was that if you

want to stop suffering the effects of stress, you need to find ways to relax. I think I might be able to help you with that." His amused grin morphed into a devilish smile.

"Oh yeah? And how's that?" I prompted.

"A glass of wine, a hot, fragrant bath, and me," he said.

My heart beat a familiar, comforting rhythm in my ears. I shut my laptop, accepted David's outstretched hand, and said, "Lead on, maharishi."

 Like different flavors of ice cream, it would be easy to think of Barbarella's various flavors of crazy as being separate and distinct from one another. However, when you get right down to it, it's all just ice cream. Barbarella's ice cream is control.

All of Barb's neuroses stem either from her trying to control the world, or the distress she experiences when she feels she is not able to. Barb is comforted by certainty. If something is uncertain, as are most things in life, she worries about it.

But Barb's neuroses are not all dreads and meds. On a positive note, the same control issues that drive her to sit with her back to the wall, and insist on being the one to pilot the car, are what motivate her to be so ambitious. She quickly rises to the top — to a position of control — of any endeavor she puts her hand to.

Barb's OCD is also a way of taking back control — she can control which foot lands first at the top of the stairs; she can make it so she doesn't step on a crack; she can tame Nature's chaos by tweezing her eyebrows; she can ensure that every bite of her sandwich has the perfect combination of flavor and texture; and if one hand grazes a cold water glass, she can touch the other one to the glass to restore balance.

I try to comfort and guide Barb through her inner storms, be they a light drizzle or a Category 5 hurricane. Nothing in this world hurts me more than to see her suffer. I still cry when reading her stories about some of the worst moments.

On occasion, I've walked into
a room to find Barb huddled in a
corner, clawing at her neck, rocking
back and forth with a crazed, wide-
eyed stare. I've watched, terrified,
as she repeatedly smacked her head
so hard I feared she'd give herself
a concussion. I've seen her punch
herself in the gut and scratch at her
eyes. And I've seen her experience
panic like none I've ever seen before.
During the worst episodes I feel
scared and helpless. I wrap my arms
tight around her to keep her from
harming herself. I rock her gently,
tell her that everything's going to
be ok, and try to exorcize whatever
demon triggered her attack. But logic
is no match for primal emotions such
as panic and fear. No matter how I
might try to explain that this week
has just as many hours in it as every
other, or that her workload is no
heavier now than it was before, her
brain won't accept the conclusion.

# Dark Night

*"If depression is creeping up and must be faced,*
*learn something about the nature of the beast:*
*You may escape without a mauling."*
— Dr. R.W. Shepherd

By the time I turned off the faucet, something within me had shifted. It must have happened while I was washing my hands because I remember feeling normal when I entered the bathroom. I removed my glasses, set them on the granite counter beside the sink, and positioned my face an inch away from the mirror, where I could see every clogged pore, every unauthorized brow hair. Fingers that seemed to belong to someone else besieged my face, pushing here, pinching there, until my reflection appeared Picasso-esque to my mind's eye — all nose, chin, and cheek, more an accumulation of features than a coherent image I would ever recognize as me. I switched off the light, felt my way to the towel rack, grasped it with both hands, and pressed my forehead against the wall.

I'm not sure how long I stood there in the dark, devoid of thought or motivation to move. But when I heard David's voice in the other room asking if I was okay, it occurred to me that what I was doing might be perceived as "not okay." I extracted myself from the bathroom and joined David in the kitchen, where he was loading the dishwasher. "Hey, there you are," he said. "How are you doing?" I smiled blankly, said I was fine. Then I caught a glimpse of the digital clock on the microwave. It read 12:34 a.m. — A.M.! Pressure must have been building beneath my consciousness because suddenly my brain erupted with thoughts, an army of words and ideas that, like so many stars in the sky, were impossible for me to keep track of.

I grabbed a sharp plastic toothpick and absentmindedly probed and jabbed at my teeth, working out broccoli bits and black pepper as I watched David finish. Once he'd wiped down the counter, David looked up and a peculiar expression came over his face. "What's wrong? What's on your mind?" he said.

Speaking around the toothpick, I said, "Nothing," and continued poking at my teeth. David waited. "I mean nothing's wrong," I said, still thrusting at my gums. "It's just that I'm looking at the time and I'm trying to figure out how to plan tomorrow — I wanted to wake up early and go to the gym before that meeting I have downtown, but now that I see how late it is, I don't think there's enough time for me to get there and get back and shower and dress, and then I guess I'm thinking about all the other things I want to get done tomorrow, all those emails I haven't responded to, those calls I have to return, and it's just, well, it's just... maybe I'm a little overwhelmed. But I feel fine; I really do."

I mustered a smile, half of which was blocked by the toothpick. David put one arm on my shoulder, and with the other, he snatched the mangled toothpick from my fingers. He turned around to throw it away, saying, "I don't know what you were doing to yourself there, but I think you're done with — Hey, hey, what is it?"

I broke into sobs, huge heaving sobs, flooding my face with tears. I shook my head back and forth as I wept — I had no answer for him. My day had been ideal: I'd attended a step class with my sister Jane in the morning, helped her out in the afternoon by silently reading a book while her baby daughter napped, then shared wine, snacks, and a slide show of our recent excursion with guests. There was simply no reason for my behavior.

I tried to escape David's embrace, turning left, then right, but his arms were always there. He repeatedly asked me what was up, but I had no words to offer him. He kept trying to catch my eye, but I glared wildly away, afraid of the care and concern I might find on his face. Words bubbled inside me, and I eventually managed to get them out: "Don't you see? That toothpick was holding everything together," I said, braving a peek at David's face. "And when you took it away, I fell apart." David chuckled.

For a moment, I was irritated with myself for the unfounded melodrama, but then a surge of emotion — a cross between anxiety and agony — washed over me, and the next thing I knew I was gasping for breath. Between gulps for air I murmured, "I can't... I can't do it... it's too much... there's no time."

David valiantly tried to keep my cheeks dry, but I was too much for his sleeves. In his naturally soothing voice, he said, "C'mon, take some long, deep breaths. Look, you don't have any more on your plate this week than you did last week. You'll get it all done. Everything's going to be just fine. Now please stop scratching at your neck." He grabbed my hand and held it. "Come on, it's late. You don't have to go to the gym in the morning; you don't have to go to the party tomorrow night. There's plenty of time for everything." I took a deep breath and let it out slowly, feeling myself calm down. "Stay right here," said David. "I'm going to go get you something to help you sleep."

Filled with neurotic energy, the idea of lying down horrified me. "I can't go to sleep," I called into the other room. "I mean, I don't want to. I'm not tired." David returned and handed me half of a Xanax. "I don't need this," I said. "I'm fine." He smiled and then proffered a bottle of water. I took it. "I still don't want to go to bed, though," I said.

"Well, what do you want to do?" David asked. I looked around, frantic for a task.

"I'll wash the dishes."

"I already did that," said David.

"No, you loaded the dishwasher," I said. "I'll wash the dishes by hand."

David shrugged and stepped aside so I could get to the sink. For 20 minutes I fixated on the hot water as I scrubbed away the demons. When I'd finished, I was physically and emotionally exhausted. I turned off the water and David appeared at my side. "Are you ready for bed now?" he asked. David led me upstairs, where I crawled beneath the comforter and pressed my face to the pillow. As the fog of sleep began to envelop me, I mumbled to David, "You don't think I'm crazy, do you?"

I wasn't awake long enough to hear his reply.

 Most people consider mental illness to be the sort of thing to keep private. But I'm not most people. Not only did I publicly share my step-by-step descent into madness, I also broadcasted my decision to get medicated. This was risky, in that I feared what people might think of me. But, despite my worries (and the occasional troll or schadenfreude-motivated hater)

the reaction to my confession was surprisingly rewarding. After "Happy Pill" was published, I received several emails from readers who wanted me to know that my confession had encouraged them to stop fearing the stigma they'd associated with the idea of needing professional help, and a few of them had already made appointments with a doctor to discuss their depression.

# Happy Pill

*"Nobody realizes that some people expend tremendous energy merely to be normal."*
— Albert Camus

I stole a glance at the elderly couple seated to my left and wondered what they were in for. Dementia? No, they looked sad, and sadness requires a certain awareness. Must be depression. Whatever it was, I knew it had to be specific. A general sense of ennui was insufficient here. You don't show up at a psychiatrist's office with a measly case of the blues; you show up with a Dumpster-full of drama.

Against the wall opposite me was a man in a highly decorated Army uniform. His presence in the cramped waiting room confused me — this wasn't a military facility. Maybe he didn't want a diagnosis for post-traumatic stress disorder on his official record. To the man's left sat a woman, watching over a child who was playing with toys on the floor in front of her. I hoped they weren't here for the kid. I don't like the idea of medicating children. Drugs are too easy a fix to mute irritating behaviors, most of which are natural for ankle-biters (loud, rambunctious, easily distracted). Chemicals don't belong in little bodies that are still developing.

The wall separating the psychiatrist's office and the waiting room was too thin. Even when the elderly couple disappeared, they were plenty audible; I couldn't make out exact words, but I was able to pinpoint who was speaking and, by the tenor of their voices, whether or not they were upset. I made a mental note to keep my voice down once I got on the other side of the door.

I nervously pinched the skin on the back of my wrists. It was two years ago that I first attempted therapy, that time with a psychologist. She had me write my thoughts on a piece of paper, after which she replaced words like "should" with less judgmental words, such as "could." I found the method patronizing, and after three sessions, I figured it would be a lot cheaper and less aggravating for me to "shoulda-coulda" myself at home.

I loathed the idea of having to do it all over again, to confess my uncontrollable anxiety to some new stranger whose methods I might consider even more asinine than repetitive writing exercises. So, why was I sitting in this chair, listening to Charlie Brown's grandparents squawking incomprehensibly on the other side of a flimsy wall? Hadn't I gone two years without this? Hell, my whole *life?* My heartbeat sped up as I contemplated leaving — the no-show fee was a small price to pay for my dignity. But then the door opened. The older couple emerged, their sadness lightly veiled with wispy smiles as they thanked the doctor. I heard my name called, and like a good girl, I hopped up, shook the doctor's hand, and followed him into his office.

I'd spent days rehearsing what I'd say to him; I didn't want to get it wrong. I approach everything in life as a test, pass or fail, and to fail is to die. It's that "life or death" feeling that finally drove me to seek professional help.

Two weeks before my appointment, I'd had an episode. On a particularly stressful day, with an assignment due and a growing list of tasks, one negative email was the bump that knocked me from a perch at the edge of my sanity. I'm not sure how much time passed before David found me standing in the corner of my office, bawling at my bookshelf. Embarrassed and exposed, I began to hyperventilate. Fearing I might never again catch my breath made it impossible to do so. Dizzy from lack of oxygen, I swayed backward, but David caught me and guided me to a chair. It was the closest I'd ever come to fainting. The most frustrating thing about the whole scene was the realization that I had not been in control of my body. The next day, I made an appointment with the doc.

"So, what brings you here today?"

It was a simple question. I opened my mouth to form the answer I'd practiced: "I have anxiety issues. I think Valium might help." But when I opened my mouth to speak, all that came out was, "I..." Something cracked in the back of my throat and I erupted, a Vesuvius of tears flowing over my cheeks, collecting at my chin, and burning through my shirt like lava.

My promise to myself completely forgotten, I sniveled and wailed without heed to how I might sound to the people in the waiting room. At the end of our meeting, the doctor expressed his opinion that I required something more serious than Valium. I was unprepared for such a recommendation. My apprehension toward antidepressants is ironic considering my liberal attitude toward recreational drugs. I told him I needed some time to think (i.e., obsess) about it. I wiped my tears, slapped an optimistic grin on my face, and bid the doctor goodbye. I did not allow my smile to falter until I reached the privacy of my car.

Two days later, I stood in the kitchen with David,

eyeing a small white pill in my hand. "What if you like the new me better than the old me? Will you resent all the drama you had to go through unnecessarily? What if I have side effects?" David stifled a laugh. "What?" I asked.

"I was just thinking that maybe one of the effects of the medication will be the loss of your 'what ifs,'" he said.

"What if I like myself this way? I mean, I do like myself. I'm afraid of not feeling like *me*."

"Maybe this will allow you to really feel like you. You know, like you were when we were on vacation in Italy — happy, carefree, not curled up in the corner crying and smacking your head," David said. He used his thumb to brush a tear from my cheek. "If you don't like it, you can always stop taking it," he said.

"What if you do like me better when I'm on it, and then I stop taking it and I go back to how I was, knowing that you liked me better another way?"

David shook his head, put his hands on my shoulders, and positioned his face so close to mine our noses almost touched. "I *love* you. Just as you have been, just as you are, just how you will be," he said. "So take your pill, and let's grab some lunch."

# Classic Barb Guy

*"Love is when you can be your true self with someone,*
*and you only want to be your true self because of them."*
— Terri Guillemets

It was two years ago this month that I sought pharmaceutical assistance for my chronic anxiety. It took awhile to get the dosage right — it was four or five visits before I could talk about my condition to my doctor without getting teary-eyed. Once I had adjusted to the meds, my threshold for handling day-to-day tasks and larger, more stressful burdens had risen so high it seemed I could handle anything thrown my way. I'd never intended to stay on the anti-anxiety meds forever, but I never really considered going off them either.

A few months ago, I sensed I was in some kind of rut. Despite the "spring forward" time change, my days had gotten shorter. This was because I was sleeping in later and later, reluctantly dragging myself out of bed at around 10 a.m. I couldn't remember the last time I'd been to the gym. None of my clothes fit, and I barely seemed to care. It occurred to me that I had no sense of urgency. The stuff that used to drive my panic-fueled engine was gone; from the look of things, it had been gone for a while.

"I want to stop taking Lexapro," I said one

afternoon while waiting for my lunch to finish microwaving. David shot me a wary look before he forced a calm, open expression onto his face. "I've been researching it," I continued, "and I'm really bummed, because from what I'm reading, the withdrawal symptoms are going to suck, big time. But if it sucks to get off of it, I should do it now rather than later, right? I mean, I never wanted to be on it forever."

I watched carefully for David's reaction, gauging every micro-expression that might convey to me what his words couldn't. Basically, I wanted to know if the most important person in my life could tolerate the old Barb, panic attacks and all.

"Let's see how it goes," David said. His face relayed the rest, or at least how I interpreted his subtle twitches: *I'm apprehensive; there was a reason you went on these meds; I worry about you.*

He insisted aloud that I taper as slowly as possible, to minimize the withdrawal symptoms. At first, I agreed. But after a full month of tapering, I grew impatient, and, without telling David, I skipped two more doses than I was supposed to. That's when I first experienced one of the most discussed withdrawal symptoms in all the forums I'd read: brain zaps.

Imagine a shock of static electricity, the kind that happens when you touch a metal doorknob. Now imagine that same sensation in the *middle of your head*, a place supposedly devoid of nerve endings. I had just run up the stairs when this sensation began — not unpleasant, but most certainly disconcerting, as I'd never experienced anything like it. I stood in the middle of the room as the sensation ran its course, and then, disoriented, I dizzily found my way to a seat.

I went back on a tapered dose for another week, and then I stopped for good. I got the brain zaps several times a day for nearly two weeks. Apparently, the zaps are so common that Wikipedia offers an elaborate definition that spans paragraphs. But I didn't mind the zaps, especially when compared to other withdrawal symptoms, such as the anger bursts. Something as simple as being unable to reach a plate in the cupboard could trigger a burst of anger so intense I had to fight the urge to grab the nearest object and smash it against the wall.

The worst part about the anger bursts was the frustrating awareness that I was not in control of my own body. At all. I made a point to wait until David was not around before I stomped my feet like a tantruming toddler or beat a pillow until my arms grew tired. I wondered if this was what "roid rage" (guys who overdose steroids) was like. After a fit of fury, I would fall into a ditch of despair. I had two panic attacks in as many weeks.

But then, the symptoms ceased. "It's like you're vibrating," David said to me while I was driving us to my sister Heather's house for Easter.

"Is that bad? I mean, I do kind of feel like I'm on crack," I said. "I don't remember my highs being this high — I just was. Is this normal for me? Is this how I was?"

"It's hard to understand you when you talk that fast," David said, but he was smiling, which reassured me.

*Oh, no,* I thought. *Why do I need reassuring? Am I worried? What if David catches on that I'm freaking out in my head right now and he wants me to go back on Lexapro?* "So, I was really subdued these last two years is what you're telling me," I said, thinking about how to spin my sudden spastic behavior in a way that would make it seem ideal. "I don't like being subdued."

Over the next few days, David made a few comments along the lines of, "Lexapro Barb wouldn't have said this or done that." I began to worry that he was not happy with my newly magnified emotions. Especially because I was really enjoying them. I hadn't realized how muted my feelings had been. Now that they were back in full force — the ecstatic and the miserable, so pleasurable, so painful, so *raw* — I wasn't about to let them go.

"I think I like my crazy," I said. We were having breakfast. I've been waking up earlier to make time for the gym in the morning. While I spoke I was also noting in my head that my coffee consumption was down by two-thirds since I stopped taking my daily dose.

"I like it, too," David said.

I took a step back and called bullshit with a warily raised brow. "But I might have panic attacks, and I worry..." I choked on the last word and my eyes began to leak. David reached out, but I took another step back and collected myself. "I don't want you to have to *handle* me. I don't want you to wake up one day and realize you can't deal with my... my *crazy*. You're going to throw your hands in the air and decide it's just not... worth it." I dropped my head in my hands and sobbed.

"Hey. *Hey*," David said. He used one hand to pull my arms away from my face while wiping my tears away with the other. "Remember, I fell in love with pre-Lexapro Barb. New Barb was sweet for a while, but now that I've had a chance to experience Classic Barb again, I've come to realize I'm a Classic Barb guy."

My body went limp at the relief I felt from hearing these words. David, who had earlier called himself the mast to my flapping sail, held fast.

 I didn't realize until I read these previous two stories side-by-side that my fears about going off meds were nearly identical to my fears going on them.

Unfortunately, it wasn't long before the bad came back with the good. Sure, I had more motivation and spastic energy, but my panic and anxiety had also returned in full force. I felt like a failure for being unable to cope with normal, everyday stresses. It was hard to admit this. It was even harder when, after writing about my first post-medicated episode in "Cirque du Crazy," I received negative comments on the story. One person (anonymous, of course) wrote: "Reading this myopic crap makes me grateful that I do not know you. David would have been better off to simply exit the car and leave you to yourself. Diva? Probably. Raving bitch? Without question."

I felt as though everything I'd feared had been confirmed — that struggling with anxiety somehow made me a failure of a human being. But when others came to my defense, their supportive words were salve on a burning wound, such as this comment: "Barbarella is a raving bitch because she is anxious? Because she is taking responsibility for her behavior? Barb, I think you are brave to admit to your broken parts in such a public form. Remember we cannot change the behavior that we don't acknowledge."

But a neurotic mind always looks for the downside, and with some clever mental Ju-Jitsu, even in what was intended to be a supportive comment. I read, "...we cannot change the behavior that we don't acknowledge," as proof that I needed to change. When I'm up against myself, I am a formidable opponent.

 If Barbarella has an arch-nemesis it is Time. Barb worries about time, well… all the time. She worries she's not going to have enough time to make a deadline. She worries that she's not going to get to the movie theater in time to get the seats she wants. She worries about when she

should go to the bathroom before the
movie starts and if she'll have time
to go back for a second prophylactic
visit before the feature begins. She
worries that we'll be late to a party — it
doesn't matter that we always arrive
early and end up sitting in the car for
half an hour suffering the suspicious
glares of the neighbors who wonder
if we're casing their house. We have,
on occasion, arrived so early that even
the hosts hadn't showered yet. This
hasn't deterred Barb in the slightest.
I have given up on asking what time
we need to be someplace and instead,
I ask what time she wants to leave.
And even then, as the appointed hour
approaches, Barb still tries to hustle me
out of the house even sooner.

Over the years we've been together,
I've learned a lot about what helps and
what doesn't. One fascinating, and
sometimes terrifying, part of Barb's
psyche that I've come to understand
is that for Barb, a plan that is made is
as physical to her as a vase sitting on a
table. If something "breaks" the plan —
a traffic jam, an uninvited guest showing

up, losing a button on her shirt just
before she needs to leave the house —
it's as traumatic as the vase crashing to
the floor and shattering. Therefore, like
trying to put the vase back together with
a few pieces missing, trying to convince
Barb that we can just modify our plan —
"No problem. It's not a big deal. We'll just
arrive a little late" — does not work. The
plan has been destroyed.

In "Cirque du Crazy," Barb writes
about one particularly priceless
"vase" that was smashed. I love
Barb dearly, and I'll always be there
for her, but I have to admit that
sometimes trying to help her can
be incredibly frustrating. No matter
how many comforting things I say,
or how indisputable the logic of my
assurances, my efforts often seem
futile. It's like trying to disarm a
ticking time bomb by talking to it. I
can't remember another time that
I've felt as frustrated and angry as I
did that day in the car.

# Cirque du Crazy

*"Anxiety is love's greatest killer. It makes
others feel as you might when a drowning
man holds on to you. You want to save him,
but you know he will strangle you with his panic."*
– Anais Nin

I have issues with time. Not the laid-back, "I'll get there when I get there" variety that seems to afflict so many here in San Diego. My time issues are more Swiss-German.

I was standing at my computer, applying makeup while scanning email, when I decided to double check the time on my Cirque du Soleil tickets. When I'd first received them, I'd noted "7:30 p.m." and assumed that was when the outside tents would be opened — the area where people perused merchandise and the concession stands prior to taking their seats.

"Oh, *shit*. Shitshitshit," I said, dropping my compact mirror and shoving items (phone, lipstick) into my purse.

David entered the room while putting on his jacket. "What is it?"

"This says *6:30*. The grounds open at 6:30. It's 6:38 right now. Oh my God, we're not going to make it — the *actual show* starts at 7:30."

"Relax, it's okay if we don't mill around, we have time," David said.

"You don't get it. *We should be there by now, and we haven't even left.* Sorry, I don't mean to snap. You're right, I just want to be sure we have time to pee and find our seats before the show starts, and then there's parking, and *fuck.* Okay, no, I'm good, you're right, let's go."

As I drove (fast, frantic), David continued to reassure me, but I wasn't hearing him. My inner monologue was deafening: *Why didn't you check the tickets? You're never going to make it. You're going to miss the beginning, and they don't seat you until the next break, you fuck-up. Why didn't you check?*

"It's just a show," David said.

"One I really want to see," I shot back. But I was beginning to calm down. It was 6:48, and we were only a few miles from the exit. We were going to make it; everything was going to be okay.

"Oh, no, No, NO, what's this?" Traffic to the exit was backed up by at least half a mile. I brought the car to a stop. I was so close I could see the tents set up at the Del Mar Fairgrounds. "This is not happening," I said. "You know when we have a tight flight connection? How when there's plenty of time I'm relaxed, and how when I know I've missed it I'm relaxed, but how I am when there's still a *chance* of making it based on when we land and how far we have to run to the next gate?" David nodded. "I can't handle that limbo," I said.

I took a deep breath. David was already showing signs of irritation — rolling his eyes, making comments along the lines of, "Let's just forget about it, then;" things that told me I needed to stave off the freak-out that was building inside of me with each passing minute. I glared at the clock as if trying to telekinetically set it on fire.

I tried to not talk, but the words just came. "This is all my fault. I should have checked. I can't believe this. We were just hanging out, it's not like I even have a good reason, and if we miss the beginning..." I sensed I was further angering David, which only made me feel like more of a fuck-up, so I stopped talking. My car inched forward. "I can see it. This is torture. So close and yet so far away, knowing we're right here and going to miss it," I said, mentally slapping myself for not holding it in.

"First of all, you need to learn to discern the consequential from the inconsequential. This is not consequential," David said in his last-resort, drill-sergeant tone. "It's not like we're rushing somebody to a hospital and can't get there — this is just the fucking *circus*."

"Cirque du Soleil," I said quietly. "It's better than the circus."

David sighed so hard I could smell the mint in his mouth. "If we get there late, they'll seat us when they're able to seat us. Worst-case scenario, we miss the first half but we'll be able to watch it on the big-screen monitors while we sip champagne." He looked at my face, which was pulled tight into a wide-eyed grimace. "Look, if it means this much, we'll just buy tickets for another night. None of this is worth being self-destructive over."

"What do you mean by that?" David looked pointedly at my arms, or, more specifically, to the fingernails I was digging into them — methodically, evenly, so that no spot was missed. "I can't..." I forced my nails away from my arms, squinted my eyes, and bit my bottom lip so hard I could feel it turning white beneath the red lipstick. My eyes started to water. It was 7:15, and we were nowhere near the light at the end of the exit.

David didn't get it — it wasn't the show, or at least it wasn't *only* the show. It was the *principle*. I have never attended an event I wasn't at least 30 minutes early for. We don't go to the movies anymore, mostly because David is sick of arriving up to two hours before showtime. When going to any theater, I need time to adjust — to relax, to buy a drink, to find a seat, to pee. I spurn those who arrive "on time," which is late in my world. Everyone knows if the show begins at 7:30, you need to be in your seat *before* then. I closed my left hand into a fist and pounded my forehead.

"I'm going to get out of this car and get a cab home if you don't stop it," David said.

"I'm sorry, I'm sorry, I just... I can't accept it. I can't let go of it. I keep chiding myself for not looking at the damn ticket better."

"You need to get over it. Because I can't be around you like this."

"And now I'm feeling more anxious because I'm upsetting you, on top of being able to see the place I'm trying to get to, but *can't reach*." I wouldn't find out how hard I was gripping the steering wheel until we almost needed to cut off one of my fingers to remove a deformed ring later that night. I still maintain it was from the clapping during the show (we made it, running through the rain, to our seats in the first five minutes) and not my death grip on the wheel.

"I hate feeling like I don't have any control," I said. "Of this traffic, of the way I'm reacting to it. I just... I hate it."

"I know," David said, softening his tone for a moment. "I know."

 The cinema of my mind is not always some doom and gloom French film with a miserable, unresolved ending. Sometimes my neuroses can take a

turn toward action/adventure. One
thing that remains true across all
genres of my mental movie theater,
is that for good or bad, it's never
boring. Boredom is the sentiment of
unimaginative people. And loneliness?
I cannot possibly be lonely when there
are this many voices in my head.

But every good action/adventure
flick has conflict. A mundane activity
such as going to the grocery store
can easily become a fraught incident.
In "Chat Locker" I detail my dread
of running into someone I know
while I'm out shopping. In this story,
the person I struggled to avoid was
an old coworker. But my fear of
unexpected small talk is not limited
to acquaintances about whom I'm
ambivalent. Even people I know and
like, people I would enjoy spending
time with, freak me out when I
encounter them outside the proper
context.

The most recent example of this
particular kind of horror went down
just this week. David and I were in
Trader Joe's (it always seems to be

Trader Joe's, I blame their intimate, diagonal, easy-to-see-everyone-in-the-store-at-once aisles), when we happened upon our friend Mike. Don't get me wrong, I was happy to see Mike, at least at first. I told him I'd been enjoying his recent travel blogs, and reported our big news (that we had just received four regional Emmy nominations). But then it happened. Things got awkward.

My eyes grew wider as it suddenly occurred to me I had no idea how to end the conversation. *How did people say goodbye again? And isn't it weird to say goodbye when neither of us are actually going to leave?*

We managed to bring the chat to a close, but then the most distressing thing happened — we ended up side by side again in the next aisle. Of course, we felt obligated to acknowledge each other's presence with what was increasingly becoming forced small talk. Mike told me it was his 35th anniversary with Damon. That was a cool bit of news, and both David and I congratulated him and said we hoped to celebrate properly soon. Then I again bid Mike goodbye with, "Well, gotta keep shopping." But I only made it to the end of the aisle, where David left me to stand with the basket while he went in search of something he'd forgotten in the previous section. *Great, so now it looks like I just wanted to walk away to stand over here*, I thought.

A moment later, Mike caught up to me, and, probably feeling obligated to say something, looked into my basket and commented on a box of rosemary raisin crackers. "I love rosemary," he said. That's when I made things weirder by becoming a pushy spokesperson for this particular brand of rosemary raisin crackers. "Really? Then you'll love these," I said, guiding him to the shelf on which they were housed. "They're lightly sweet, and the rosemary isn't overwhelming, they're great with most cheeses, and they have this satisfying crisp to them, even though they look like little bread slices." I couldn't stop talking about the rosemary raisin crackers. Mike grabbed a box and put it into his cart. I worried that I had somehow made him feel obligated to get them, as though it would have been a direct affront to me if he did not grab a box, especially after I had made it so very clear how wonderful they were.

Supermarkets are hard.

# Chat Locker

*"On this shrunken globe,*
*men can no longer live as strangers."*
— Adlai E. Stevenson

People think time is fixed, an immutable truth like the laws of mass and energy. They're wrong. Seven days of vacation are over in an instant, while 20 minutes in a dentist's chair is an eternity. To the other shoppers it appeared that I simply and swiftly entered Trader Joe's, but for me, time was moving Neo-in-*The-Matrix* slow. Before my second step had landed on the linoleum, I'd already made a survey of my surroundings, spotted a threat, and formulated an avoidance strategy.

The hazard was standing near the veggies, so I veered

from my normal route and bee-lined to the bread, leaving David to fend for himself like a fawn in a forest clearing. I grabbed a package of mini wheat pitas and stood there, paralyzed with indecision. *Backtrack to David, who'd seemed puzzled by my sudden flight? Or proceed around the corner of the aisle?* So preoccupied with keeping myself out of sight while tracking the source of my trouble, I wasn't aware that I'd taken cover behind two employees until they paused in their box-stacking and raised their brows at me as if to say, "Yessss…?" *Proceed it is.*

I ducked around the corner and grabbed four containers of yogurt with the haste of someone snatching up rolls of duct tape before the hurricane hits. Balancing the tubs of yogurt with the pita in my arms, I determined my next move would be to reconnect with David, carrier of the basket.

It wasn't that I disliked the person I was avoiding — she'd been a great coworker, one of my favorites. We even hung out a few times outside of work. She was always complimentary, funny, and easy to be around. But it had been a handful of years since I'd last seen her, and this was supposed to be a quick trip to the market. I did not want to get trapped in an awkward grocery-store catch-up session, the kind that never ends gracefully.

It was during my CIA-esque scoping of the store (Operation Surgical Strike) that I detected her profile, half hidden by a wisp of hair, and then the matching profile of the little girl in her cart. The kid was the clincher.

Like a clairvoyant, I saw the potential conversation unfold before me in a vision: "Wow, Rose, is that you? No way, how have you been?" *Listen to superficial answer, nod and smile. Must acknowledge the child.* "Is she yours? That's what I thought, she looks just like you!" *Force enthusiasm over the kid's cuteness, then engage kid directly — make a crazy exaggerated grin and hope she smiles back because if she cries at that freaky face, you're obligated to stick around until she's been soothed into silence. Then, eyes back to the mother.* "What's her name? Oh, that's a beautiful name."

She'd ask me what I've been up to, and I'd have to decide what to share. "Not much" would be rudely vague, but anything positive or negative could be perceived as bragging or complaining. I'd settle on "You know, working, having fun, same old." She'd ask if I had kids, and I'd have to select a mother-friendly explanation for why I don't — something like "They're great, just not for me." The whole time, I'd be worrying about our respective perishables, calculating how long each item could survive without refrigeration. She'd say we should hang out, and I'd think, *Why,* but I'd say, "Totally." And so on. Time would crawl.

I'd prepared myself for the polite chitchat with the checkout person, the "Fine, thank you. Yes, we found everything we needed, thank you." But I did not have the energy for a whole catch-up sesh, especially with someone whose world revolves around a different sun.

David found me shivering by the frozen foods, pretending to read labels. "What are you doing?" He had a bemused, slightly irritated look on his face.

"Can you go back around that corner and grab two more yogurts? I could only hold four," I said. He turned to leave, but I stopped him so I could unload my arms into the basket. "Rose is around the corner," I explained. "I can't let her see me. I don't want to get stuck talking. I don't want to have to be on right now." David sighed, rolled his eyes, and set off on his mission. I envied him as he passed the free-samples booth at the far end of the aisle I dared not tread. I wondered what they were offering up this time. I imagined it was something I hated and wouldn't want to taste anyway, something with lots of mayo and cilantro. *Ew.*

David returned with a full basket. "Is that everything?" he asked.

"Yeah," I said, distracted, my eyes darting left and right. "Come on, this way." I led him on a circuitous path to the checkout line I'd scouted earlier, safely tucked behind a pole and a kiosk full of impulse buys.

Compensating for the guilt I felt for avoiding the acquaintance, I was super-cheery with the checkout guy: "No, *you* have a great weekend!"

We'd been in the store for no more than ten minutes. For me, the seconds had stretched, each minute dragging like fingernails on a chalkboard.

"Whew, that was a close one," I said, once we were

in the car. "I was worried she'd see me; I really wasn't up for the whole charade of pretending like I care what preschool her kid goes to when all I want to do is go home and chillax."

"I could tell," David said. He seemed to be stuck deciding whether to take the path of censure or consolation. I was hoping he'd settle on the latter. "You acted like they had just vented radioactive gas in that part of the store," he said.

"I didn't want to deal," I whined. "There should be some societal rule about how long you have to maintain polite small talk when you run into someone — you know, like the five-second rule for food on the floor. We're all in the middle of errands, not at a bar. Forced pleasantness takes too much effort." At this, David widened his eyes, as he waited for me to catch on to the ridiculousness of what I'd just said in light of what I'd just done. "Yeah, well, it's a different kind of effort," I said.

David guffawed and said, "The world is a scary place for you, isn't it."

# Creatures
# Big and Small

Despite the countless times David has told me not to try and touch wild animals, it's really his fault that I ended up in an emergency room for trying to pet a squirrel. It was David who surprised me, on a trip to Morro Bay, with a huge jar of nuts. David who found the "beach squirrels" by the water, David who told me how "friendly" they seemed, David who took pictures of me as I sat in the dirt and rocks and handfed the squirrels that swarmed my lap. David who chuckled with the satisfaction he gets from making me happy, as I gasped in awe when one furry forager allowed me to stroke its back with one hand as it stuffed its cheeks with the peanuts it found in my other hand.

It was because of that experience in Morro Bay, the one David gave me, that I thought it would be okay to try and pet a squirrel in Balboa Park.

 Barbarella and animals go together like kids and candy — if candy had sharp claws and could rip your face off. She is irresistibly drawn to them. Like Snow White and Sleeping Beauty, she desperately wants to be able to communicate, commune, and cuddle with them.

I cannot overstate this — Barbarella is a total dork when it comes to animals. Her appetite for cute puppy videos, photos of squirrels with their fuzzy cheeks stuffed with nuts, and pretty much anything to do with raccoons, is boundless. It doesn't matter where she is or what she's doing, if Barb catches sight of some furry creature, she is immediately transfixed. We could be having some serious discussion:

"Wow. A mass of 125GeV was a totally unexpected finding. It puts the Higgs boson right between what's predicted by either the Standard Model or Supersymmetry," I'll say.

"Yeah, but it's not entirely inconsistent with the Standard Model," Barb replies. "There may be a number of different decay OHHHH LOOK AT THE PRETTY PUPPY! YOU'RE SO FLUFFY! OH YES YOU ARE! I JUST WANT TO SQUEEZE YOU!"

It wouldn't matter if she was receiving a Nobel Prize for Literature from the King of Sweden — if a big, fluffy, white Husky appeared nearby, or a raccoon standing on its hind legs with its tiny, hand-like paws outstretched, the King would have to wait.

Barbarella's fixation with animals would actually be kind of cute and harmless if only she wasn't so obsessed with touching them. If an animal looks even remotely fluffy (squirrels, raccoons, big furry dogs, wombats, polar bears), Barb wants to cuddle it. If it's pretty

(hummingbirds, cats) or has big
anime-style eyes, or little hand-like
paws (skunks, ferrets, lemurs, sugar
gliders), she wants to lure them into
our home where she imagines they
will sit on her shoulder while she
works. No matter how many times
someone reminds her that squirrels
are rodents, that a cuddly koala
could claw her eyes out, or that polar
bears are *bears*, Barbarella will not be
deterred.

There's nothing wrong with
wanting to pet some fluffy creature. I
get it. Once, because I knew it would
delight her, I even introduced Barb
to some tame squirrels in Morro Bay.
And how am I rewarded?  When Barb
wound up in the emergency room to
be treated for a squirrel bite, she tried
to blame me. But it's not my fault —
Barb's been trying to pet wild animals
for far longer than she's known me.

# Don Squirreleone

*"If you have any doubts, go to the emergency room.*
*Don't worry about embarrassment —*
*it's better to be embarrassed than dead."*
— Richard Stein

"Wow, look at all of them! There's so many," I said in awe. Jenny folded her small green towel in half and set it on the ground. "Let's sit here," she said. I folded my white towel in the same fashion and sat next to my younger sister in the damp grass beneath a handful of trees, the leaves of which filtered the sunlight to create a warm dappled glow around us.

I opened the can of unsalted cashews and, like kittens reacting to the sound of a can opener, dozens of squirrels began descending from the trees and making their way toward us.

"There are so *many!* And they're coming so close! I feel like Sleeping Beauty," I said, and began to hum a tune from the old Disney film.

"I don't like it when they come up behind me," said Jenny, shooing away a squirrel that had been sniffing at her back.

"Look at this one. He looks like the Godfather." Jenny and I snapped pictures of the fat squirrel to the left of my foot. "He's just so cute and pudgy! I love how they hold their food with both of their little hands like that."

"I'm feeling uncomfortable, Barb," Jenny said with a hint of hysteria. There were easily 20 squirrels in front of us.

"I don't know why you're worried, Jen. They're here for the nuts. Besides, aren't they fun to look at? The closer they come, the better our pictures will be. This one's about to take the nut off my shoe." I paused in conversation to get a shot of the furry Don Corleone collecting the cashew.

"They're coming too close, it's freaky," said Jenny.

"Don't be a scaredy-cat. It's cool. Don't you do this all the time?" This was the first time I accompanied Jenny on her walk to Balboa Park to feed the squirrels — she goes every weekend. "Man, I just can't get over how cute and cuddly this big one looks. I want to touch it."

The Godfather squirrel was fearless; he sat on his haunches and munched on a nut as I snapped pictures less than a foot away. It would be a lie for me to say, "I don't know what came over me next." I know exactly what came over me and, as is sometimes the case, my hands were much faster than my brain. I grabbed a cashew and held it out.

The next few moments were a blur, reminiscent of Alfred Hitchcock — the adorable fur ball took two steps toward my hand and then it must have jumped up and onto me, because suddenly I was on my feet, trying to shake it off. My left middle finger was in its mouth and its claws were clutching tightly to my forearm as I shook, shook, shook, and then it came loose and hit the ground running faster than a squirrel that fat should be able to run. Blood was flowing freely from the tooth-deep slice through the middle of my fingertip and, shaking, I snatched up the white towel and wrapped it around my wound. Throughout the quick ordeal, I was vaguely aware of Jenny's and my combined screams.

"Holy shit!" I shouted.

"Are you okay?" Jenny was laughing, but it was her nervous laugh. She was just as scared as I was. Being bitten by a wild, potentially disease-ridden rodent didn't worry me until I realized how much of my skin the little beast's teeth had broken into. "Shoo! Shoo!" Jenny stomped around to give us a wider berth, but the squirrels hardly seemed fazed, so we walked quickly away from the area.

My first thought was to call David — if he thought it wasn't serious, I wouldn't worry. But if he did, I would panic. He did. "You should probably get to a hospital," he said.

"Will you come and get me?" I asked in a shaky voice. Before he could answer, I remembered the car keys in my purse, which meant David was without transportation.

I called the number on my insurance card to find out which urgent care I should go to. The man who answered asked, "What is it you need to be treated for?"

"I was bitten by a squirrel. I think I need to get a

shot or something," I responded.

"Huh," he said, and then, in an amused tone, "that's never happened to me. Say, what does it feel like, to be bitten by a squirrel?"

"What do you think? I've been bitten, *I'm bleeding*, it fucking hurts!" Exasperated, I ended the call. A minute later, I got a hold of my friend Nathan, my hero, who arrived within minutes to collect us and drop us off at the emergency room at Scripps Mercy Hospital.

As the sharp pain in my finger dulled to an uncomfortable throbbing sensation, I began to relax. Jenny, who hadn't stopped laughing since we got into Nathan's truck, kept me in good spirits as I waited for my name to be called.

"I told you," she said. "There was something off about that one. He was crazy in the eyes. They don't just sit there like that, that close to you, unless there's something wrong with them. You know, he could have taken your whole fingertip off."

"This isn't helping, Jen."

"Sorry. Can I see your phone? I feel like I need to tell people. It's just so funny."

I handed it over and listened as Jenny, through chortles, explained to my sisters and mother what had just happened to me. My head jerked up at the sound of my name, and I followed an attractive blonde woman through the door to triage. She had a weird smile on her face. As soon as she began speaking, I recognized her smile as that strained expression one gets when attempting to withhold laughter. She looked at the paper on her clipboard as she spoke.

"You were bitten by a squirrel?" She choked on the word "squirrel."

"Yes."

"Were you, uh, trying to feed it?" She was no longer able to control her smile; her lips curled up at the ends between each question.

"No, it just attacked me out of nowhere," I snapped sarcastically. "Okay, okay. I was trying to feed it."

"Squirrels are rodents, you know," she pointed out.

"Yeah, so I've heard." She looked at my finger, which had stopped bleeding, probably a result of the pressure I'd been exerting on it as I waited.

"A doctor will have to see you, I'm not sure what the protocol is in this situation. If at any time, however, you feel that your wounds are... [suppressed laughter] life threatening... [more suppressed laughter], then return to this window."

"Go on, let it out," I suggested. "It's okay, you can laugh."

"I'm sorry," she said, beginning to giggle. "It's just, you know, we usually get people here who are withdrawing from drugs or suffering from violent crimes. It's refreshing to treat someone who was trying to do something nice. And it's funny."

A young man in light blue scrubs led Jenny and me

to the exam room. On the way, he turned to me and said, in that familiar, strained tone of voice, "Feeding squirrels today, eh?" I shrugged my shoulders. "I'm sorry, it's just, uh, well, it's pretty funny. Wait here and the doctor will be right with you." I could hear a muffled staccato laughter as he walked down the corridor.

Jenny and I waited in that little room for almost an hour, testing everything from the foot-pedal sink to the "are they or are they not locked" file cabinet drawers (they are not). The doctor, in dark blue scrubs, appeared in the doorway and said, "So, I hear you were feeding... Ha! Ha! Ha!" He was much freer with his laughter, and even finished up with a little "Ho, ho!" before he managed to speak the word "squirrels."

"Gee, I'm so happy I can be such a source of amusement for the emergency room staff today," I said in a snarky tone. He could read from my smile that there was some truth to my words — what's a little squirrel bite if you can make a bunch of hardworking health-care professionals laugh for a day?

"Squirrels are rodents, you know," said the smiling doctor.

"Yup."

"Don't worry, you can't get rabies from them. But we're going to give you a tetanus shot and some antibiotics to ward off any infections." The doctor disappeared and another woman who was obviously informed as to my predicament came smiling into the room to give me my shot.

While she prepped the needle, the doctor popped his head in the door and said, "I just want you to know, I had a really hard time dictating that. I had to keep stopping the tape while I laughed."

"Thanks for letting me know," I said, but he was already off to see another patient, and then there was a needle in my arm. Jenny was laughing quietly as she scanned through her pictures. When she came across the picture of the chubby rodent that attacked me, she held it up for me to see. "He looks so cute and fluffy," I said. "Don't you just want to pet him?"

 Okay, so I'm obsessed with the desire to touch fuzzy animals. But on the flip side is my underlying urge to annihilate all creepy crawly insects. I may squeal with delight when I see a fluffy dog, but I screech with terror when I think I just saw a mosquito. David rolls his eyes when I "overreact" to an insect. He doesn't understand the panic that grips me. In "Them," I write about one of my more horrific encounters. Had David been home, I would have screamed for his help, but he wasn't that day, so I was left to fend for myself. I admit I took some pride in this.

 Wild animals with razor claws, sharp teeth, and maybe the Bubonic Plague? Barb is perfectly at ease trying to lure them to come sit in her lap. But when she sees a harmless spider roughly 100,000 times smaller than her, just minding its own business, she freaks the fuck out.

# Them

*"Fear is not the natural state of civilized people."*
— Aung San Suu Kyi

If the morning had been anything other than unremarkable, I might have been better prepared for the terrible onslaught that was to come. As it was, however, the sky was neither clear nor cloudy, and the temperature inside was maintained at 75 degrees. I'd eaten my oatmeal, selected something caffeinated from the fridge, settled into the ergonomic chair at my desk, and slid into the quotidian business of checking e-mail and scanning headlines. While purging the night's accumulation of spam, I sensed movement in my periphery. Tearing my gaze away from the computer screen, I located a gossamer strand catching the light. One end was floating in the air, and the other appeared to be attached to the far side of a dust-covered copper sphere — part of a small fountain that has sat inactive on my desk since the water evaporated a year ago. I watched the silky string dance in the air for a few minutes and then brushed it away with a Max Mara catalogue.

Sometime between *cnn.com* and the *Drudge Report*, I again sensed motion, this time to my right. A miniscule spider, such a light green that it appeared transparent, was traversing a credit card statement. I'm no Jain. What little guilt I occasionally feel for murdering insects, bugs, and other pests is fleeting. My weapon of choice — a pad of paper — was the closest thing I could grab. I set it gently atop the wispy creature and returned my attention to the words on the screen. I must have been *too* gentle, for a minute later I glimpsed my victim scrabbling over a stack of papers a few inches away from the pad that was supposed to have killed it.

Without a second thought, I lifted the pad and struck the bug with a resounding slap. It was then that I noticed the remnant of spider that had already been under the pad. The first one hadn't survived after all. The vision of not one, but two little squash marks instilled in me a hint of trepidation, but I shook it off and retreated, yet again, to the Internet.

As a touch typist, my eyes remain on the screen while my fingers do their thing. I was updating my blog when, like a snowflake, the silhouette of another spider drifted down in front of my screen and landed squarely on the 7 key. I jerked my hands back and gaped at the invader. As I stared, momentarily paralyzed, two horrific realizations burned at the forefront of my mind with the icy heat of liquid nitrogen: 1.) There are many of them. 2.) They are *above* me.

Had he been home, I would have screamed for David. Instead, I held my breath and considered my options. I crushed the creature with a piece of paper when I saw it make a move toward the 6 key. Releasing the air from my lungs, my sigh became more and more vocal, until it reached a desperate whine. It occurred to me that, if these things were dropping onto my desk, they may very well be dropping onto *me*. Thus, I tore my ponytail loose and flailed wildly at my head with both hands.

After this brief and violent episode, I sat and stared at my keyboard, resisting the knowledge that the only way to gauge the severity of my predicament would be to look up. I was convinced that the moment I tilted back my head, their little leader would give the signal and my face would suddenly be covered by hundreds of bloodthirsty spiderlings. I fought hard to convince myself that the reality couldn't be as bad as the B-movie version playing in my imagination. I knew I had to look before another one fell, but my head wouldn't budge. It wasn't until one of the diminutive green devils, whose silk had caught a puff of air and floated right to left past my face, that my mind checked out and my body reacted. Like an overdose victim who'd just been jabbed in the heart with a needle full of norepinephrine, I jerked to a standing position and my head snapped backward.

I was relieved to see nothing but the white ceiling and the tops of the sage-colored walls. But then, after my eyes had adjusted to this new perspective, I began to distinguish them — dozens of moving, microscopic dots — from the shadowy, spackled texture. There were only a few on the ceiling. Most of them lined the 90-degree crevice where ceiling met wall, as if they were taking up positions in preparation for a SWAT-team-style assault. I was surrounded.

I can't remember if I screamed as I ran from my office to the closet that houses the vacuum. I must have been making some kind of noise, because I do recall the vibration in my throat and chest. Touching my ankle is painful confirmation that I dropped the vacuum on my foot after I fished it from the closet; and a dull throb in my head is a constant reminder of how many times I bumped it as I fumbled to attach the long hose and find a suitable stool to stand on.

Armed with household appliances, I scrambled around the room, jabbing every inch from corner to corner with the broomy end of the vacuum hose. I lifted the blinds and shrieked when I found more baby spiders on the window. I could feel the sweat beading on my brow from my exertions, but I could not rest. Not until I knew they were all dead. Then I saw it: a huge, shriveled exoskeleton lying on the floor at the base of the window, next to a bundled up ball of what looked like flimsy gauze.

Fragments of scenes played through my head — all of my spider associations colliding in a hodgepodge that included bits from the cartoon movie *Charlotte's Web*, the horror flick *Arachnophobia*, and hours of Nature Channel documentaries. Finally, the pieces joined to make one solid conclusion that I could have sworn was spoken aloud to me in a British man's voice: "The mother spiders are devoured by their newly hatched spiderlings, after which the young will climb to the highest point and let out their silk, letting the air carry them away." I extended the hose in my hand as if it were a sword, and sucked up the sac and carcass.

I don't know how long I stood in the center of the room, vacuum in hand, nostrils flared, eyes wide and darting every which way. I sighed a breath of relief when I heard David at the front door. He paused at the entrance and then followed a trail of detritus that had fallen from the closet and been dragged down the hallway to my office by the vacuum's cord. David stopped at my door and looked around the room. Furniture was overturned, hoses and cords were scattered about, and my desktop was disheveled. My eyes were crazed and stuck wide open, and my hair was deranged from having been let down and slapped silly.

"Something traumatic happened while you were gone," I said, by way of explanation.

Looking me up and down, David smiled and choked back a laugh. "Let me guess," he said. "It involved the vacuum?"

 Even more traumatizing for Barb than spiders are germs. At least she can *see* spiders. Germs, however, are invisible and they maliciously lurk everywhere. Barb's entire family is made up of germaphobes. Her father won't touch his shoelaces if they've touched the ground. Her sister Jane is an obsessive antibacterial abuser — she even has a small bottle of Purell hanging from her keychain in case any germological emergency should arise (i.e., she's touched something). All of them either press the walk button with their elbow or knuckle, or they simply wait for someone else to press it. And though I've been making progress with Barb, the rest of them still insist that their eggs be hard-cooked, their meat be desiccated, and that expiration dates are the Word of God.

# Germ Warfare

*"There are always germs, and you're never going to get rid of all of them."*
— Cheryl Mendelson

I scrutinized the underside of David's shoe as it dangled in the air. The sole and its host of pathogens revealed itself as David leaned back in his chair and lifted his right leg to rest his calf on his left thigh, thus positioning shoe-borne flora and fauna within inches of the platter of cheese on the low table between us. I envisioned millions of germs as microscopic, distorted humanoids jumping off of the shoe, sounding inaudible germy screams as they hurtled through the air and landed on my cheese, where they would bivouac on the rind until they received orders to invade the soft, gooey part that was allocated for my cracker.

"What?" David said, studying my face as I inspected his foot. I shrugged, my eyes looking deep into his sole, wandering from toe to heel and back again, finally settling somewhere in the middle, on the most offensive blemish on the black rubber — remnants of a splotch of gum, rendered unsticky by dirt and what I realized were bits of hair protruding from the buildup.

"*What?*" This time, David's tone was more impatient.

I tore my gaze from his shoe and met his eyes as I considered how much to tell him. After a moment, I settled on, "Your shoe is grossing me out." He uncrossed his legs and brought both feet to the floor. "It's nothing," I said in response to his interrogatory frown. But David can always tell when I'm withholding something. "Okay, *fine*," I said. "Your foot was so close to the food, and I could picture shit jumping off of your shoe and onto my cheese."

"That's ridiculous," David said.

"Is it? Well, even if germs can't jump, it was still unappetizing to look at."

"Unappetizing is one thing, but germs absolutely do not jump," David said.

"How do you know? You can't see them," I said. "For all you know they could be climbing up the side of the table right now."

I learned long ago that not only do most people seem to not have the same concerns as me, but they also tend to think mine are peculiar. Maybe I was trying to defend the rationality of my aversion to shoe bottoms or to mitigate David's derision for what he thought was my misguided perception of biology. But whatever my motives, I soon found myself revealing the details of a private episode that had occurred that morning, and I began to regret the words the moment they tumbled forth from my mouth.

I had been applying my Lancôme liquid eyeliner, with the applicator in my right hand, when I sneezed in the general direction of the open container I held in my left hand. I relayed to David that as soon as the *choo* part of my sneeze escaped, I began to visualize colorful cartoonlike amoebas sailing through the air and diving headfirst into the container, their tiny cilia pointing forward like arms. Then in my mind's eye I beheld an animated sequence of my spit molecules reacting with the chemicals in the eyeliner and multiplying into some superbug with the power to blind me. "And now," I concluded, "I'm not sure if I can use that eyeliner again. And I just bought it, and it wasn't cheap."

"Wow," David said. "On so many levels… wow." He leaned forward, spread some Brillat-Savarin onto a square of multigrain flatbread, then sat back, began to cross his legs, seemed to think better of it, and popped the presumably polluted soft cheese into his mouth.

When he finished chewing, David said, "First, that you would think that you could actually sneeze something directly into that little bottle is just remarkable."

"I sneezed right on it! Millions of little God-knows-what flying directly onto, *into,* the container," I argued.

"Second," David continued, "to think that anything can possibly live and flourish inside the chemical miasma within that bottle is unthinkable. That after you sealed it, you'd think anything that got in there would grow and multiply using the eyeliner as *nutrition*."

"Then how do you explain pinkeye? I got that, and the doctor said it could have been from my pencil eyeliner. That means it had to be *living* on my eye makeup for months!"

"Third," David said, disregarding my argument, "that you would think that once you open it again and put it on your eye, that it would be *bad* for you."

"You never know," I said. "Pinkeye."

David scanned my face with the same intense look he has when he's working on a pivotal Scrabble play. "Your brain is so preoccupied with bizarre shit, it's no wonder you have so little left over to cope," he said.

"This isn't make-believe," I said. "I remember biology class in high school, when we did the Petri-dish project. That shit grew from swabs taken from the bottom of my shoe, from my backpack — to think I used to put my face on that bag! But never again, not after I saw all the gunk that lived there with my own eyes. I don't even like to put my face on the pillows we keep on the couch."

"Your germophobe thing is so arbitrary," David said. "I mean, do you even know what the germiest place in the house is?"

"The kitchen sink," I said with confidence. "That's why I'm always running our sponges through the dishwasher. I saw it on the news, during one of those 'Now Fear This'–type segments."

"That's not it," David said.

"Don't," I said. "I don't want to know. You're right. It's arbitrary. So, the less I know, the better."

"It's the shower," David said.

"I don't touch the walls or the curtain when I'm in there, so I'm —"

"It's the shower head, actually," he clarified. I couldn't tell if he was attempting to cure my neurosis with logic or if he was being sadistic. I decided on the former when he continued, "Germs are good for you."

"*Jesus*, David, how am I ever going to shower again? Is that what this is? Are you trying to tell me you have a thing for stink? I mean, the walls I can avoid; the curtain, sure; but the *head*? I can't avoid that. What am I going to do now?"

"Germs are what your immune system thrives on," David said, speaking faster to match my hysteria. "Like the flu shot, they —"

"That's why I don't *get* the flu shot," I shrieked.

David cracked a smile. I'd been wrong. This was sadism. "You're evil," I said. He offered me a piece of cheese and did not seem surprised when I refused to take it. "Just for that, I'm going on a shower strike," I warned. "You think that cheese is funky? Just wait."

David laughed and called my bluff. "Go ahead... won't bother me. If anything, you'll be building up your immunity."

# One Terrific Pig

*"How about 'Pig Supreme?' asked one of the lambs.*
*'No good,' said Charlotte. 'It sounds like a rich dessert.'"*
— E. B. White

When my friend Sara announced the impending arrival of her new pet — a miniature painted pot-bellied piglet that would grow to be the size of a large cat — I became dizzy. She might as well have told me that a unicorn, with its glittery horn and the power to grant wishes, was munching on a patch of grass in her backyard. I was geeky with anticipation to see the little porker.

I received the text on a Monday night. Sara and her boyfriend Hanis had returned from a day at the Del Mar Fair and invited me to pop over to meet the newest addition to their clan (they already had the "incredibly growing" desert tortoise and Doogers the rambunctious Spaniel). I'd seen tusky warthogs and pygmy pigs at the zoo, but always from a distance on the other side of a barrier. This would be my first time going nose to snout with a pig.

I was there before they'd finished unloading the car. Dropping my tact along with my purse on a chair, I walked right past Sara to Hanis, who was holding the piglet in his arm like a football. I hadn't expected it to be so tiny. He was lighter than my multiple-rep dumbbells and not nearly as long. "He's growing fast," Sara said from behind me, "but even at his largest, he won't be more than 15 to 25 pounds. He was the runt of his litter, just like Wilbur."

Hanis set the runt on the grass. Both a chef and farmer, Hanis raises pigs (the kind for eating) on a shared farm in Alpine. Though this little piggy will not be going to market, Hanis named him Carnitas.

The pint-sized hog waddled around straight-legged on his hooves, looking ballerina-like on his tippy-toes. His tail — also straight — wagged like a dog's, and his rotund tummy was wider than the rest of his body; he grunted as he poked at the soil with his snout, his oinking a testimony to his serenity.

"Can I hold him?" I asked. Sara nodded, and I smiled like a junkie about to land a job as a pharmacist. I reached down and put my hand around his softball of a belly. A piercing squeal filled the air — a desperate, miserable cry more alarming than a hungry infant's — while itty-bitty piggy legs flailed about. I withdrew my hand and looked to Sara for help.

"He does that when you just grab him," she said.

"You think?" I said. Sara laughed off my sarcasm and demonstrated how tapping the pig's bottom would encourage him to bound into my arms. I sat beside him, touched his bum, and Carnitas trotted onto my leg and into my arms. He buried his snout in my elbow, rooting for comfort, driving his nose into my flesh with the perseverance of Sisyphus. It felt as if someone were poking me with an index finger. Hard.

"He did that to me for over ten minutes last night," said Hanis. "Actually gave me a bruise."

But I didn't mind. It was a bearable pain. I was willing to put up with a whole hell of a lot for the opportunity to cradle the exotic creature. Something about him burrowing into my arm kindled in me a latent need to nurture.

I paused from stroking the animal's back and looked up after Sara mentioned something about the Gay Pride parade. It wasn't mere talk of the upcoming festivities that had tugged my attention away from the piglet. "Did I hear you say you're going to be *in* the parade?" I asked. "And Hanis is going to be working? Does that mean you need someone to watch Carnitas?" It was at that moment — as I envisioned those peewee pig hooves traipsing around on my hardwood floors — that I realized just how boar-besotted I was.

I don't baby-sit, I don't dog-sit. I don't water plants. I don't feel the urge to volunteer myself to assume other people's chosen responsibilities. On the occasions that I've agreed to look after my niephlings or scoop a friend's Kitty Litter, it was because I was beseeched as a last, desperate resort. But pig-sitting, now that was different.

"Are you sure David would be okay with him in your house?" Sara asked. "I won't be able to come pick him up right away; it might take us a while to get out of there."

"He'll be fine," I said. "Won't you?" I held a wild gaze on David, scaring him into the nod he finally provided. "See? No problem," I said.

"Well, I just want to make sure," Sara said. "I know how you guys are. You don't even allow kids in your place."

"Well, yeah, not until they're old enough to hold a conversation or operate a corkscrew," I said. "Toddlers are like ferrets, they get their little hands into everything. And babies are boring. They just sit there until they scream bloody murder because they need to be filled or emptied."

"But I thought you didn't let animals up either," said Hanis.

"Well, no, not historically," I said. "Dogs can be

destructive." I looked down at the strange bundle in my arms. "But this little guy, he's harmless. And entertaining. I'll take him to the parade, and then he can kick it at our place until you're ready for him."

The morning I collected Carnitas, I walked away with two armfuls of Hanis-prepared care packages comprising food, treats, water, spray-on sunscreen, a quilted carrier, and Carnitas's bed. Hanis appeared ever the fretful father as he watched us leave. I set the pig in his small bed on my passenger seat and tweeted a few photos, my face aching from my huge grin.

After torturing the poor pig with spray-on sunscreen (his sad squeals of protest still haunt me) and then giggling for a while as he scuttled about, failing to find traction on our polished granite counter, I packed him into the carrier and headed out the door with David and my father.

The street was packed. Dad parked his beach chair (with its attachable solar-reflective umbrella) in a searing shadeless spot on the grass between the sidewalk and the asphalt. David and I continued on, trekking through the throngs until we found respite on a grassy knoll beside a sushi joint, where palm fronds offered protection from the sun and occasional puffs of cool air carried over from the restaurant. But our chief reason for settling there was the raised planter against the wall behind the grass. The planter was narrow and contained plenty of mulch for a curious snout.

"Can you see from down there?" I asked David. He was seated on the edge of the planter, scratching Carnitas's belly. The pig was stretched out against David's leg, enjoying the massage.

"It's okay," said David, keeping his eyes on the content piglet. "I'm good right here."

 My videos featuring Carnitas the mini pig have over a million views on YouTube. I even got the little porker interviewed on our local NBC news. Now, his parents (my friends Sara and Hanis) are about to open the second location of their nationally renowned restaurant, which they named after their porcine pet: Carnitas' Snack Shack. When they first got Carnitas from a farm in Texas, Sara and Hanis insisted that their "miniature" pot-bellied pig would never grow to be larger than 20 pounds or so. Today, he's knee-high, packed tight and round, and tips the scale at nearly 60 pounds.

The tiny piglet has grown into a belligerent, alcoholic boar — seriously, he really likes beer. At parties, guests are warned not to leave their drinks anywhere near the ground because Carnitas will knock over the cup or bottle and lap up the carb-y booze, and the moment he's buzzed, he becomes very pushy in his quest for more of the good stuff. That pig has got a serious monkey on his back. Sara and Hanis don't let Carnitas around people much any more, but I'll always remember playing with itty-bitty, sweet Carnitas when he was a baby, and, despite his being a little asshole now, he still comes to me when I call him.

# Deep Thoughts

Barbarella is an inquisitive, reflective, and contemplative person. Scrutinizing everything for its deeper meaning and subtext, she leaves no statement unturned. If I happen to mention I'm chilly, Barb's mental code-breaking supercomputers leap into action. *Does he want me to turn on the heat?* she'll wonder. *Maybe he wants me to get him a sweater? Or, worse, maybe he's trying to tell me how much he hates our cold, drafty apartment and that he wants us to move. Then again, he might just be trying to get me to cuddle with him.* The truth is, all I meant was that I was chilly. That's it — a simple, objective, observational fact with absolutely no subtext. When I try to explain to Barb that my statements are exactly as they seem, with no hidden layers of meaning, she stares at me, puzzled and uncomprehending, as if I had suddenly started speaking Icelandic.

Barbarella doesn't just analyze everything, she pre-analyzes and then post-analyzes. If, for example, we have to go to shopping for groceries, Barb will first try to predict how crowded the store might be based on the time of day, day of the week, meteorological conditions, whether or not the Chargers won the day before, and a host of other factors she feels are somehow relevant.

Barb is always searching for order in the chaos. She feels that if she can see *why* things happen the way they do, she'll be able to control them, herself included. I, on the other hand, have a more laissez-faire attitude and can accept a degree of randomness in my universe. If I need groceries, I just go. There are always people at the store — sometimes more, sometimes fewer. Even if I could predict with certainty how many people will be there, I'm not going to go shopping at 8:30 in the morning just to save 15 minutes in the checkout line. To me, trying to divine the laws that govern such large, complex, and inherently unpredictable systems, especially ones of little consequence, seems like a pointless expenditure of energy.

As bewildered as I am by Barb's never ending analysis, she is equally baffled by what she calls my "Zen" approach to life. But here's how I look at it. For any given situation either: A) I already understand how the system operates, in which case I don't need to think about it; B) I realize that the system is inherently too complex to understand, in which case there's no point in thinking about it; C) I feel that, with enough research, the system may be knowable, but there is little practical consequence that comes from not understanding it, in which case I won't bother thinking about it; or D) Yeah, okay, maybe it's important enough to think about. Of all our daily activities, only a very small percentage ever fall into category D, and figuring out the best time to go to Trader Joe's is not one of them.

It's not that I'm not curious about the world — I have a lot of curiosity, and I love knowing how things work — it's just that when I'm contemplating the universe, I'm usually doing it for pleasure rather than out of a feeling of necessity.

Barbarella spends an awful lot of energy trying to make sense of the world, but for all the time she spends trying to figure out what makes things tick, she spends at least as much time gazing inward, trying to figure out what makes her tick. Socrates would be proud.

# Confessions and Epiphanies

*"Journal writing is a voyage to the interior."*
— Christina Baldwin

I looked around for something to throw. The thought of lashing out physically caused my heart to skip a beat in anticipation of such animalistic satisfaction. In a panic to find a release for my mounting frustration, I considered each object around me: *Boa? No, too flimsy; a wimpy, feathery flutter will only disappoint. Paperweight? Too heavy, I'm upset, but I don't want to break anything. I could hit something, but that might hurt my hand.* While scanning my bookshelves for an inanimate victim that I could chuck to the ground, my eyes fell on the topmost right shelf, where my journal waited for me to notice it. The last words spoken by my sister echoed in my head. She had disconnected the call with cruel swiftness during the first syllable of my response. I wanted to finish my thoughts, express how I felt, whether or not she was willing to hear it. I needed to know what was beneath the anger and rage simmering inside of me; perhaps more frustrating than not having the chance to explain my position was that I didn't really know what my position was. As I reached for my leather-bound confidante, my face began to cool, the blood that had rushed to heat it returned dutifully to my veins and organs.

I held the book in my hands, and its weight — whispering the promise of inviting blank pages — transmitted a calm that began in my fingertips and spread its soothing warmth through my body, causing the tension in all of my muscles to dissipate. It is always the same when I turn to my journal — irritation and emotions build until I want to explode, but I know, as do the pages already covered in my scribbled ink, that transforming my feelings into words is the one true remedy.

I went about converting the room into a space worthy of confessions and epiphanies. I lit a candle and stared at it. This was my favorite candle, a cylinder of deep burgundy hinting at the berry fragrance that will emanate as soon as the wax around the wick begins to melt. Later, when I extinguish the flame with a gentle, focused breath, the scent, mingled with a swaying stream of smoke, will deepen in complexity, and its sugary sweetness will become musky and heady. The following morning, upon waking, I will breathe in its faint memory to trigger the sensation of serenity my brain will forever associate with the aroma of writing.

I sat in my favorite chair, a dark wood-framed brocaded rococo armchair more suited to a Victorian-era tearoom than where it was settled, in the corner of my office, facing a room filled with contemporary furnishings. I selected a blue ballpoint pen — I had let go of my preference for consistent-colored ink years ago, when I decided the only things that really mattered about a pen were the way it felt in my fingers and the fluidity and ease with which the ink ran from its tip onto the paper.

My best friend lay closed on my lap. I hesitated to open it, savoring the righteous taste of anger, because I knew once I lifted the front cover, I would have to surrender to the truth beneath my mask of rage and embrace the part of me that is as insecure and uncertain as the feeble old wizard cowering behind the curtain. I thought of my father's new-agey theory that anger does not exist, that no emotions exist outside of fear and love, and that every other feeling we think we have can be boiled down to one of those two common denominators. In the case of sibling rivalry, I reasoned, it's a mixture of both.

It took me two years of journaling before I was honest with myself for the first time, honest in that ugly, poorly lit naked way in which we are petrified of seeing ourselves. I was 19, and though I cringed at what I saw reflected back at me through this mirror of words, I soon became addicted to the clarity and peace of mind journaling gave me and used it as a form of self-medication.

As the candle began to emit its intoxicating essence, I opened the journal and flipped through the pages before stopping at June 21, 2002. The words were uneven, messier than the entries surrounding them: *I have that feeling of lonely despair; I know I've felt this before. You know the drill: I'm surrounded by people, friends, family, coworkers, etc. — and I feel so unbearably alone. I feel like nobody gets me. Like as close as they think they may be to me, they are kept by me at arms' length.*

But I wasn't alone, I thought, running my index finger over the words, as if I might be able to touch the very pen that spilled this black ink years ago. I turned to the first blank page toward the end of the book, the fourth of its kind, its predecessors filled from cover to cover with my ranting, raving, and soul searching. Suddenly, with the same disbelief I experience when emerging from a dark movie theater to see that the sky is still lit by the sun, I realized the last of my anger had vanished.

I allowed my stream of consciousness to pour forth, my pen a funnel through which only one word could fit at a time, forcing order and sense from what would otherwise remain a jumble of ideas muddying up my mind. I transcribed the argument and, once it was down in blue and white, I did my best to explain how the argument had affected me, to question the true source of the white-hot anger that had coursed through me 30 minutes earlier.

I gave myself over and without discretion to the pen in my hand, allowed it to write every thought that entered my head. *I feel like... if only I knew how to finish that sentence*, I wrote. *I guess I don't know myself as well as I thought I did.* It is amazing how candid one can be when all potential for judgment is removed. Right and wrong are ideas I attribute to myself as I consider my thoughts. *I don't want to see her hurt. I love her. She's tense. She's quick to anger. She's a lot of wonderful things as well — but I'm starting to forget what they are. And that's just tragic.*

One phrase continued to repeat itself in my head as my hand danced furiously over the page — it's okay. Anything I write is okay, because this is mine, these are my thoughts, and only I can say if they're good or bad. It's okay if my opinion of others is not always glowing. It's okay if I admit I am afraid or in pain or angry for reasons I would never share for fear of being labeled as petty or judgmental. It's okay to feel, and it's okay to document those feelings and attempt to figure them out. *I really need to find the balance between what I think I should be doing in terms of family obligations, what I'm willing to do, and what that means about me.*

After I'd recorded two pages worth of self-revelations, I sat, spent, in my chair, and stared at the undulating flame. A few minutes later I returned my journal to its home, and, with a quick puff of air, extinguished the candle. I inhaled and smiled as the smoky perfume filled my nostrils, and then I went to bed.

 Have you ever stared into a mirror so long you started to lose all concept of your own identity? It's probably not good for you.

# Reflections of Self

*"Identity would seem to be the garment with which one covers the nakedness of the self, in which case, it is best that the garment be loose, a little like the robes of the desert, through which one's nakedness can always be felt, and, sometimes, discerned."*
— James Arthur Baldwin

I stare at my face in the bathroom mirror and silently ask my reflection, *Who are you?* I consider my nose, the skin dry and peeling. I raise and drop my brows, paying close attention to the horizontal lines that appear and disappear on my forehead. One short white hair, the first of its kind to grace my body, is partially hidden among the finer brown strands at my hairline. I pucker and smile, pucker and smile, until my lips take on a life of their own, my mouth a nomad roaming across my face instead of the permanent resident it should be. Gazing into a mirror until I no longer recognize myself is a practice I picked up when I was ten years old. The first time I did this was by accident. The electricity had gone out and my family was gathered in the living room, playing board games by candlelight. I had to pee, so I grabbed one of the candles and made my way to the bathroom.

The darkness didn't scare me. I finished my task

without incident. But when I turned to wash up and caught my flickering reflection, I froze with fear. The left half of my face, fallen in shadow, deviated with the light, my features appearing to toggle between my own and those of an old lady. As a superstitious kid who avoided stepping on cracks because I was convinced doing so would compromise my mother's spine, I assumed this strange half-face was a ghost, and that I had been chosen as her conduit to communicate something crucial from the other side.

When I returned to the living room, I was surprised no one asked where I'd been for so long. Apparently, what must have been five hours in the dimly lit bathroom had been five minutes in the living room. As I resumed my position at the Monopoly board, I told myself I'd spill all at the slightest provocation but would not volunteer anything about my unexpected meeting with the ghost in the mirror. My sisters didn't seem to notice that I was distractedly going through the motions of the game while my mind was racing with the encounter I had just had at the other end of the house, a dimension away.

Off and on for the next few years, I tried to summon the old lady. Who was she? What did she want? Would I be able to help her? Sometimes I would try facing myself in the dark. Once, I stole a match from above the fireplace and lit a candle, hoping no one would notice that the power hadn't failed. Having considered the possibility that the lady might not be able to appear in the same place more than once, I alternated mirrors in my attempts to reconnect with her.

As I entered adolescence and gave up all things childish, the silly idea that ghosts exist disappeared along with my Barbie dolls. But the girl in the mirror still intrigued me. On some mornings, after showering, I would linger in the bathroom and stare at my flipped-around self.

I was 15 when I had my first out-of-Barb experience. During a routine stare, I gave in to the sudden urge to speak my name out loud. "Barb." The word sounded strangely foreign to me, something used to describe a sharp, inanimate object, not a person. "Barb," I tried again. "Barb," I said over and over until the sound, beginning and ending with a short burst of air through my closed lips, lost all meaning. My sense of identity escaped from my mouth along with the now peculiar sound of my name. "Barb." Who was this Barb? What did she want? Would I be able to help her?

Most people reach middle age before they experience a crisis of identity. My perplexity regarding what makes me *me* has been as much a part of my day-to-day life since childhood as brushing my teeth. I realize now, staring at this one white hair, this small reminder of mortality that helps frame this face in the mirror, that I am still in the early stages of getting to know who Barb is.

I have allowed my circumstances to define me at

different times in my life. In the clouded bathroom mirror of my apartment in Los Angeles, Barb is a single, 22-year-old woman who likes to do drugs and go dancing; her eyes meet mine in a desperate stare that always say the same thing: "I want people to like me." In the tall, narrow mirror nailed to the back of my bedroom door in my parents' house, Barb is 18 — she doesn't have a job, she doesn't have many friends, and she often says to me aloud, "I don't like you." In the gold-framed mirror that hangs in the entrance of my father's condo, Barb is 27, and the confident sheen of her eyes tells me she is experiencing one of those rare moments in which she is sure of who she is. The moment soon passes.

Here I am, in the master bathroom of the home I share with David. Barb is 29. She hates loud bars and shallow people, and loves to travel. Her eyes locked on mine, she says, "If you're who I think you are, I like you. And I don't care what other people think." But I detect the familiar hint of doubt in her voice.

The American Heritage Dictionary defines the word "identity" as "the set of behavioral or personal characteristics by which an individual is recognizable." Such characteristics are difficult to identify by staring at one's face. There are few things that all of the Barbs in all of the mirrors of my life have in common: we all love to read, we have a weakness for animals, a need for attention, an eye for beauty, and a tendency to be judgmental. However, all the "significant" aspects of my life — behaviors, opinions, and careers, or those things around which most people form their identities — have changed with each passing year.

More than a decade has passed since I thought of the ghost. Usually, David is standing next to me as we brush our teeth and get ready for bed, but tonight he is still downstairs, catching up on his e-mail. I flip off the light and everything reflected in the eight-foot-long mirror on the wall above the dual sinks blends into the background — the tub and shower behind me, the towels, even the green carpet and walls of the bedroom to my left, take on a blue cast. From the downtown buildings in the distance, red, yellow, and white dots, like stars, fill the circular window above my head.

My features are difficult to discern. My face falls in shadow, but I continue to stare at my reflection. A thought enters my head — *I am not a ghost.* My eyes widen with surprise and awareness, and then the muscles beneath my skin relax and fall calm. Perhaps there was an old lady after all — not a supernatural being trying to travel through dimensions, but merely a Barb I have not yet met, standing before a mirror I have not yet seen, and wondering if who she is has anything at all to do with me.

For the first handful of years David and I were together, we were living my idea of a fairytale life. We traveled, we wined and dined, and we bought our first home — a swank, million-dollar penthouse in a newly constructed luxury condo building. The bulk of our income came from David's artwork. But then, the real estate bubble burst, and we entered the first (and hopefully only) major recession of my lifetime. Everything changed. People scrambled to shore up whatever assets they owned. Luxury purchases, such as fine art, stopped with the abruptness of someone shutting off a water tap.

We thought we were doing pretty well, but it turned out that we didn't "own" much of anything — the dealership owned the first new car David and I had ever purchased, and

Bank of America owned our home. Ours was one of those superjumbo loans they talked about on the news, the kind for which the broker said, "We don't need to check your records, just write a number on a piece of paper and slide it across the table and we're good." It was sketchy for sure, but we wanted that penthouse, so we just considered ourselves lucky to not be subjected to all kinds of audits and red tape.

As our credit card bills mounted and our bank accounts dwindled, it became devastatingly clear that we could no longer afford to live in our condo. It's no coincidence that this realization coincided with my escalating anxiety and depression. "Just a Place" reveals my turmoil, and ultimately, my acceptance of the situation, and my realization that life is about more than the things we have.

# Just a Place

*"You can never go home again, but the truth is
you can never leave home, so it's all right."*
— Maya Angelou

Forget marriage — my commitment with my man was consummated the day we followed street signs into a development company's office and set our eyes on their latest building model. Up until that point, I'd been carving out space for myself in David's Kensington apartment. It was his place, not ours. I wanted us to create a home together.

I joke that our condo was nothing more than a drawing on a napkin when David and I decided to buy. Though it's true that we signed the papers with no more than a blueprint and a huge hole in the ground to go on, the floor plans weren't actually presented on a napkin, and it's an outright lie to say the place was "nothing more" than a drawing. It was everything.

We were among the multitudes to invest near the top of the market, right before the bubble burst. When it did, many of our neighbors stopped paying their mortgages and bailed on their units. We stayed, hoping if we could hold on for a few more years, things would turn around — with the economy, with the market, with the world.

It took us a week to decide to buy our place; six months to decide to sell it. The recession rippled slowly toward us, past friends and family, eventually arriving at our doorstep. David is an artist, and art is one of the first things people cut back on when times are tough.

When a person gains weight, it happens slowly, barely noticed until, one day, those pants are hard to breathe in. I felt the same way the day I surveyed my finances and realized the balances on my credit cards were higher, the amount in my checking account lower. The majority of our income was going toward paying the mortgage.

"It's just a place," David said during one of the many discussions that led to our decision. It had begun as a hypothetical pondering, idle "what if" chitchat. But after a few months, the talks had become serious.

"It's not 'just a place,'" I said. "It's *our* place. I've been the HOA president for over five years, ever since the building was first finished — this is more than just a financial investment for me."

David's face lit up. "You wouldn't have to be on the board anymore."

"That does sound like a big weight off," I said. My gaze drifted into space as I imagined how great it would be to surrender the responsibility that comes with giving a shit. I was about to enter my sixth year serving on the board, and I knew just as well as David that I would never relinquish control if I stayed. Not only because no one else in the building seemed interested in replacing me (more than once, I had to recruit members) but also because I wanted to be involved in any decisions affecting my home.

"You have to admit," David continued, "We've been in a rut these last few years. Time is just going by, and we're doing the same things day after day." I nodded. "I've had plans for years to move our furniture around, but it's still the same."

This was the longest I've ever lived in one place. As a kid, my father's naval career had us moving around a lot. As an adult, 23 months had been the best I'd ever managed. "I do like change," I said. "It might be fun to get to know a different neighborhood."

"This condo costs too much for us now," David said.

"Yeah, but now that I think about it, even if we were flush, and the mortgage wasn't crippling, we'd still be pissing money into something that's not going to give us any great return. I'd much rather spend that on other things, things we do."

"That's part of it," David agreed. "Quality of life. Say we weather these few really bad months, then what? Think of how much extra we'd have if we rented a place at half the price of what we now pay to stay here."

There was no arguing with that. Dreams were being put on hold. It didn't make sense to stay anymore. We were no longer discussing the possibility of selling; we'd moved on to justifying our decision to sell. For the first time since I began taking anti-anxiety meds, I had a full-blown panic attack: hyperventilation, tears, David chuckling softly as he comforted me because he knew I'd soon be doing the same — laughing at my overblown reaction to something that, in the grand scheme, didn't matter.

As he stroked my hair, David said, "If selling our place and moving into an apartment is the worst thing we ever have to worry about, we're doing okay."

I knew he was right, but that didn't stop my tears. "It feels like something's dying," I said between sobs. "It's so stupid, I know, but it's our home. We made it ours."

"We have each other," David said. Again, he was right.

"We could have fun figuring out where we want to go," I said. I wiped my face and suddenly brightened. "If we rented a house with a yard, we could have a garden and maybe even get a dog!"

"Don't get ahead of yourself," David said.

I took a deep breath and looked around the room. "We had a great time here."

"And we'll always have those memories. And we'll make new memories wherever we go."

"It's going to be hard," I said.

"We'll have our ups and downs, but we'll get through it."

"It's just a place." I realized these words would have to become a mantra until I'd convinced myself they were true. I looked David in the eyes. "One thing I know for sure, even now," I said, cupping his face in my hands, "is that home is wherever you are."

 Eleanor Roosevelt once said, "No one can make you feel inferior without your consent." I do my best to keep these words in mind as I go about my life, but it's not always as easy as it sounds. As a child, I was embarrassed to admit to being bullied, because I thought it was akin to admitting I had failed to be strong and not let the cruel words or deeds of my peers affect me. As a grownup, I admit that knowing better doesn't mean feeling better, and that bullies are just as prevalent off the playground.

# Shark Tank

*"People who love themselves, don't hurt
other people. The more we hate ourselves,
the more we want others to suffer."*
– Dan Pearce

Every so often I find myself confronted by a seemingly innocuous phrase that rubs me the wrong way. This week, the offending line is "Don't let it get to you," a sentiment that simultaneously comforts the recipient while displacing the blame. It has a way of scratching into one's psyche, leading one to believe, *I let that get to me, therefore any hurt feelings I'm experiencing are my fault.*

The simple fact of life is that people can be jerks. The interwebs have increased the average person's exposure to jerks by an order of magnitude. If I could have bought stock in internet trolling, I'd have a few planes by now. From the playground to the office to the comment thread, at some point we all have to deal with a generally unpleasant person who derives pleasure from putting others down.

If Psychology 101 taught me anything, it's that those who lash out at others (trolls, bullies, abusers, whatever your name for them) are unhappy and insecure. But that's only a salve to slap on a sting while the poison gets under your skin and spreads.

I was bullied mercilessly in junior high. I had a tier of tormentors. It wasn't the ruthlessness of the lone individual at the top that got to me, but rather the number of people who jumped on the bully-Barb bandwagon. My main tyrant — a 13-year-old sadist — wasn't the worst of my problems. Sure, he made me dread showing up to school — taunting me with unflattering nicknames like Bar-Barf, putting melted chocolate in my backpack, and Vaseline in my shoes. But even in the eighth grade I could tell he had issues. So, as irritating as he was, I could write it off as, *That one's not right in the head.*

It wasn't the name-calling or the physical harassment that ruined junior high for me — it was the psychological agony that stemmed not from my being targeted so much as my being tested. I had a close-knit group of girlfriends and a few "best friends." One day, without warning, I found myself unwelcome at the lunch table and told to go away if I was walking too close to the group in the halls; it was as if I'd ceased to exist. It was a collective shunning — I was like a diseased monkey being pushed out of the troop.

Meanwhile, my friends welcomed the new girl I'd introduced to them. She'd been a midyear transplant from another school and, until then, I'd been the only one to reach out and offer my friendship. Even she joined in on the shunning. Too embarrassed to sit alone, I began to take my lunches with a teacher whose work I helped grade.

At the end of the school year, one of my "friends"

was passing out invitations from a giant bag on her shoulder for her end-of-the-year party. There had to be at least a hundred of those little scrolls. I thought it was so cool she'd thought to roll them like that. As I stared at the bag expectantly, a girl named Sarah stepped forward to shoo me away and said, "Don't think about asking for an invitation. You're not invited."

That summer, I spent a lot of time crying. My mother and sisters did their best to cheer me up, from deriding my ex-friends to attempting to rebuild my shattered self-esteem. I smiled and pretended their antics were working so that I didn't seem like such a miserable chump.

It wasn't meant to be cruel, what those girls did to me. When school began again, we were all friends like nothing had happened. It wasn't until senior year that one of my besties finally shared the answer to the question that had plagued me for years: Why?

To my surprise, the answer had nothing to do with my failings as a person. "I just wanted to see if I could get them to do what I wanted," she explained. "I told them to stop hanging out with you, just to see if they would."

My friend's revelation conjured images of a documentary I'd seen in which lion cubs tackled and tumbled, unknowingly honing their predatory instincts as they played. I didn't blame my friend for her little power trip; she was just unwittingly preparing herself for the shark tank that is adulthood. What I didn't realize at the time was that rather than being just a victim, I, too, was growing — developing and hardening my emotional armor.

Sometimes I feel like I live on a little island inside of my head. I'm on this island, and there's a giant ocean between my shore and the physical me that interacts with other people. My survival mechanism is to detach myself emotionally. But, words... they're such good swimmers.

I live my life in the public eye, a lifestyle that invites commentary. It's one thing for someone to disagree with my opinion — I respect and value disparate points of view. That's cool. It's a big world with room for a lot of different ideas. However, when all talk of opinion is tossed aside, when people revert to their scared, confused, still-figuring-out-the-world middle-school personalities and resort to name-calling when there's no objective defense, what's left? "I'm rubber, you're glue, whatever you say bounces off of me and sticks to you"?

"Don't let it get to you," David will say after I read him a message that has already gotten to me.

"I just... I don't understand *why*," I respond, wiping a tear from the corner of my eye and then huffing at myself for caring what some person on the internet thinks about me. In that moment, I hate myself. Not because a part of me fears that every terrible thing that is written about me might be true, but because I allowed those words passage across my ocean and onto my island. I let them get to me.

# Becoming Worldly

Had I bothered to do a little pre-relationship research, Barbarella and I might never have gotten together. It wouldn't have been her OCD or her neuroses, or her endless worrying about *every little thing*. (For example, as I am writing this, Barbarella is worrying about the possibility that there may be microscopic tardigrades, a.k.a. water bears, living inside her body. The answer is probably not; they prefer the outdoors, though she may have ingested some at one time or another.) No, all of that would have been, and still is, absolutely fine. The deal-breaker, had I been forewarned, would've been Barbarella's severely narrow idea of what she considered to be acceptable food, which at the time was: chicken breast, pasta,

Hunt's tomato sauce, Heinz ketchup, broccoli, and a few of the less challenging items from Taco Bell.

For me, food, and the exploration and enjoyment of it with friends, is one of the primary joys of life. Whether it was the molded Jell-O 1-2-3 cake I made as a little kid for my mother on Mother's Day, the Hungarian food I'd introduce to my college housemates when it was my turn to cook, or the clam that Barbarella spit out into my hand on our second date, I have always loved sharing food with others.

About that clam — for our second date, I thought it would be nice for me to cook. After all, anybody can go to a restaurant and plunk down a credit card. Where's the effort in that? Taking time to make something special shows you really care. So, as I do whenever cooking for someone, I asked Barbarella what things she liked and didn't like. She told me she liked chicken and pasta, and that she did not like fishy things.

I honestly didn't think that my Thai stir-fry with mussels, cockles, scallops, and shrimp was "fishy." It had always been a crowd-pleaser, but in hindsight I now see that chicken and pasta might have been a more prudent option.

Had I known then what I know now I would have also realized just how much Barb liked me. To even allow me to put the small clam in her mouth was tantamount to someone with severe arachnophobia acquiescing to having a live tarantula placed on their face. I'm not sure she would have done that for anyone else.

 Oh, come on! Who in his right mind asks a woman what she likes and doesn't like, and then serves her something on the "doesn't like" list? I will never understand why David thought it was appropriate to prepare a seafood dish after his date pretty much said, "anything but seafood." I was shocked and horrified when he opened that pot of steaming shellfish.

But I could tell he was proud of the dish, and he'd mentioned how it had taken him all day to put together. I wasn't used to a man going to such lengths for me. He insisted I try it, no matter how hard I shook my head or how much of the white was visible in my eyes. "Just taste it, it's really not fishy at all," he said. I hadn't told him about my texture issues yet. He seemed so sure I'd like it, that I allowed him to pop the chewy, briny bit into my mouth even though I have never liked clams. I was mortified when I couldn't keep myself from gagging the moment it touched my tongue, but I am forever grateful for how cool David was about the whole thing. He put his hand out, probably so I wouldn't eject the bivalve onto his clean floor, but still. He put his hand out, he caught the clam, and he learned his lesson.

 Barb doesn't cook. We joke that all her recipes begin with "pierce plastic film several times with a fork before heating"

and that she won't even microwave
something if it's going to take more
than five minutes, but that's actually
true.  What kind of bizarro family
has four girls, none of whom cook?
Fortunately for Barb, and all her sisters,
they married men who do.

Barbarella's editor knew that she
didn't cook and thought it would be
hugely entertaining for her readers if
she were to try baking a cake. She was
right. It was great fun for everyone
but poor Barb. Frustrated, she pleaded
with me to help her, and I wanted to,
but I knew I couldn't. All I could do
was giggle-laugh, which Barb did not
appreciate. I wasn't laughing at her, or
even at her expense — it was the only
reaction my body could conjure as I
fought my desire to jump in and rescue
her. In the end, I did help her out with
a couple of the finer points: What are
soft peaks? What is a double boiler?
And, Do I really need to fish the bits of
eggshell out of the batter? (Yes.)

I watched the whole 3-hour ordeal
from behind a video camera. Barb
swears that no one will ever see that

tape, but I'm hoping that at some point, perhaps years from now, she may feel nostalgic enough to pull it out, or be willing to auction it off for the benefit of a charity that teaches kids how to cook.

 No one will every see that tape. On a related note, these ten years later ("Let Them Eat Cake!" was one of the first columns I ever wrote), I think it's hilarious that I put quotations marks around the word "foodie."

# Let Them Eat Cake!

*"Baking — Messy but reliable method of taking a complete kitchen inventory by removing and covering with a sticky batter every single utensil, implement, and container from every drawer, hook, cabinet, or shelf in the kitchen."*
— Beard & McKie, from *A Cook's Dictionary*

I was raised on chicken and pasta. My mother, catering to my father's persnickety palate, had a limited repertoire from which she chose her recipes. Hunt's

Tomato Sauce poured over frozen ravioli, Ragu passed through a sieve (who wants to be surprised with the random crunch of an onion?), the occasional vegetable — canned corn or green beans, frozen broccoli, and mashed potatoes from a box. Given this history, it's no surprise that my sisters and I grew up to be finicky women with no kitchen know-how.

Shortly after my sister moved out, she phoned me in frustration: "Hey Barb, I'm trying to boil these eggs, and I don't know what to do! Do you put the eggs in *before* or *after* the water boils?"

Confident in my *eggspertise*, I said, "Alright, calm down. What's happening now?"

"I put the eggs in, and now there are bubbles coming up from under them," she said.

"Are they big bubbles?"

"Kinda… I mean, I don't KNOW! Wait, okay, it's boiling right now, lots of bubbles, so I let it go like this for 20 minutes, right?"

Taking a moment to consider our options, I responded, "I think as soon as it starts boiling, you're supposed to take it off the burner and let them sit in the water until it cools."

"Ah, okay. Awesome. Thanks so much, Barb."

"Anytime, Faye." Faye is my nickname for my sister Heather (Feather Head became Faye Haye, and now it's just Faye).

Years later, while living in L.A., I called *her* with an

inquiry: "Hey Faye! Just a quick question: does it make me *more* white trash if I put the ketchup directly *on* the macaroni and cheese? Like, is it better if I keep it on the side and dip my fork in it instead?" This time, it was she who was all-knowing. "Either way is white-trash, Barb." With no one around to call me out, I squirted red on yellow for the first time in my life (and not the last).

Our calls for help diminished as the people in our lives filled us in. Heather's husband, Sean, introduced us to red and green peppers — novel! My best-friend Stephanie taught me that broccoli could be eaten uncooked. Who knew? Slowly, we each learned from outsiders that there was more than one way to cook a chicken.

My lover has shown me much in the way of gastronomy, and considers himself a "foodie." I like the taste of many things, but I've had neither the patience nor the interest to *make* them. I have a thing about textures, and most raw food triggers my gag reflex. Issues aside, I decided I would leaf through the many shelves of David's cookbooks and find a cake to make my friend George for his birthday. I found my recipe on Wednesday, which gave me three days to prepare it for Friday's party. I'd made cakes before (with the help of Betty Crocker and Duncan Hines) but never had I done more than open the box and add water (fancier cakes needed milk and eggs).

This time would be different — I'd make a cake from *scratch*, sure to impress the birthday boy, along with a handful of friends who know of my aversion to anything domestic. Wednesday I read the ingredients for the Panamatorte, a chocolate-almond flourless cake invented to commemorate the opening of the Panama Canal. I chose the recipe for selfish reasons (I love chocolate-almond-anything, and the ingredients were few — this would be a piece o'… well, you know). This all seemed so easy! I wondered why I had avoided recipes that didn't begin with "pierce film cover several times with fork to vent." Granted, all I had done was read the ingredients, but how hard could it be? It's just following directions, and I'm an intelligent woman. I wasn't worried in the slightest.

My shopping list was short, manageable: eggs, bittersweet chocolate, almonds — easy. Springform pan? Okay, whatever that is. Breadcrumbs? Weird, but I'm game. When Vons turned up dry in the pan department, I went to the only place I knew sold cooking stuff — Williams-Sonoma in Fashion Valley. A hundred dollars later, I left with two pans, a bar of chocolate, and a small tube filled with white icing (for writing). I had everything I needed. Except experience.

Friday morning, I went downstairs to find that David had laid my ingredients neatly by the pans after straightening up the kitchen. *Aw, how helpful he is.* I looked down at the recipe: 7 large eggs, *separated*. When I asked David to fetch me seven little bowls — one for each of the eggs — he laughed out loud. "So they don't go in separate bowls? What's it mean, then, that I should separate the eggs from the shells?" His answer: more laughter. *Hey, you shit! Help me!* Through giggles, he managed to say, "This is *your* cake, babe. Anyway, it's much more fun watching you try to figure it out." When I finally guessed that I was to separate the yolk from the white, I read in his face that I was on the right track. Encouraged by this new information, I began to separate eggs. *Um, EW!* I held back a gag every time that slimy snot touched my fingers. Everything about the process disgusted me, and each time I touched egg white or yolk, I ran to the sink and rinsed my soiled hand with scalding hot water. David kept right on laughing. *Asshole.*

I have as much patience as a hummingbird. I choose Lean Cuisines based not only on flavor, but also on how many minutes they require in the microwave — six is pushing it. Eggs all "separated," I was ready to beat. The recipe said, "Beat until you achieve soft peaks." What are soft peaks, and how does one *achieve* them? David was no help, so I switched on the electric mixer. Fifteen seconds later, small bubbles rose in the bowl. "Are those peaks?" Blank stare. "Don't make me hurt you. Are those peaks? Why don't they just call them bubbles like everyone else?" Frustration was evident in my tone. He said, "I don't want to help you, because this is so entertaining, but I'm torn because I like George and I don't want his cake to suck." He had said the same thing when he insisted that I remove those small pieces of shell before mixing shit together. I got him to spill: Peaks can be seen when, after lifting the mixer, the beaten whites pull away from the beater and flop over, forming "soft peaks." And I was supposed to *know* this? These weren't directions. This was CODE.

I almost cried with relief when I read that I could melt the chocolate in the microwave. Fortunately, because my man is such an avid chef, his kitchen is stocked with everything a cake-baker could want. Unfortunately, despite 22 months together, I never bothered to learn where he keeps his tools of culinary creation. Most of my time was spent muttering curses as I dug through cupboards, drawers, doubtful that I would recognize a "rubber spatula" upon seeing it. There should be a little picture of each item required to make a cake right next to the recipe.

After figuring out how to open the food processor (an adventure in itself), I struggled to chop the almonds until they were "a fine powder, but not oily." Shouldn't there be a gauge on these things? I turned it on and off in two-second intervals until the nuts looked like small gravel — good enough. With everything mixed and folded, I poured my concoction into the pan and turned my attention to the frosting. The Pillsbury Dough Boy giggled in my head, taunting me with ready-made. So close to completion, I resisted the urge to run to the store and fake the finish. I had no idea how much butter went into frosting. I melted more chocolate (thanks to the microwave), and added two sticks of butter (a tablespoon at a time, to fully emulsify). Butter alone, like mayonnaise, is an emetic to me, but I beat away, and voila! Like gold spun from straw, icing appeared from the butter bowl.

I squeezed a crude "Happy Birthday George" from the white tube, and pressed toasted almonds (one at a time) along the sides of my labor of love. I sat back, behind the digital video camera David had set up to tape the drama (blackmail, I know it), and asked, "Now why the FUCK would anyone EVER want to do that?!" My answer came later, in the form of moans and groans, followed by compliments and gratitude from friends, and most importantly, the birthday boy.

You know, I've got enough ingredients to make another one.

 When I first started writing my column, my life experience had been limited to partying. I could name the best bars and dance clubs from Hollywood to Tijuana, but outside of that, my level of sophistication didn't even register. Many of my early columns reflected my disdain for anything I considered to be gourmet fare, or as I referred to it, "snails and shit." But I'd gotten together with a serious foodie, and David was determined to expand my horizons. In the span of five years, I went from defending my right to put ketchup on my mac 'n' cheese to opting for the "chef's whim" tasting menu. I even started writing restaurant reviews — a vocation that the obsolete "no thanks, I only eat chicken and pasta" version of me would find preposterous.

It all began with cheese.

# A Matter of Taste

*"Laurie got offended that I used the word puke.*
*But to me, that's what her dinner tasted like."*
— Jack Handy

Last week, David received a package Fed-Exed overnight from New York. Curious about a possible gift for me, I hovered over him as he sliced open the box with a razor. When he cut through the space-aged, climate-control wrapping, I nearly passed out from the stench of what smelled like a combination of sweaty sneakers and vomit.

"The cheese has arrived!" David declared. "We need to act quickly, there's no time! This cheese is at its peak of perfection!" I gazed into the box at the source of my sudden nausea. Five small hunks — the first of four cheese installments David ordered through the *Rosengarten Report* — stared back. David Rosengarten is a food expert, and my David subscribes to his newsletter.

Rosengarten and a team of experts aged a selection of cheeses with the precision and care of J. Lo's handler. Every hour, according to their individual needs, the cheeses were brushed with salt, spritzed with grappa (an Italian brandy made from grape skins), patted down, and rubbed with oil. We rushed to the store for cheese accessories — wine for pairing, fruit for nibbling, crackers, and baguettes from Bread & Cie. Our final stop was Whole Foods, where we procured the same types of cheese under the assumption that the Whole Foods cheese had not undergone the rigorous East Coast training program. This cheese would be placed next to its pampered counterpart for comparison.

When we returned home, David grabbed the landline, I grabbed my cell, and we began dialing. I called Grace (who hates cheese) because she'd enjoy the wine while her husband Ben sampled the flavored curd. David was on the line with his friend Jamie when I made contact with Kip. "Kip, we have a cheese emergency! Can we count on you?" He didn't even ask for an explanation before confirming himself and Renee. There was no need to call Ollie — he was sitting in the chair next to David. We tried to limit the number of people for the emergency cheese fest, for this was the beta test of what is to be a total of four parties (one for each of the monthly cheese installments).

Finished with his calls, David labeled the cheeses with the little plastic cards that came with the package. I decided the outfit I was wearing — black velvet pants and a pink sweater with a pink rabbit-fur collar — would suit the occasion just fine. While David designed the spread, I went hunting to find and light the candles he'd placed around our home. Ollie "helped" by following me around and blowing out each candle as I lit it. "Stop it!" I'd light another one. *Ffoooof,* out it would go. "STOP IT!" I'd light another one. *Ffooof,* out it would go. Our argument came to a halt when we had pushed our way into the kitchen, wrestling over the long, red click-stick lighter.

"Would you two..." David snapped, yanking the lighter away from us.

Tea lights in small glass containers lined the wooden staircase. I found more candles by the windows, in the bathroom, and throughout the kitchen and living room areas. Cheese biographies were spread around. These information sheets, as thorough and specific as the information one might receive upon "adopting" an Ethiopian child for a dollar a day, had also come in the package.

David poured wine for friends as they arrived. "You're going to try the Stilton? Here's a glass of port. Goat cheese for you, Ben? Try the Sancerre, I think you'll appreciate the combination." I stuck with Stilton, a kind of sharp blue cheese. After a bite of the Stilton we had gotten at Whole Foods, I understood the importance of aging: there was no comparison; Rosengarten's Stilton was divine. Moans of appreciation escaped the mouths of our guests. As the wine and cheese flowed, I found myself relaxing for the first time in over a month.

David, my beloved food snob, has been trying to broaden my taste-bud horizons ever since our second date; he refuses to accept that it is possible for someone to be content with a limited experience in any facet of life. For this I love him, but as one who is quite happy with her tastes, I admit that his pushing for me to have the same zest for food exploration as he does can sometimes get annoying.

David was happy to see me enjoying the fancy tastes, but he noticed I hadn't touched either of the two stinky cheeses.

"Come on, just a bite," David prodded.

"Absolutely not. That smelly crap is going nowhere near my nose, let alone my mouth," I said.

"You might like it."

"Highly doubtable." A few heads nodded in agreement with me.

"You won't like it, Barb," Stephanie said from behind David. "You should stick with the Stilton."

David's frustration was evident. Gesturing toward the runny, repugnant, and offensive comestible, he said, "What if you tried this and you really liked it? It might be your new favorite food!"

"No way." I was steadfast in my conviction that if it smells bad, it will taste bad — something I'd learned years earlier when Stephanie insisted I try kimchi, a Korean dish prepared by seasoning cabbage and burying it in a hole where it is allowed to rot until it's ready to be dug up for serving. I brought this up in my defense, but David, a kimchi eater, stood his ground.

Trying a new tactic, he said, "It's too boring to eat the same thing all the time. Would you watch the same movie over and over?"

"I have."

"Yes, but would you watch only one movie for the rest of your *life?*"

"My food intake is not limited to one movie," I said, following his analogy. "Let's say a chicken dish is like a chick flick. You can serve chicken a thousand different ways, but in the end, I know I'm getting chicken, and I know that I like chicken. In a chick flick there's going to be conflict and maybe I'll cry, but in the end, I know the girl will get the guy. Beef could be action flicks — the hero *always wins*. See where I'm going with this?"

Our friend Jen chimed in, adding, "Kimchi is subtitled!"

Still stating my case to David, I said, "You refuse to watch horror movies. How do you know there's not one that you'll love? Hmm?" I had him there. "Not wanting to try food I'm convinced I'll spit out is like you not wanting to watch a movie you're convinced will scare you and give you nightmares. I'll eat that cheese if we can go rent a horror movie."

Laughing, David said, "Fine, you win this time. But remember, you promised me that you'll try wild boar when we get to Venice."

"I may have to renege on that," I teased. "Unless, of course, you can assure me that there will be chicken nearby in case of an emergency. Now, how about some more of that port?"

 I did try the wild boar in Italy (not in Venice, but in the Umbria region), and I loved every bite. By the time we went,

David had been working to expand my palate for a few years, an endeavor that has served us both well.

But developing sophisticated tastes is only one part of becoming worldly. The word itself implies travel. In that sense, I had a semi-worldly upbringing — my parents were born and raised in Brooklyn, so I got to spend time with extended family in New York. We crossed the country in our orange VW bus a few times, so by the time I was in high school, I had passed through most of the states between New York and San Diego. As a kid, I lived in California, Alaska, and Rhode Island. But this was all domestic travel, and fairly low rent at that (we'd stay in Navy housing, cheap motels or even sleep in one of the hammocks in the VW).

David had traveled internationally before, but when we met, I didn't have a passport. Together, we began to explore the world (the clean, safe, non-humid, unbuggy parts, that is).

Many of our trips have been in relation to David's photographic art. Whenever one of the galleries

representing him has an exhibition
of his work, they invite us to attend
the opening reception. In "Bud-Weis-
Art" I detail my introduction to the
art world, and my budding interest in
art that later blossomed into a fully
art-centric life. It was during that trip
to David's exhibition in Houston that
I procured my first piece of original
art. Since then, I've amassed a modest
collection of word-themed pieces, and
have become so involved in the art
scene that I even produced and hosted
a weekly television show to highlight
regional artists.

The next trip we took for an
exhibition of David's work was also my
first time off the continent — we went
to Zurich, and it was this international
excursion that left me hungering to
see more of the world. In the course of
our travels I developed a nasty luxury
boutique hotel habit, to the point
where hotels are now as much (and in
some cases even more) of a destination
than the towns they're in. I blame
David for spoiling me — he introduced
me to the lavish experiences that have

made it impossible for me to accept
the sorts of accommodations I'd once
found satisfactory. Bad David.

# Bud-Weis-Art

*"It is the spectator, and not life, that art really mirrors."*
— Oscar Wilde

Watching Catherine shift her weight from foot to foot, I rejoiced in my decision to wear practical shoes. It took only two gallery openings, where I need to be standing — and pleasant — at David's side for three hours to teach me that wearing heels is just plain stupid. As manager of the gallery, Catherine was on her feet long before we'd arrived, hanging the last of the show, cleaning up, purchasing a box of generic white wine and cans of Budweiser.

This was my first time to David's gallery in Houston, one of the nine that represent him nationwide. Since my life as a paralegal abruptly ended, I've found myself available to accompany my love to all his shows. Of all the cities I've visited (Los Angeles, Seattle, West Tisbury on Martha's Vineyard, and New York), this was the first time I'd seen patrons offered beer. Most galleries serve red and white wine or champagne; in West Tisbury, of course, it's an open bar.

After David had finished adjusting the lights ("It has to hit the print *just* right"), we waited for prospective collectors. We did not have to wait long. A man walked in, company ID badge dangling from his neck over a pot belly, and beelined toward David. Ah, a techie. When these guys approach, I suddenly find something interesting to look at over there — "there" being anywhere other than where the techie is.

Techies are men (always men) who want to talk shop; they ask David about his camera, his process, his printing, down to the grainiest of grainy details. I picked up a great line to use when this situation occurs: "Let me know when you guys are done sniffing each other's butts." With David's extensive technical knowledge drawing techies like preteens to *Playboy*, my snappy retort is frequently put to use. The unfortunate thing about techies, aside from their terrier-like tenacity to take up the bulk of a featured artist's time, is that seldom are they buyers.

I've seen David's work before, so I tend to pass time at these functions by watching attendees. Distinct species of gallery-goers remain consistent from city to city.

Drinkers make up the greatest number of gallery exhibition visitors. I have seen people walk into a gallery and stride right past the art, straight toward the free drinks. They return again and again for refills of wine. At evening's end, their lips and teeth are stained purple, their movements loose, and their voices loud.

The Houston gallery was set betwixt other galleries, all showing work on the same evening. This is a great setup for drinkers — more free booze, more drink options. I left David alone to answer the techie's questions and joined Catherine in the back, where she was pouring beer from cans into plastic cups. Only men chose beer when given the two options (three, if you count Bud Light). As the room filled up, a woman approached Catherine with arm extended, empty cup in hand. She asked for a refill of red. "We only have white here," Catherine answered.

"What? Only white? *Pshhh*. Well, I guess I'll have *white* then." The drinker pushed her red-tinged clear plastic cup into Catherine's hand as though she were doing the manager a favor. As the pouting woman walked away, Catherine screeched, "These people are unbelievable!" With a southern Texan twang, she went on to give specific examples of audacity: "Once, this woman came up to me and said, 'Do y'all have any water?' and when I told her no, she said, 'There's a bathroom here, right?' I said, 'Yes, there is, right over there,' and she was, like, 'Well, can't you take this cup and fill it up in the sink?' Can you believe that? I told her, 'No, but *you* can. '"

Another drinker came by and, when informed that red was not an option, made a comment under his breath. To demonstrate my loyalty to an ever-reddening Catherine, I said, "Next guy who has an issue with our free selection will be directed to the local market to buy his own goddamn wine." She agreed with a *"Thayat's raaaht!"* Not surprisingly, the drinkers rarely set down their cups to enjoy or purchase anything on the walls.

Without missing a beat in her conversation about contemporary art, an elderly woman grinned our way. Looking her up and down, I concluded that she fit into my "eccentric old lady" category. Complementary to the techie, this broad is refined, reserved, and extraordinarily wacky. Her large, colorful earrings were purchased at an artisans' fair or museum gift shop, and a brooch the size of a kitten perched just beneath her shoulder proclaims her panache. She smiles through orange or fuchsia lips as she makes her way about the room, stopping only to take in the art or strike up a conversation about local theater.

Eccentric old lady is on the scene for every art-related event — museums, theater, galleries, craft fairs. Creative energy is the air she breathes. She is always in a good mood, because somewhere beneath her cashmere pashmina, within her wrinkled, ring-laden hands, she holds the answers to life's impossible questions. She is here to appreciate. However, only a few eccentric old ladies ever go home with a photograph.

I made my way back to David. A middle-aged couple greeted David in such a way as to make me assume they were related to him. He grabbed my arm and said, "This is my partner, Barbarella. Barb, this is Mr. and Mrs. X, they own one of my prints." They fit into my final category: collectors.

Collectors often come in twos, a husband and wife with an appreciation for the arts that goes beyond a gallery opening or a museum benefit. I've learned through friends (most of whom support local artists) that collectors are not necessarily wealthy. To have art in their homes, some collectors make arrangements to pay off the cost of a photograph or painting over time. For them, original art is a necessity. Because he produces an average only four new images a year, David's collectors tend to seek out his openings to view this year's new work. Regardless of whether they add to their collection, they always want to greet him, as if by purchasing one of his prints they not only acquired a work of art but also adopted a son.

The night was winding down — the last of the drinkers huddled around Catherine for the remaining alcohol. The eccentric old ladies had traipsed off to another event, I'm sure, because who wants to go to bed when there's art to be seen? Two techies were left, one-upping each other with examples of how *their* equipment excelled in various situations.

We left without seeing the work in neighboring galleries but returned a few days later (it's easier to see art without an opening-night crowd standing in the way). At the gallery three doors down, a piece on the wall caught my eye. I've seen art before, even some that I liked, but never had I wanted to buy anything. I stared at the square board. It was covered with tea-stained pages of Braille, and in the center was a large vertical rectangle composed of words that had been cut out of a novel and placed, hundreds of them, every which way. These words, forming the rectangle, disappeared at the top into a horizontal black cloud. At that moment, I fell in love with art for the first time.

I bought the piece, even though it was out of my price range. Handing over my credit card, I thought of how my father would blanch if he knew what I was spending on something so impractical. Once, he fell in love with a piece of art — a vase sculpted by my friend Gabe — but he couldn't bring his frugal side (98 percent of him) to justify the price. I ended up giving it to him for his birthday and, as I expected, he was delighted to have it. Looking at my art, I wondered, does this make *me* a gallery-goer? If so, which kind? I considered the free drinks but decided that drinkers are too tacky. No, I thought, as I reflected on the outfits I wear to openings

— feathers, fur, vibrant reds, and jewelry from museum gift shops. I'm definitely an eccentric old lady. Now I need to find the perfect brooch.

 David's parents, both born in Hungary, eventually settled on Martha's Vineyard, the hoity-toity island off the coast of Massachusetts. All I knew of the island before my first visit was that it was where Jackie O had her estate, and where famous people "summered," along with anyone else who had enough money to use the word "summer" as a verb. But after several trips to the island, where David and I would stay in a room at his parents' humble abode, it became clear to me that Martha's Vineyard wasn't a luxurious resort so much as it was a place for the moneyed to slum it.

# Roughing It

*"Give me the luxuries of life and I will
willingly do without the necessities."*
— Frank Lloyd Wright

For every five people who hear me say, "I'm going to
Martha's Vineyard for a few weeks," at least three
will respond, "*Ooooh, Maaahtha's Viiiineyaaahd*," and
nudge the end of their nose skyward with the tip of a
finger. Martha's Vineyard — summer playground of
the rich and famous — is an island three miles off the
southeastern coast of Massachusetts. Unlike Ibiza or
St. Tropez, where notable nymphets gather for clubs,
raves, and drug binges, the Vineyard is a magnet for
über-wealthy clans (e.g., tribes brandishing the names
Kennedy, Forbes, Clinton, and Gates) looking to get
away from the hubbub of life and enjoy some good
clean family fun. Each summer, they flock by air and
sea to the quaint island, where traffic lights and chain
stores are forbidden, and time is measured in days
rather than hours or minutes. For me, one who has
grown accustomed to fast-paced urban life with its
24-hour conveniences, visiting the Vineyard is a test
of endurance. To keep things in perspective, I remind
myself that it's not as bad as camping. I don't camp
well. When I want to gaze admiringly upon nature, I

prefer it be from a safe distance — like through a glass window or in high-def. My friend Stephanie once lured me to the Anza-Borrego Desert with the promise of a four-star experience. Upon arriving at our designated clearing, Stephanie set me up in a canvas chair with a cup of freshly brewed coffee, propped an umbrella over my head, and went about constructing our three-room tent. It wasn't until my friend was puffing away to inflate my air mattress that the full implications of "no plumbing" sunk in, sending a chill down my spine.

The only thing worse than peeing behind a bush is going in a port-o-john. Perhaps my most traumatic encounter with the nasty blue boxes was at Burning Man — the annual seven-day counterculture party held in a godforsaken desert 100 miles from the nearest running water. The portable outhouses, baking in the sun, would have benefited greatly from an hourly disinfection regimen. Instead, those foul plastic water closets (shared by tens of thousands of mind-altered iconoclasts) were serviced just once a day. Determined not to die of dysentery, I transformed one of my coolers into a chamber pot and my tent-mate into my chambermaid.

I am perplexed when prosperous people pay a premium to be inconvenienced. After watching the DVD our friends Paul and Sarah created to document their stay at the Ice Hotel in Canada, I made it clear to David that I did not want to follow in our friends' snowshoe-steps. "If you want to visit one day and check it out, that's fine," I said. "But sleeping there is out of the question. Did you see how many layers they had to put on before they went to bed? That's just ridiculous." The hotel wasn't cheap, but our friends weren't paying for comfort; they were purchasing a new experience. Like braving the subzero winds of Antarctica, fighting off creepy crawlies in whatever rainforests are left, or getting stabbed in the eye with a screwdriver, there are certain experiences in life I am quite content to live without.

In the weeks leading up to our summer trek to David's annual show at the Granary Gallery (known as the "Red Barn" to islanders), I switch my maintenance setting from its usual "high" position to "low." While packing, I tell myself I do not need Arizona Diet Green Tea (or the hundred other brands I will not find in the island's tiny grocery stores) and that the world won't stop on its axis if I limit myself to only four pairs of shoes. Upon arriving at David's parents' house, we are surrounded by a verdant landscape lush with trees. Sure, they're nice to look at, and I suppose they do their share in creating the remarkably pure, fresh air for which the Vineyard is famous, but for me, they're a glaring green reminder to pop a Claritin for my allergies. I don't even want to begin thinking about the bugs.

Everyone seems to adjust to the pace more easily than me. After attending receptions for David's work in Zurich, New York, and Tokyo, I had forgotten that on the Vineyard, "formal" is casual. "Preppy" is not a part of David's and my vernacular. For the opening of his show, David wore a black, stylishly crumpled linen/viscose blend jacket by Theory over a black Banana Republic tee and beige linen pants. I went for a '50s pin-up girl look with a red floral dress, black patent leather peek-a-toe shoes, and ruby lips.

The first moment my four-inch heels touched down on the Red Barn's wooden floor, it was apparent I'd painstakingly primped for naught. Making a quick survey of the room, I counted five Ralph Lauren ponies, three Izod alligators, a pair of pants festooned with the silhouettes of whales, and a plethora of sweaters tied around necks. Well over a hundred people attended the two-hour opening, maybe three who wore makeup. A few girls, with matted hair and mesh shirts over tanks and shorts, seemed to have come directly from the beach. I'd glammed it up for the art gala, just to find everyone else suited up for a sunny day on the yacht.

Back in the city, I walk barefoot along the plush carpet outside my door and down the hallway to chuck my trash into the chute, after which it disappears forever. Strolling just a few blocks from the front door of my building I can find numerous restaurants serving a wide variety of exotic cuisines, two coffee shops, two supermarkets, a wine bar, a cheese shop, and so on. It takes me ten minutes to get to any one of three shopping malls, and an extra five to reach Fry's Electronics.

Things are different on the Vineyard. Life is supposed to be easy on the island — slow-paced and simple. That's what they say. What they fail to mention is that "simplify" in this context means, "do it yourself." David's parents have to put their trash *in their car* and *drive it* to the dump. Five of the seven towns on the island are "dry," so we must remember to bring our own bottles of beer and wine when dining out. Restaurants are few and far between, and none of them deliver; movie theaters do not have stadium seating or DLP projectors. There's no Whole Foods, no Trader Joe's, no Nordstrom or Ann Taylor. No streetlights line the long, winding dirt roads. My phone gets no reception. Sure, the eggs are fresh, the water is clean, and the air is thick with oxygen; the neighbors are friendly, and people stop their cars to let you pull yours out into what traffic there is; but what if I have a middle-of-the-night craving for sushi? How did Jackie do it? Perhaps most distressing of all is the fact that if I needed to replenish my black liquid Lancôme eyeliner or SPF 30 facial lotion, the nearest department store is a 20-minute drive, a 45-minute ferry ride, and a 90-minute bus ride away. If that's not roughing it, I don't know what is.

# Home Sweet Home

*"What is more agreeable than one's home?"*
— Marcus Tullius

I opened my eyes and turned my head to face David, my hair trailing across the white pillow beneath me. This time it took only two seconds, rather than the disorienting five or six more common on recent days, for me to realize where I was: *guest bedroom in Ellen and Kirby's house, Boston.* In a voice soft enough to coax a wildcat into submission, David said, "Two left," then yawned and smiled, extended his arm around my waist, and pulled me closer to him. "Mm, yeah, two," I mumbled into his neck. Eight flights down, two to go. Three gallery openings attended, four cities briefly inhabited, one new passport broken in, three suitcases overpacked, and two people exhausted from 28 days on the road.

The sweet silence of slumber had almost reclaimed me when I noticed how light the room was. "What time is it?" I shrieked, and then thought, *Time, ha! I don't even know what day it is.*

I jerked upright and looked at the floor, where clothing, shoes, and toiletries seemed to have been spewed forth from my luggage as though the large plastic case had found my wardrobe unappetizing.

"I'm not sure, check your phone," answered David.

"Doesn't matter," I said, "Whatever time it is, it's time to get going."

Yanked from his mellow morning mood by my nervous energy, David shed the warm fluffy blanket and flung his legs off the side of the bed. "I guess we should pack," he said in a reluctant tone. "It will be nice to sleep in my own bed again. We had a great time, though, didn't we?"

"Yeah, beh beh, we sure did," I said, pausing from folding a pair of pants to return his calming smile with a pathetic smirk. "So much so that I am as disappointed as I am relieved to be going home." I longed for the feel of my bed and craved the permanent organization of the drawers and shelves in my closet and bathroom; but I couldn't stop thinking of the other things awaiting my return, things that are not so comforting yet all too familiar — like the mountain of bills and notices requiring my "prompt attention" that was waiting for me at the post office. Like the manila envelope leaning against my door, the one that contains the agenda for a homeowners' association meeting that I, the association's current president, must be prepared to facilitate in two days.

The thought of one task would remind me of another until my mind was racing uncontrollably and, overwhelmed by their simultaneous weight, I had the urge to say, "Fuck it," and crawl back under that fluffy blanket. Twenty-eight days is the amount of time it takes someone to make or break a habit, which is why most rehab programs operate in that time frame. In 28 days, I had become addicted to my peripatetic escapism, which is similar to heroin in that it offers immediate pleasure and eventual pain.

Traveling offered me an escape from routine responsibilities. "I'm out of town" was the *coup de grace* that won me temporary triumphs over external stresses. Once those words were uttered (or emailed), nobody pushed or questioned — they understood the futility of doing so and respected the almighty absence in a way they never would if I had simply said, "I don't want to deal with this for a few weeks. Why? Because I have *other things* going on."

But even the best procrastination device can backfire. Before embarking upon this latest adventure, I had become overly dependent on one dangerous sentence — one that I have continued, like an idiot, to employ while away: "Yeah, sure, I can do that... when I get back." Now, sitting on the last two flights, I try to keep track of all the things I must do upon my return. I realize I have 28 days worth of shit to get done within the next *three*, and I am beginning to freak out.

David, unaware of the paralyzing thunderstorm raging inside my head, turns to offer me an almond from the small crinkly bag in his hand. I stare at him, wide-eyed and unmoving. "What's up?" he asks, his hand withdrawing at my silent declination of his offer. Unable to answer, I furrow my brows.

"Just think about how wonderful it will feel to sleep in our bed tonight," David says, intent in bringing me back to the moment. He kisses my forehead and briefly rests his cheek on the same spot. When he leans back and searches my face with those penetrating, impossible-to-deceive blue eyes, I say, "I want to traipse around Soho without a worry in the world. I want to relax with a drink outside that cute Italian café near our hotel in Zurich. I want to listen to the rain as it lands on the green leafy canopy outside our room at Ellen's." I know I'm whining, but I'm unwilling to stop until the truth of it is on my lips: "I don't want to deal — I want to stay away from everything."

"Ah, but that's not possible," states Mr. Obvious, before giving my hand a conciliatory squeeze.

"Don't patronize me," I snap. My lower lip juts forward in frustration and my brows droop dramatically.

"Are you pouting?" David sounds amused.

"No," I mumble, mentally kicking myself for allowing the weariness of travel to turn me into a grumpy five-year-old.

"Look," David says, poking me with the word as though it were a sword prodding me to walk the plank. "There's a ton of stuff for you to look forward to at home." Slapping an eager expression on my face, I implore him to convince me. "We'll get to see our friends," he tries.

"Man, I've got so many calls to return," I complain.

"There's probably some bad movie from Netflix involving a unicorn waiting with our mail," he says.

I perk up a little, but decide this is no good. "Yeah, but you won't want to watch it, so it won't be as fun," I mutter.

David thinks hard as he pushes the snack wrapper through the mouth of his empty soda can. "You have that new V.I.P. membership to Rama! We'll hang out downtown and eat great Thai food. And don't forget, Ellen and Kirby will be here in less than a week, so we'll get to show them around red-carpet style." I raise a brow. Yes, this sounds good, this is what I need, something to look forward to, a procrastinatory light in the middle of the responsibility tunnel.

"We can go to the zoo," I offer, forgetting David has zero interest in watching me watch animals.

"I can think of something even better," he says, a devilish smile appearing between dimples. "Once we're home, we can run around the house naked." He lifts my hand to his face and kisses the tip of my index finger. "We can..." now the tip of my middle finger, "escape to our bedroom..." ring finger, "and we can be..." thumb, "*terribly* naughty..." pinky, "and –"

"Shhh," I say, cutting him off and stealing a kiss from his teasing lips. "Alright, you win — I can't wait to get home."

Barbarella and I love exploring new countries and experiencing new cultures. We just prefer to do it in relative comfort. Bugs, humidity, communal toilets, and camping are deal-breakers.

You might think that traveling with someone as neurotic as Barb would be challenging, but she is surprisingly easygoing when we're on the road. She still has her issues with time, of course, but so long as we arrive a couple hours early for anything scheduled (airline flights, restaurant reservations, etc.) she's very cool.

The only time she freaks out is when we're running late, and there's still a slim chance we'll make it on time. Huffing and puffing as we sprint through an airport to make a tight connection is definitely not Barb's happy place. But like the Hulk transforming back into Bruce Banner, once it's certain we either will or won't make it, Barb is fine again.

When we first began taking trips together, it surprised me that Barb seemed content to have me make all our travel arrangements. That was until I realized that if Circle A represented Barb's control-freakishness, and Circle B represented her patience, then researching flights and booking hotels didn't fall within the intersection of Barb's neurotic Venn diagram. Her lack of patience exceeds her need for control and, like shopping for televisions, external hard drives, or anything else that benefits from hours of mind-numbing comparison research, Barb just doesn't have the patience for it.

After days of research, I'll have narrowed the number of potential hotels down to three. I pull up their websites on my computer and ask Barb to have a look. They all look the same to her and, as her eyes begin to glaze over, she points to the first one.

"That one looks nice," she'll say.

"But what about the others? You didn't even read the descriptions describing the amenities!" I blurt.

"Yeah, they all seem good."

"Seem good? But they're all different! Each one has its pros and cons. I don't just want to pick one, I want to pick the *right* one." I reply, a bit overly obsessed and brain-fried.

Everyone has their own style of travel. Some folks want to hit all the famous "THEs" — *the* Eiffel Tower, *the* Grand Canyon, *the* Pyramids, *the* Empire State Building. Some are drawn to the organization of guided tours, while others prefer the freedom of itineraryless backpacking and crashing in hostels. Millions of travelers love visiting museums and cathedrals, and I have heard it said that the world can be divided into two types of people — those who like cruises and those who don't.

No matter what your own particular style, the most important thing is to have a compatible traveling companion. Fortunately for us, Barbarella and I are in alignment in this regard. We love great food and unique hotels. Barb even wrote a story titled "Hotel Fetish." We have a limited desire to see museums, cathedrals, or the main tourist attractions, opting instead to visit a supermarket or hang out at some small café and soak in the local culture. After hitting up some of the world's great cities, we've come to realize that our most satisfying travel experiences have been the ones where we have ventured to small towns off the beaten tourist map. Our primary objective is to try to catch a glimpse of life as seen from the perspective of the locals.

 A few months after we eloped, David and I went on our biggest trip yet. Over the course of five weeks, we stayed in ten cities in four countries, and saw many more in between. For me, it was a crash course in worldliness.

It was in France that I first began to loosen up about my food phobias. David, a quintessential gastronome, was delighted at my new attitude toward food, because this meant we could share serious foodie adventures, such as the time we went to Japan for the sole purpose of doing a ramen crawl after reading about the Tokyo

Ramen Gods in the first issue of David's Chang's *Lucky Peach* magazine, or when we went to Montreal for authentic poutine; or when we went to Rioja, Spain to taste wine made from the local tempranillo grapes, and vegetables grilled over burning grape vines; or the handful of times we've returned to New Orleans for the rich regional food that is among David's favorite. All experiences I never would have had, if it weren't for David pushing me to try new things.

# French Food

*"To the sober person, adventurous conduct seems insanity."*
— Aristotle

I awoke to the same rhythmic rocking that had lulled me to sleep seven hours earlier. I could hear David stirring on the bunk above, an indication that it was safe for me to open the blinds and let the morning light fill our cabin. We dressed and brushed our teeth, folded the top bunk to reveal a decorative reproduction of a Victorian-era sketch of Paris, and converted the bottom bunk into a couch. We were relaxing, watching the landscape flash by, when there was a knock at the door. It was the steward of our first-class car delivering breakfast. He seemed to be avoiding eye contact. I presumed it was because I had inadvertently made him blush the night before, when I had asked him about a white container kept in one of the cupboards. There was a hole at the bottom of the cupboard that drained to the ground below. The vessel turned out to be a chamber pot, or, as the man had explained while turning rouge, a receptacle "for in the night." Breakfast consisted of espresso and a pastry sealed in a plastic bag. I downed my espresso, but refused the rest. I had been served stale pastry for breakfast three mornings in a row at the Venetian bed and breakfast we had left hours before. I'd slept better on the train than I had in three nights, and I was feeling optimistic about the day ahead. We'd soon be pulling into the station in Nice — I could wait for real food.

By the time we'd collected our rental car, found our way out of a crowded and hectic Nice (with the help of several moped-riding locals and the map given to us by the rental-car agency), and reached Chateauneuf Villevieille (a small village in the mountains), it was lunchtime. We decided to stop for food, as check-in at La Parare, the B&B that was to be our home for the next two nights, wouldn't be for another few hours. In the village, we chanced upon two restaurants — one on the main road and one behind a crumbling stone church. We chose the latter, having found a parking spot near its entrance. A few children, their mothers looking on, laughed as they played among olive trees. Red flowers dangled from pots on the ledges above.

We followed the signs to the restaurant one floor up. A woman greeted us at the top of the outdoor staircase. She had the weathered face and scraggly hair of one who is accustomed to a life of hard work. She smiled, revealing a few missing teeth, and gestured for us to choose our seats. I glanced into the dining area, where two older men were drinking and smoking at a bar while a television blared, and then, shrugging off the steadily increasing chill in the afternoon air, I chose one of the pre-set tables on the outside terrace.

I turned a blind eye to the layers of dirt on the white plastic chair and took my seat. I had decided when I woke up that morning on the train that this would be a *good* day, which meant I could hardly allow myself to get worked up over a little filth before taking my first bite of French food. I turned over my plate, which looked as though it had been face down on the canvas tablecloth for weeks. I could sense David watching me carefully, the way someone might eye a priceless vase teetering on the edge of a shelf.

"This is great, isn't it?" I said, wondering if the high

pitch of my voice gave away my encroaching sense of panic.

"I particularly like the ceramic animal statues," David said, showing his dimples.

"I mean, we're at a restaurant in *France*, where even the simplest food tastes great... Right?" I was looking for reassurance. Before David could give me any, the woman appeared at our table. Between David's high school French, the woman's rudimentary English, and my mediocre miming abilities, we managed to order a charcuterie plate, cheese board, and two glasses of white wine.

When I realized we'd be drinking from the dust-covered glasses on the table, I told myself that everything was going to be okay — after all, I was in another country, and people in other countries lived differently, so I had to be flexible. David had forewarned me that in France, not everything comes sterilized and shrink-wrapped. I tried not to tremble when I noticed a spider climbing the tablecloth to my left and forced a stoic expression as I used my napkin to wipe the *terroir* from my glass. Because the air was humid, my efforts resulted in more of a smear than a wipe. I tried to convince myself that the French dirt would add complexity to the flavor of the house wine we'd ordered, an inexpensive Montrachet.

"How are you doing?" David asked after wine had been poured into my dirt-streaked glass and the food was set before us.

"Are you kidding me? We're in *France*, beh beh. I'm great! We have fresh, French mountain air, real French cheese, and—"

"Hey there," David said, addressing the two mangy dogs that had rushed him. The smaller dog, its long shaggy hair matted with burrs, resembled a homeless Benji. While David showed the mongrels some love, I seized on his distraction to douse my silverware with the hand sanitizer I keep in my purse. I tried not to think about the grease and organisms living beneath all that fur that David was touching. I wanted to insist that he disinfect his hands before sharing the food with me, but I was trying so hard to prove to him that I could adapt, that I could be flexible and cool, that I didn't always have to freak out over something "so silly" as a few germs. I kept my mouth shut but my eyes wide open, memorizing every place his fingers touched and taking care not to eat anything within the vicinity.

A man who appeared to be the chef showed up with our check. I strived not to count how many times he wiped his running nose with his bare hand. I kept a smile plastered to my face all the way to the car, and let it fall away only when I was sure David was focused on the road.

Our room at La Parare was perfect — tucked into a hill, nature's splendor on display outside, but not inside (meaning I would not have to contend with creepy-crawlies), and linens that were plush, white, and clean.

"I knew today would be splendid," I said, kicking off my shoes and falling onto the bed with a book.

"Hey, there's a little scrapbook here," said David. "It's a guide compiled by our hosts."

"Yeah? What's it say?"

After reading tips on places to visit in the surrounding area, David came upon a section about local restaurants. "It says the place on the main road has good food, but, ha! — that the poor decor should be overlooked. And then... *huh.*"

"What?"

"Nothing," David muttered.

"No, really. What is it?"

"It says here that they strongly *un*-recommend the place behind the church."

"What? Why?" My heart was pounding with apprehension, but a grin remained pasted on my face. "Really, it's cool, I don't care what it says. I mean, the food was good and we had a great time, right? Go ahead. Tell me."

David studied my face for a moment, decided to believe me, and said, "It says not to go there because they don't meet basic hygienic standards."

"Oh, that's it?" I said, wondering if my grand shrug had been a bit too melodramatic. "That's nothing." To keep from gagging, I thought happy thoughts about glitter, unicorns, and Prada, while conjuring images of the sparkling clean dining establishments I'd dined at in

Tokyo. Then, changing the subject so as not to give in to an overwhelming urge to vomit, I said, "What do you say we go have an espresso and pretend we're French?"

# French Fashionista

*"Clothes make the man. Naked people have little or no influence on society."*
— Mark Twain

She looked amused. Or terrified. It was hard to tell. I had only spent three, maybe four hours with her, tops. Rather than pausing to gauge her reaction, I pushed forward, sensing on some animalistic level that if I did, she would give me what I wanted. "Open it," I said in a firm but friendly voice that said, *I am not here to judge, I seek only to understand.* "No, I can't," she replied for the seventh time, but in a coy way that told me that her refusal was just for the sake of appearance. Or maybe I was wearing her down. Either way, it was clear to everyone in the room that she would succumb to the pressure, and soon.

She'd been introduced to me as Bérengere, but I couldn't pronounce that, so I referred to her as "Berry." Because the name of her husband was just as vexing, I had dubbed him "Armoire." David and

I sat on a couch in Berry and Armoire's fashionable apartment, located in the ultrahip Marais district of Paris, sipping champagne from jewel-colored flutes as we hounded our generous hostess to stand aside and open the cabinet door behind her. She hadn't meant for us to see anything when she had carefully cracked the door to just the width of her arm. She wanted only to illustrate a point in conversation by showing us one small object. She obviously had not foreseen my natural inquisitiveness and brazen American nosiness — a common mistake made by those with whom I am not well-acquainted.

As my mouth formed the words, "Come on, open it, I've already seen what's inside," I silently chided myself for being so barbaric. After all, this was the third occasion in as many cities that a member of Berry's family had magnanimously donated their time to enrich our European experience. David and I met Berry's parents, Pierre and Nicole, at the bed and breakfast in Venice. When they learned we were heading to the South of France, they invited us for lunch and a tour of Château Beaulieu, their extensive vineyard in Provençe. We came to know Berry a few days later, while enjoying a French interpretation of *chili con carne* and sipping a delicious rosé produced by Pierre's winery a few miles away. Nicole had unexpectedly been called away so Pierre had invited Berry to join us as the feminine representative of clan Guénant. Directly following lunch, Pierre, a busy man who employs 11,000 workers amongst his many ventures, gave us a personal tour of the Beaulieu estate. As David and I tasted the Cabernet Sauvignon her father had named after her, Berry was already winging her way home to Paris. It just so happened that Paris was to be our next destination, and before dashing off to the airport, Berry had graciously offered to meet us in the city, show us around her mother's art gallery, and take us to one of her favorite spots for tea.

When we met up in Paris, Berry had brought her husband with her. Sitting at a window-side table in Ladurée, the rich, exotic aroma of the rose tea, the small, elegantly decorated *Marquise* cakes, and the clamor of patrons at the pastry counter made for a delightful afternoon; for a few short hours, I felt Parisian. Unfazed by our American "charm," Berry and Armoire invited us for an apertif in their home the following night. It was there, relaxing on the couch with a bit of bubbly in me, that I engaged in one of my favorite hobbies — coercion by means of incessant, playful badgering.

Berry was a down-to-earth kind of girl, or so I thought. Her long dark hair was thick and shiny and fell perfectly down to the middle of her back. Her make-up-free face was fresh and beautiful, and her big eyes were like pools of chocolate. She dressed like a Boston collegiate, in solid colors and conservative cuts. She had once driven a jeep through Africa giving safari tours. But when we met up in Paris, something was amiss — it took about an hour for me to answer the age-old question I had silently asked myself — "What's wrong with this picture?" Today she wore blue jeans and a snowy white button-down that hung out loosely from beneath a dark cardigan. Her hair was brushed straight and the most she could have been wearing on her face was a smear of Chapstick. But like an ornate, jewel-encrusted vase filled with cattails, at the bottom of her plain, unassuming ensemble she wore metallic, baby-blue lamé high-tops. Confused at first, I decided to consider her choice in shoes an endearing quirk. That was before I realized just how deep Berry's fashion affliction ran.

It seemed to David and me that fashion sense came with the Paris postal code. Sitting at a sidewalk café off the beaten path, consuming a typical French breakfast of baguette, coffee, and orange juice, we watched Parisians as they went about their normal lives. All of the men sported jackets, designer shoes, and matching "murses." Regardless of whether they wore leggings or leather, all of the women appeared elegant. People didn't pedal as much as they cruised by on their bicycles like Audrey Hepburn, so smoothly that the wind could not knock a hair loose from their luscious coiffures; they looked more like they were sitting motionless on a prop with a film of the passing landscape running behind them. We had never felt so awkward and poorly put together.

Over tea, we learned that, prior to acquiring his job at Louis Vuitton, Armoire had never been much into fashion, and that he only wore the high-end runway duds because he happened to be the same size as the prototypes. I could buy that. Together with Berry's no-nonsense attire, I thought I'd finally found some different sort of Parisians, a couple who were not so preoccupied with being stylish. Perhaps it was my insecurity from those two days of exposure to perfectly attired people that precipitated my inappropriate reaction to Berry's secret, the one she now guarded with her entire body.

It had been the mention of my surprise at seeing those shiny blue high-tops on Berry's feet the day before that prompted Berry to tell us about a new pair of shoes she'd purchased just that afternoon — multicolored Adidas sneakers that were difficult to describe, so she'd just show them to us. But when she opened the door, I saw more than one pair of crazy-looking shoes.

Finally beaten into submission, Berry stepped aside, and I leapt off the couch and over to the built-in shelves that were piled with shoes. They were not just any shoes — these were Fendi, Prada, Louis Vuitton, Chinese Laundry, Miu Miu, and more. And

they weren't the kind you could get in the store —
these were psycho-colored, limited editions. "I have
a problem," Berry confessed as I dug through the
shelves and handled each shoe, reeling at the sheer
impracticality of trying to match any of them with
clothing. There were no simple colors, no black or
red, the two boring basics that comprise my wardrobe.
This went beyond fashion. This was *cutting edge.* I
felt betrayed somehow. "I've never even worn most
of them." She said this as if it were supposed to make
me feel better. Then she explained that this Imelda
Marcos-worthy treasure trove was but one-sixth of a
collection housed in three homes.

At a loss for words, I did the very thing I'd
promised I wouldn't do — I pointed and laughed. I
held up a clear acrylic heel in which plastic flowers
were entombed and said, "These. I mean, *these are
ridiculous.* "Turning the shoe over and over in my
hand, I acknowledged to myself that my joking
cruelty was born of envy. I had not the gumption to
purchase, let alone wear, such an audacious heel. I
looked up at Berry, who was staring at me, perhaps in
expectation of more ridicule. "Too bad my feet are a
size bigger than yours," I said, by way of concession.
"Because I would love to steal these and wear them to
my next wine-and-cheese party."

# Non Capisco

*"I speak two languages, Body and English."*
— Mae West

Exposed as I was to the elements, I was relieved it wasn't raining, but I was thankful for the clouds, which muted the sun's glare just enough so that if I squinted, I could make out the words on my laptop screen. Since my arrival in Trevi a few days earlier, I'd learned two important life lessons: not everybody speaks English, and not every town has Wi-Fi. As consequence of my ignorance, I was crouched on a curb in the one-street suburb of a medieval hilltop village, hijacking bandwidth from an unwitting Italian. The Wi-Fi was not found by accident — in each neighborhood we'd entered, David set out on foot with his iPhone, surveying the air for a signal. The awkward spot was not ideal, but desperation had made me less finicky. Apparently, Italians have yet to embrace the Internet with the fervor of Americans. After staying a week with our friends Urs and Gudrun at their home in Sweden, the four of us hopped a flight to Rome. For three days, we frantically darted around the city and then, mentally and physically exhausted by our breakneck sightseeing, we piled into a rental car and drove two hours north to the more sedate Umbria region. Umbria, the "green heart of Italy," is the area north of Rome and south of Florence characterized by a lush landscape of silver-leaved olive trees that blanket the region's rolling hills. Perched on several hillsides are small villages founded nearly 3000 years ago with stone walls that have been standing since the 1200s. A short drive from the more popular towns of Perugia and Assisi, Trevi (the village in which we were staying) is so off the beaten path that many maps of the region don't bother to mark it.

I was overwhelmed by the vast rural beauty and delighted by the charm of our apartment in *Residenza Paradiso*, a villa that has been inhabited by the family of owner and operator Emiliana for hundreds of years. When I walked in the door and across the room to the shuttered window that framed a Disney-esque, magical kingdom sort of view, I knew relaxation was but one deep breath away. I was just about to take that breath when a horrible realization struck. "*Ohmygod!*" The note of panic in my voice caused David to jerk his head my way and instinctively tense his body for fight or flight. I pointed accusingly at my laptop — the first thing I had unpacked — and said, "There's no Wi-Fi!" Because my eyes are accustomed to searching for such things in foreign accommodations, I had already ascertained that there was no Ethernet jack. David dropped his shoulders, sighed, and, for the umpteenth time in the four weeks we'd been in Europe, he put his arm around me and, in a soothing tone, said, "Don't worry, it's all going to work out just fine."

He didn't say, "It's all going to work out just fine if you set up shop on a street curb a short drive away," but there I was. At our request, Urs and Gudrun left David and me on the curb where David had detected Wi-Fi the day before. We'd asked our friends to go and do whatever they wanted for three hours; that way, we could check our email and get our net-surfing fix without the pressure that comes with knowing others are waiting for you.

When he'd had his fill of the Web, David decided to amuse himself by filming my plight with his new toy, a Canon HV20 he'd acquired to document our adventures. Minutes after David pointed his camera in my direction, an old man pulled up in a white station wagon. Leaving the engine running, the octogenarian stepped from the car and walked toward me. When he was close enough to be heard over the rumble of his motor, the man began talking. David asked him if he spoke English or French. Disregarding the question, the man kept speaking Italian and sweeping the air with his arms.

While we listened uncomprehendingly, David turned off his camera and I closed my laptop, convinced that we'd been busted for filming without a license and stealing broadband. Noticing my blank smile, the old man's face scrunched beneath his pale brown cap with the realization that I hadn't understood a word of what he'd said. For a moment he remained frustrated, but then he raised his brows, shrugged his shoulders, and continued talking, only this time he was much more animated. He gestured to his left, where a car was parked. "No, no, that's not our car," I said, but the lack of understanding was mutual. It suddenly occurred to me that I had the ultimate tool for bringing strangers together, sitting right there on my lap.

I held my hand up to the man in the universal signal for, "Please, wait a moment," and I opened my laptop and clicked on Google's "language tools." A moment later, I said, "*Questa non è la mia auto.*" Only I shouted it, because that's what you do when talking at someone who doesn't speak English; and, because I had no idea how Italian pronunciation works, it sounded more like, "KAY-STA NON AY LA MEEAH AW-TOH." The man's bushy white brows furrowed in confusion.

"Tell him our friends have the car," David said.

I typed in, "We are making a personal film, we are waiting for our friends," and pressed "Translate." I saw the words, "*Stiamo facendo un film di personale, Siamo in attesa per I nostri amici*," and said, "STEEYAMO FACKENDO UN FILM DE PERSONALAY, SEE-A-MO IN AH-TESA PURR EE NOSTRI AMICKEE."

The man looked baffled. He continued to speak to me in Italian, and I kept smiling, shaking my head, and saying, "NON CAPISCO." After ten minutes of this, another tech-related idea popped into my head. I would translate what he was saying! Only, it sounded to me like he was saying, "*Blah-oh, blah-ay, bambino, blah-blah-oh, tedesco blah-ay.*" I seized on the words I caught between the "blahs" and came up with "German," "war," "boy," "beautiful woman," and "five kilometers down the road." Like playing Mad Libs, all I had were a handful of nouns and verbs compiling a nonsensical story. I was beginning to feel I had it all figured out when Urs and Gudrun finally returned. "Oh, thank God, Urs!" I cried. I pointed at Urs and shouted toward my new friend, "ME AMISEE PARLA ITALIANO." To Urs, I said, "I think this man is trying to tell us a war story and something about a restaurant down the road called Bella Donna."

Urs and the old man chatted, gestured wildly, and laughed, while David, Gudrun, and I waited quietly on the sidelines. As abruptly as he had arrived, the elderly Italian returned to his car and drove away. David and I looked to Urs for an explanation. We expected him to confirm our Google-aided findings, but it seems our deciphering abilities were as deficient as my pronunciation skills.

As Urs explained, while I was yelling, "THIS IS NOT OUR CAR" in a language that hardly resembled the old guy's native tongue, he was trying to tell me that I reminded him of his wife when he first fell in love with her. While I was screaming, "OUR FRIENDS DROPPED US OFF AND

WILL RETURN SOON," he was telling me a story about his German friend who lives up the street and has a pretty wife, but that his friend's wife is not nearly as beautiful as his. Apparently, the old man had also told us a story about his youth, when he and some friends hid three deserting German soldiers in a basement for three months, supplying them with news, food, and water. And when I was pleading our case for making a personal film, the smiling gentleman was speaking of my hair, and how his wife, despite her mature years, still has long, dark locks. While chatting with Urs, the man had added, "and her tits are still up to here," making one of the many wild gestures followed by laughter that I had watched without comprehension.

When Urs finished relating the information, David and I — two thieves driven to apprehension by our guilt — exchanged embarrassed glances. We had assumed the man wanted to complain about our actions and shoo us on our shameful way. But in reality, even after he learned we could not understand him, the archaic gent just wanted to borrow the ears of two foreign travelers who happened to catch his eye and regale us with his life's stories.

 When we travel abroad, Barbarella and I try to be good ambassadors for our country. We're keenly aware of the bad impression left in the wake of

The Ugly American, so we try not to be one. Regardless, cultures differ, and we *are* American. One of the greatest rewards of travel is that you come home with a better understanding of yourself. We've never been more aware of our Americanism than when we were surrounded by non-Americans.

Every time I read Barb's sweet story, "Non Capisco," I can't help but laugh at how American we really are — specifically how uptight we can be. We had sniffed out an unprotected Wi-Fi signal so that Barb could dispatch her latest column to her editor. When an old Italian man saw foreigners with a laptop sitting on a curb in his small town, was he suspicious? Was he concerned that we might be terrorists? Did he think we might be CIA operatives trying to hack the national banking system? And even if he didn't peg us as CIA, was he certain that we must be up to some kind of no good? No. He just wanted to be friendly, say hello, and regale this beautiful woman sitting on the curb with some stories from his life. Not understanding what the man was saying, our very American reaction was to immediately assume that he was coming over to tell us that we were doing something *wrong* — hijacking Wi-Fi, videotaping in the wrong place, parking in a reserved spot, etc. I think we could learn a thing or two from that guy.

 My two most deep-seated food aversions are fishy flavors and snotty textures. I can handle innocuous, "light and sweet" seafood, such as halibut and sea bass; I even enjoy scallops and shrimp. But fishy fish ocean weeds, slimy snotty oysters, or rubbery clams and mussels, most of which harbor that briny, sea-funk flavor, are just not appealing to me. So of course I was a little freaked out about my potential food options when David and I first went to Japan. Despite a few fish-related traumas, upon arriving home, instead of immediately jonesing for a burger or a taco as I expected I might, my first food craving was for sushi.

We loved Japan so much that we vowed to go back as soon as we could. And we kept our promise — a few years later, we went again, this time not for an exhibition of David's work, but just to eat some ramen and spend a week in a rented Shinjuku apartment to experience what it might be like to live there. It was on that trip that we made some interesting discoveries of Japanese history, one of which, in "Kappa," I delighted in describing.

# Fish Food

*"Thy food is such as hath been belched on by infected lungs."*
— William Shakespeare

I don't know what I found more disturbing: the words, "It can be difficult to keep the live octopus in your mouth," or the accompanying illustration of a man seated at a table, his eyes locked open in terror, with eight tentacled arms stretching from his mouth and attaching themselves by suction to every corner of his face. I'd seen this before in the movie *Alien*. Snapping my head in David's direction, I begged, "PLEASE tell me we're not going to have to see anything like this in Japan." David ignored me and turned the page. Color drawings of raw eggs, chicken innards on a skewer, and slices of something pink did nothing to quell my fears. *Two weeks of this weird shit*, I thought. I tried to put a positive spin on the impending ordeal and told myself, *Hey, maybe I'll lose a few pounds.*

My food horizons have expanded exponentially since I met David. Before, I considered extra ketchup on my Kraft mac 'n' cheese adventurous. Expensive dishes in which food was carefully arranged in aesthetically pleasing designs were referred to as "fancy crap," and anything French was dubbed, "snails and shit." Though I haven't wavered in my aversion to the rich sauces and slimy fare of "high-end" French restaurants, I am now more likely to taste exotic cuisine (like cheeses that come with a rind), and I have learned to appreciate food that looks as good as it tastes.

Despite my growth, however, the idea of eating in Japan made my jaw clench in apprehension. See, I don't like fish. Unless it is a skinned and boneless chunk of halibut that has completely taken on the flavor of whatever it's been drenched in, I don't even want to see it on the table. Should it end up there anyway, I will avert my gaze and breathe through my mouth until it disappears. It's not just fish, either, but anything fish-related — the sight, smell, or texture of ocean plants, fresh or dried, triggers my gag reflex. In short, I was about to enter a foreign land that specialized in my culinary nightmare.

The month before we left, David and I undertook a cultural crash course. We ate at Japanese restaurants all over San Diego County. I ventured beyond teriyaki chicken and experimented with cucumber rolls, ramen, udon noodles, and even the esoteric *katsu-don* — a breaded chicken cutlet served in a bowl over seasoned rice and grilled onions and topped with a fried egg. I insisted on eating a burrito the day before we left, and I savored every bite as if it were my last.

"I'm not worried anymore," I said to David during the hour-long bus ride to our hotel in Tokyo. So far, everything had been safely Western — back at the airport, I had even purchased a latte from a vendor that sold hot dogs. I was lulled into complacency by the smiling face painted on the brightly colored, human-sized statue of a hot dog that stood next to me while I waited for my coffee.

But it turned out that navigating food wasn't as simple as avoiding fish — every item, even innocuous-seeming ingredients like chicken and tomatoes, was suspect. Apparently, anything I happen to find disgusting is a delicacy in the land of the rising sun. Things like gristle, skin, and fat, or fruit and veggies soaked in fish oil. I learned this the hard way, after I'd confidently passed through an entrance over which was painted a giant chicken — a familiar symbol that imbued me with a false sense of security.

Upon glimpsing our whiteness, the waiter handed us an English menu, a gesture that left me feeling both offended and relieved. I ordered some kind of chicken meal deal (or "set," as they call it), which came with an appetizer, soup, chicken, and rice. When the food arrived, my second impulse (the first had been to choke back bile) was to look for cameras. *This has to be some kind of joke they play on foreigners*, I thought. In a shiny, hand-painted, ceramic dish sat a raw chicken leg. That's right, that sick bastard served me the salmonella special. Beside it was my "soup" bowl, which smelled like funk and contained a tepid, nearly opaque liquid with a raw egg floating around in it. The entrée was no better — glistening gristle-covered bone on a bed of white rice. While I glared at the abomination of a feast before me, David chowed happily on his fish-flake surprise.

Like any big city, Tokyo offered plenty of dining options. I sought refuge in tofu, curry, and noodles. But as Murphy would have it, the day I finally found my culinary groove was the day we were to leave for Hakone, a small resort town a few hours away. It was in this quaint traditional village that I suffered the greatest food effrontery of all.

Because I had been prepped for what lay in store — David had explained that we were staying at traditional Japanese inns for two days and would have no choice when it came to what food would be brought to our room for dinner and breakfast — I stocked up on red bean buns at the train station.

Dinner was to be served in our quarters at 7. Our server, a friendly woman named Kazuko-san dressed in a beautiful kimono, brought each of the 11 courses to our private dining room, each time announcing herself before sliding open the shoji screen and entering the room on her knees. Our first course included an entire fish — head, bones, skin and all. It was three inches long. "I can't do this," I said. David smiled and popped his fish into his mouth and chewed.

The next item to arrive was a seaweed salad. Then sashimi. Then something brown and slimy looking. After Kazuko-san gracefully placed a course before us and then disappeared to let us eat, I would suspiciously inspect her latest offering. I would sniff it cautiously, look up at David, and say, "Taste this. Is it fishy?" David repeatedly answered me with a nod. In desperate, whispered pleas, I begged him to eat my food so that my dish would be empty when Kazuko-san returned to replace it with something even more horrific.

Finally, a bowl with a lid was placed between us. After Kazuko-san had backed out of the room, I said, "You open it."

"Nope, it's all you," said David. He'd been drinking chilled sake and seemed to be enjoying my agony.

"Fine. I don't care. It's probably more fishy crap anyway." I lifted the lid. "Hey! Pasta! Ha!"

Like a mirage convincing a lone traveler wandering lost in the desert that an oasis is mere steps away, I had seen what I wanted to see in that dish because the reality was too terrible for me to fathom. I clutched my chopsticks and raised the bowl. It was then that I caught a whiff of the stench — a salty, something-rotting-on-a-beach sort of smell. The mirage of pasta faded away and another image came sharply into focus. Tiny eyeballs, hundreds of them, were staring back at me. I dropped my chopsticks onto the table and stared into the bowl with grotesque fascination. "What the fuck? Are those... *baby eels*?"

I was stunned into silence when David doused the freaky little things with soy sauce and ate them with rice. When he was finished, David rubbed his belly like a happy Buddha.

"I'm starving," I complained.

"Look," David said, in an attempt to find a bright side for me. "At least we didn't have to pry any tentacles off your face."

# Kappa

*"If you reject the food, ignore the customs, fear the religion and avoid the people, you might better stay at home."*
– James A. Michener

"What is that, a duck?"

David followed my gaze to the green-painted humanoid statue. "Looks more like a turtle," he said.

"Turtles don't have beaks. And look at its head — maybe it's some kind of monk, that looks like a Friar Tuckish crown around a bald patch." We continued walking. After a few minutes, we passed a similar figure, only this one was doing some kind of handstand. "Maybe we're both right — it's a turtle-duck."

As we ventured further down Kappabashi-Dori — the area nicknamed Kitchen Town, which is Tokyo's go-to kitchen supply district for the world's largest city's 80,000-plus restaurants — I noticed tiles in the sidewalk, engravings on signs, depictions on banners, and more carvings, all versions of the same creature. Some of them were embracing a golden ball.

"I wonder what that thing has to do with cooking," I said. David shrugged. We'd already marveled at the specialized stores (some shops sell only those utensils and items necessary in the preparation of a single recipe, such as *soba* noodles), and salivated over the super-realistic plastic representations of ramen, sushi, ice cream, and any other prepared food I could imagine. After hours of exploring Kitchen Town, we were now in search of real food, which, ironically, was nowhere to be found.

As we backtracked down the sidewalk toward the train station (where we were guaranteed to find sustenance), I continued to wonder about the neighborhood's mascot. "It's Kappabashi-Dori, which means Kappabashi Street, but there are other streets that start with the word Kappa," I said. "Do you know what that means?" David shook his head.

Before leaving the country, I'd purchased a few Japanese language apps for my iPhone, one of which is an extensive Japanese-English dictionary. I typed in "kappa" and 21 related definitions popped up. "Ah, this makes sense. The first definition is 'kappa,' mythical water-dwelling creatures.' Also means 'excellent swimmer.'" I scrolled down, reading the additional definitions as I went. "Raincoat, vigor, printing, mythical —what the freak?"

"What?" David swiveled his head to make sure my suddenly shrill voice hadn't annoyed any natives.

"Check this out — one of the things that comes up under 'kappa' is, 'mythical ball inside the anus that is sought after by kappa.' Freakin' *weird*, right?"

Bafflement continued to dog us as we ate our curry and rice, as we rode the train back to Shinjuku, as we stared at the elevator doors all the way up to the 21st floor, as we entered our temporary home, one of myriad high-rise apartments in Japan with a distant view of Mt. Fuji. Once inside, I went straight for my laptop.

"Listen to this," I said. David retrieved a bottle of water from the fridge, kicked off his shoes, and joined me on the bed. "Kappa means river child or water sprite, which seems accurate, given how adorable and cartoony they are. Nothing about anus balls... oh wait, this is kinda close: 'Kappa are usually seen as mischievous troublemakers. Their pranks range from the relatively innocent, such as loudly passing gas or looking up women's kimonos, to the malevolent, such as drowning people, kidnapping children, raping women,' *Jesus*. This isn't Donald Duck we're talking about."

Wikipedia had some illustrations of the creature; they looked nothing like the sweet Teenage Mutant Ninja-ish mascot of Kappabashi. I pointed to one particularly disturbing image — it was like Gollum meets Godzilla. "Look at those long sharp teeth, scaly skin, and crazy claws."

"Leave it to the Japanese to make that thing cute," David said. "I'd like to see their pictures of the Devil, with big puppy dog eyes. Next thing you know they'll be coming out with a *kawaii* Adolph Hitler."

"It's funny 'cause it's true," I said. I returned to my search. "Here we go. Apparently, these things were invented to explain away drownings and surprise pregnancies. Ew, I didn't really need to know this, but now I'm going to tell you — when someone drowns, their butthole becomes distended, so villagers surmised some kind of ball must have been sucked out. They call it the *shirikodama*. Oh, and get this — you know the kappamaki?"

David nodded. *Of course I do*, his face told me. The kappamaki, or cucumber roll, is one of his usual orders when we're out for sushi.

"Well, it's named after this monster-turned-pet.

When it wasn't eating kids and anus balls, it was said to be after cucumbers. Women would carve their children's names in cucumbers and throw them in the river to appease the creatures. And that whole bald, Friar Tuck head-top? It's a container-of-sorts for some kind of liquid that allows the kappa to leave the water. Despite its horrific pursuits, the kappa is supposedly very polite, so one of the ways to debilitate it or send it back to the water is to bow, because it will politely bow right back, thus spilling the liquid."

"Yeah, weird's the right word for it," David said. We took a moment to digest this newly discovered folklore. After a few minutes, David said, "What do you want to do for dinner?"

"Duh. Sushi," I said. "Thanks to all this research, I'm totally craving kappamaki."

*Teleportation,*
*Old People on LSD,*
*and Other*
*Completely Normal Stuff*

# Connection

*"And God said, 'Let there be light,' and there was light,*
*but the Electricity Board said He would have*
*to wait until Thursday to be connected."*
— Spike Milligan

I was sitting in the coffee shop across the street from my building when my cell phone began to vibrate and skitter across the table. To avoid annoying my fellow caffeine junkies, I answered in a whisper: "*Hey beh beh. What's up?*" Only ten minutes had passed since I'd seen David, ten minutes since I had told him I was heading over to the Urban Grind with my laptop for a change of scenery and would be back in an hour. It wasn't like him to bug me with minute-by-minute updates (that's my department). I detected a note of despair in his answer. "I can't believe this," he said. In the moment before his next words, several possibilities flashed through my mind — *someone's sick. No, worse, dead. No, don't think that. Maybe he just has to get back to someone regarding an appointment and needs me to check my calendar, or maybe someone's sick or dead. No, stop that. Maybe he just needs my car key.*

"The Internet is down." Like a cold autumn wind, his words blew through my thoughts, scattering them like leaves.

"That's it?" I whispered. "It's probably just a glitch. Why don't you go into my office and see if you can pick up one of our neighbor's connections?"

"Good idea, let me try that," said David, his voice flickering with hope. I stared at the other patrons, wondering nervously if they could hear my whispers over the acid jazz, while I waited on the line to see if David could pick up a signal. "Nope. Doesn't work. Maybe you'll have better luck with yours," he said.

"Did you call Cox?"

"Yeah, I did." The hope I'd heard in his voice a moment before had been usurped by desperation. "They said they can't see our modem, they can't do anything on their end, and they'll have to send someone out here, but that no one is available until Saturday. I can't *live*," David moaned.

"WHAT?!" I shrieked, ignoring the heads that suddenly jerked up to look at me like irritated prairie dogs. "SATURDAY? That's ridiculous, that's *two* days from now." When the initial shock wore off, I realized David was probably taking this much harder than me, and said, "I'll be right there, beh beh."

I figured once I showed David that my laptop's superior reception capability would allow us to piggyback on someone else's broadband for a few days, he would realize we had nothing to worry about. I walked through the door, flashed a confident smile to a dejected looking David, and marched into my office. When I opened my laptop, I smiled at the five small black lines that indicated a strong signal. David hovered over me. I launched my browser and held my breath. With each passing second, my hope faded. As though it had been reluctant to let me down, my trusted digital friend waited for what seemed like an eternity before finally, like a doctor who lost a patient, it delivered the tragic news: "I'm sorry. I did everything I could," although the way it actually read was, "Safari can't find the server."

"That can't be," I said. David nodded to confirm the sad truth. He had already visited denial, stopped by anger and bargaining, and was now rearranging the throw pillows in depression. It was clear he wouldn't be setting out for acceptance any time soon. "What will we do?" I wondered aloud. Then, slipping into anger,

I snapped, "What about all the people who work from home? *Saturday?* How will waiting until the weekend help *them?* Or us?" David was patient until I offended his intelligence by saying, "Are you sure you talked to the right person? Maybe I should call."

When David (who had graduated from an Ivy League college with a degree in electrical engineering) had finished lecturing me on his superior comprehension of everything computer, we plopped down on the two chairs in the living room and stared at each other. When 20 minutes had passed, David suggested that we go get the mail.

"Great," I said, jumping to my feet with a newfound sense of purpose.

Someone had placed a notice in the elevator. We weren't alone. Under a typed paragraph asking if anyone else was having trouble connecting, a list of unit numbers and increasingly frazzled notes were scrawled from various pens: "#606 — Went down last night, called Cox, someone coming today"; "#108 — Can't connect, appointment tomorrow"; "#210 — Can't get on, been two hours, still calling"; "#611 — Down, way down. Coming Saturday." I was amazed at how quickly the community had gathered to solve the problem. I imagined it was no different 100 years ago when the well ran dry and the kinfolk would band together to find a solution, because otherwise, they would surely die.

People wandered the hallways like disaster victims. "You too?" they'd ask each other, bonding in their misery and loss. With mail in hand, David and I got back on the elevator, which was occupied by a short, stocky man with mahogany tinted skin and prominent Aztecan features. He sported a wiry black mustache, a heavy-looking tool belt, and a tag with the name "Jesus" embroidered in a florid script. I gestured at the notice and the man nodded. I opened my mouth to speak, but he had already read my mind and answered, "I'm not sure yet."

I directed Jesus to the control room that services the cable to our floor and the one below. David and I observed him closely, hoping to read (from the twitches in his cheeks, the lift of a brow, or a "Hm" versus a "Huh") just how dire the situation was. People followed our voices into the hallway and a crowd soon gathered. It was mid morning in the middle of the week, which meant all these people probably worked from home and, like us, had nothing better to do than hang out in the hallway and hope for a miracle when the main line went down.

"They told me I'd have to buy a new modem," said our neighbor Bruce.

"That's funny, I was told there was an outage in this whole area," countered Ron.

"They told me it was our building and that the first person wouldn't be here until Saturday," said David, raising a quizzical brow in Jesus's direction.

The conversation paused as we all watched our neighbor Bob walk toward the elevator lobby. "I can't take this," Bob said in answer to our questioning looks. "And I don't have wireless, either, so it's not like I can just go to a coffee shop. I'm taking this baby," he raised his briefcase high, "to a friend's house. She'll be able to hook me up."

Jesus disconnected and connected. He sauntered away to make phone calls at the opposite end of the hallway, where he could be free from our nervous chattering. When he finally turned to face us, our silence was immediate. "I'm going to have to make a report," he said. "Once a report is made, it takes up to 48 hours for the issue to be resolved."

"But what does that mean? When will we be okay?" I asked.

"By Saturday," Jesus answered. "I'm sorry, really. I did all I could do. You should keep your appointments anyway, you know, squeaky wheel and all that." We nodded sadly, thanked the nice man for his time, and dispersed, each of us moping back to our own units in search of something else to do.

I decided to make the best of my time by carrying on with my Japanese language lessons. I stared at my laptop and repeated the phrases spoken by a female voice to describe the pictures that appeared on my screen. That's when I heard it — a soft, happy-sounding chime notifying me of a new e-mail message. "David! Come here! It's happened! It's working!"

When he was standing beside me, I launched the browser and my Yahoo! home page popped up, faster than ever. "It's a miracle," David said in awe. "Our Jesus has turned wire into WAN!" Then he vanished from my side and I could hear him skipping across the hardwood floor on his way to check his e-mail.

# Cyst-ers

*"The art of medicine consists of amusing
the patient while nature cures the disease."*
— Voltaire

I shivered with cold, or was it nervousness? Every object in the dark room was bathed in the red glow cast by the large Asian lantern that hung in the corner. An obese gray and white cat sat staring up at me from the wooden floor. To think I had considered taking my problem to a real doctor — that instead of relaxing on this experienced blue velvet couch, someone I hardly knew could be scrutinizing me in the harsh light of a sterile examination room. I looked to the bald man on my left for comfort as the bald man on my right took my left hand in his. I turned my head away in apprehensive anticipation. *Ohmygodthisisgoingtohurt! What am I doing?* My heart beat faster, my breaths came quicker, and my teeth clenched involuntarily. Then I thought of Renee. She had undergone the same treatment, and not only did she survive the antiquated remedy, she had also been healed. But did I need healing?

It was almost two years ago when I first noticed a lump the size of a Milk Dud under the skin on the top of my left wrist. As a hypochondriac in denial, I assumed the lump was cancerous, and therefore decided to ignore it. My plan worked until I took up the piano, at which point the lump began to grow and make itself noticeable to others.

"What the hell is that?" my friend Ollie asked.

"A lump. It's been there for a while," I answered.

"Jesus, it's huge! Hey, if you draw a little face on it, give it a hat and a purse and take it shopping, I'm sure it will be your new best friend," he snickered. I didn't want a lump for a friend. Since denial was no longer an option, I decided to do online medical research.

According to *emedicinehealth.com*, my new "best friend" was a ganglion cyst, defined as "a tumor or swelling on top of a joint" that "looks like a sac of liquid. Inside the cyst is a thick, sticky, clear, colorless, jellylike material." Ew.

Up to 75 percent of these cysts disappear on their own. The woman who answered the phone in my doctor's office told me I would only be referred to a specialist who would either drain my ganglion or surgically remove it, and that neither procedure was covered by my insurance. Since my new friend seemed harmless, I chose to welcome it as I would a houseguest for an unspecified amount of time.

At parties I flaunted my cyst, enjoying the sensation of my mouth when it formed the word, "ganglion." Many of my friends were grossed out. Some were curious. One was angry: three months ago, Renee marched up to me at an art show, thrust her arm before my eyes and snapped, "Are you happy?"

"Huh?" I had not yet noticed the little lump jutting out on the dorsal side of her hand where thumb meets wrist.

"All I know is, first you have one, and now I have one. You jinxed me. Are these contagious?"

"Renee, they can happen to anyone, at any time. But mostly to women between ages 20 and 50," I said, remembering statistics from my research. Thinking myself quite "punny," I shouted, "Hey, now we're 'cyst-ers!'" Before the night was through, I managed to talk Renee into touching her cyst to mine, thus forming a powerful superhero bond.

Last Saturday, this bond was broken. Or, to be more accurate, it was whacked away. I learned of the severing via an excited phone message left by Renee's husband, Kip. It sounded something like this: "Barb, it worked! It's gone! I can't believe it! Tim whacked it!" Upon hearing his message the next day, I couldn't punch Kip's number into my phone quickly enough.

"What do you mean, it's *gone*?" I said when Kip answered, not bothering with time-taking pleasantries, like "Hello, how are you?" Kip didn't miss a beat.

"Brandon was going to hit it with Spain, but Tim just grabbed her hand, massaged it a little, and then whacked it! You should get him to do yours!"

I had read in my research that ganglion cysts are also known as "Bible bumps" or "Gideon's Disease," for in the old days (around the same time they used leeches to cure headaches) doctors would prescribe smashing such a cyst with a large book, the biggest of which was usually the Bible. In Renee's case, the biggest book on hand was a travel tome about Spain.

"Let me get this straight," I said into the phone, in my most sarcastic voice. "Tim *punched* Renee's wrist and her cyst just *went away*?"

"Yeah!"

"Is she in pain? Did it hurt? Wait a minute, what am I saying? It doesn't matter, it's not like I'm going to ask Tim to whack me, that would be just plain stupid."

In the days that followed, I paid close attention to Renee. Her wrist seemed fine, and she swore up and down that the whacking hurt no more than someone poking you in the arm. Maybe calling Tim wasn't as stupid as I had thought.

"Alright, Barbie," Tim said, in response to my

request that he work his magic and doctor my cyst. Then, in the manner of a surgeon prepping for a face transplant, he announced, "On Wednesday, I whack."

David was against it from the beginning. He was convinced that Tim, an athletic guy who is higher on life than Rodney King has ever been on PCP, was going to break my wrist. "Do what you want," David said. "It's not like you ever listen to me anyway." But each time I mentioned the impending whack to a friend, David would roll his eyes and shake his head back and forth, his nonverbal communication for "You are an idiot."

I had thought, given Renee's success, that this would be a sure thing. But now, in the face of invited danger, I beseeched David for help with my eyes and received only an "I told you so" smile. I cringed in fear and tried to pull my hand away from Tim, who was caressing my cyst as though it were a child in need of comfort.

"I think this is going to work," Tim said. "I'm going to whack it... right about now."

I held my breath and took a peek. Tim's hand was made into a fist with his middle knuckle protruding. He lifted it and brought it down quickly, but not very hard, upon my cyst.

"Well that didn't work," I said, after letting my breath out in a blow of air. "I could hardly feel that."

"That's how hard I hit Renee," said Tim. He looked perplexed, but determined. "Let's try it again."

"I don't know, maybe I should — OW!" This time it

was more a knuckle-punch than a whack. "Okay, thanks, but I don't think it's going to work. My cyst is a lot older than Renee's, and well, it's clearly more resilient."

In a sudden burst of cooperation, David reached over and held the growing lump on my wrist with his thumbs and forefingers. "There, try it now," he said. "I think it was moving away when you hit it." I looked at him in horror. Either he no longer believed Tim was going to break my wrist, or he was out to get me. Another whack.

"AAHHH! OKAY! Really, you guys, it's not going to work," I whined. Tim jumped up and, in two long strides, reached the other side of the room. After rummaging around in a corner, he found what he was looking for and raised the object — a huge sledgehammer — high above his head.

"That settles it. You are categorically *insane*. There's no way I'm letting you take a swing at my wrist with that thing," I said, cradling my arm, which was beginning to throb. "And *you!*" I snapped at David. "I thought you were afraid I'd get hurt! How could you condone this?" Tim handed the sledgehammer to David, and my lover taunted me by brandishing it in my direction, perhaps as a mocking form of punishment for not listening to him in the first place.

"Thanks, Tim. You tried your best, but I think I should go to a real doctor now."

"No, no, Barbie, this is what we'll do. Give your

wrist a week to heal, and then we'll try it again, with the hammer. I know I can do this," said Tim. I looked into his eyes, ice blue sincerity. He sounded so confident.

"Yeah, sure," I said. "I'll think about it."

 The damn thing is actually back right now, hanging out on my wrist like that last person at the party who just won't go home. I did get rid of it before, all by myself. I was sitting at my desk at home, contemplating whether or not to go back to Tim, when I suddenly grabbed a flat, round eyeshadow container from my makeup bag and gave the bump a focused smack. I was equally surprised and satisfied when, like the Wicked Witch of the West, the bump dissolved and melted away before my very eyes. But that whack doesn't always work. Just now, I tried the same trick, but the bump remains, and my wrist is sore. Ouch.

Sometimes, when my deadline is pressing in upon me and I am without a topic to explore in my column, David and I will open a bottle of wine and brainstorm ideas. We'll talk about what's been on our minds, maybe consider current events — anything to get me out of freak-out mode and into buzzing-creativity gear. "France in an Instant" was one of those stories. It's also a snapshot of what it's like to be on the couch beside David and me on a typical afternoon.

# France in an Instant

*"With great power comes great responsibility."*
– Voltaire

"D id you see the headline from China? They teleported photons over *60 miles*," I said. When David shook his head in the affirmative, I felt a sense of pride in my worldliness. "Yeah, it was in *Forbes*. I didn't read the story, but it was right there in the headline — 60 miles. Crazy, right? The future is *now*, beh beh, *teleportation*. Could you imagine if we get to a point in our lifetimes when they can actually teleport people and stuff?"

"You know, that's my chosen superpower," David said.

"Didn't you have two? What was your other one?"

"Invisibility."

"Oh, right. That's creepy. Stick with teleportation."

"What do you mean, creepy? Why do you always have to go negative with stuff?"

"Negative? Tell me one thing you'd use the power of invisibility for that *isn't* creepy."

"Say there's a famous painter and you want to see how he works, and —"

"*Creepy*," I said, punctuating the word with a shiver to let David know how much I meant it. "Either he's cool with you hanging out and watching and learning or you're sneaking around and he doesn't know you're there, which is totally creepy."

"What you're saying is invisibility can only be used for creepy or nefarious purposes, that there's no positive for invisibility."

"Yes," I said. David fell quiet, presumably because he couldn't think of any valid, noncreepy reason for skulking around unseen.

We were seated in the living room, on opposite sofas, with a bottle of wine and a bowl of jalapeño Kettle chips on the low table between us. David leaned back, studying the reflection of a flickering candle in his wine glass. "So, what would you do if you could teleport?"

"I'd figure out how to defend my space; you know, make some kind of protective shield so that nobody could just pop up in front of me," I said. I thought this was clever. It was hard to tell what David was thinking, from the fragmented syllables he was sputtering to the random muscles that twitched around his face. He leaned forward, waved one hand in the air, and let out a *phfft* of incredulity. "What is *wrong* with you?"

"Me? What's wrong with ME?" David expelled a few more incoherent sounds before collecting himself. "You have this amazing power, and all you think about is negative stuff," he said. "You could go to France in an instant!"

"I don't think it's negative, I think it's practical," I said. "Say I teleport to France, and then someone pops into my house, steals my shit, and pops out, all before I get back."

David looked at me the same way he did the time I answered two different phone lines — one on each ear — with the same, "Hello?"

"I thought I was being creative," I said. "Travel is a *given* when you talk about teleportation. I was taking it to the next level."

"I would certainly use it to travel, mainly to go to restaurants and bars, but there are so many layers to that," David said. "There are places you won't visit in the world because they have bugs and humidity — if you wanted to, you could just pop in to, say, Thailand for five or ten minutes, experience the view, and then bail."

"I'd still be away from home," I said. "You can't have an amazing power without people who are going to abuse it."

"What if you could send your shit away directly out of your ass so it doesn't stink up the bathroom?"

I laughed. "That's disgusting," I said. "And then I would really need to protect my space, to make sure other people can't literally shit all over me."

"That's your dad talking," David said. "Always looking for the danger in every situation."

"Not true. My dad loves to travel. He'd be all over teleportation."

"You told me he would read the police blotter out loud to you and your sisters every night over dinner as an object lesson," David said. "Anyway, if you don't think he'd come up with the same kind of answer as you did for teleportation, then you're more your dad than your dad."

I rolled my eyes and held out my glass for a refill. "You could make a cake and teleport half of it to Stephanie in England and you could have the other half here and it would be like you're sharing cake on her birthday."

"If I could teleport, why wouldn't I just bring the whole cake to her and we could eat it together?" I sighed. "Listen, beh beh, every invention has a downside. I'm just thinking beyond that. I'm coming up with a way to capitalize on the need people will have for protecting their things."

"I'm the one who thought about teleporting your *poop* out of the bathroom. It doesn't get more innovative than that," David snapped. "You'd probably have to have a password-protected poop shield around your house so that other people's poop doesn't get teleported into your home."

"I'm hearing a lot on the poop front," I said.

"If you're at a restaurant and you have leftovers, you can teleport the leftovers to some starving person in Africa, and you don't have to take them home."

"You keep thinking of good ways to use this, but I keep seeing holes in the system," I said.

"That's because you're crazy."

"No," I said, "I'm *practical.*"

"Your dad would be proud." David smiled to himself. I stayed quiet, letting him have that one, because the idea of making my dad proud, in any capacity, sat well with me.

We sipped and crunched for a few minutes, left to our own thoughts while we checked in with the world via iPhone. "Aha! I got it!" David's spine straightened with the energy of his epiphany.

"Jesus, you almost made me spill," I said.

"What if you're observing gorillas in the mist?" David beamed.

It took me a second to realize what he was talking about. "You mean being invisible to observe nature for the purpose of science?" David nodded. "Okay, you win."

# Nothing Left to Lose

*Reality is a crutch for people who can't cope with drugs.*
– Lily Tomlin

I've got drugs on the brain, mostly because of my current surroundings. I'm on the island of Martha's Vineyard, to attend my man's annual photographic art exhibition at the Granary Gallery and visit my in-laws, as I have every summer since I began dating David ten years ago. It's not the island itself, nor is it the dense summer population of visiting students, politicians, New York attorneys, and the private-jet class that has left me all med-minded. By "surroundings," I'm referring to my in-laws and their friends, the people with whom I interact most when I am here. Bridge players and retirees who all have one thing in common — they're old.

I don't mean over-the-hill, midlife-crisis old. I'm talking blue hair, senior, septa- and octogenarian, Betty White and Buzz Aldrin old. The kind of old I hope to make it to some day. Unfortunately, with experience comes wear and tear. Parts give out. Three months ago, David's father went in for a check-up and didn't leave the hospital until he'd had a quintuple heart bypass. Hip replacements, shoulder and back surgeries, and biopsies — rare is the conversation on the island that doesn't include some kind of medical update. Each time David and I visit, we learn of another bridge player's passing.

"It's so depressing," I said to David. He was driving me from Oak Bluffs to Edgartown, part sightseeing, part errand-running. David raised his brows in question. "You know, the daily — scratch that — the *hourly* reminders of our mortality. Watching helplessly as people we love are declining in health, some slow, some fast. It's no wonder there are so many drinkers here. At your show last night, most of the old folks went straight for liquor — plastic cups filled to the brim with whiskey or vodka, no tonic. I don't blame them." David listened in silence.

The canopy of trees lining the road broke on my side to reveal a field of wavy green grass speckled with patches of flame-colored flowers. "They should all be on drugs," I mused as I gazed at the meadow.

"Hm?"

I tore my gaze away from the view to find David's face scrunched in confusion. "I mean, how great would it be if we gave your parents and their friend 'shrooms? They should be running naked through that field, frolicking and laughing, without a care in the world."

"They'd get sunburned," David said.

"Oh, my God, I just had a brilliant idea." I paused for effect. "We could create a camp, like a summer camp, but for older people, where they could try all kinds of drugs in a safe setting with a counselor — you know, someone sober who knows his shit — to make sure they don't hurt themselves; someone who could talk anyone down from a bad trip and guide the whole group into a positive, mind-expanding, joyful experience. Think about it!"

I sat forward in my seat fast enough to catch the lock on my seatbelt. "People who are aging and depressed could feel safe in the knowledge that their experimental drug use would be way safer than anything they might find on the street. We could provide pharmaceutical grade MDMA — that's ecstasy," I clarified for David, whose knowledge of medications both legal and controlled is as limited as my grasp of kitchenware. "They would have no fear of dangerous kitchen-sink chemicals because everything would be pharmaceutical grade, just like the dozen or so prescribed pills most of them already take every day."

"You'd have to do it somewhere like the Netherlands,

where they're lax about drugs," David said.

"It's stupid that this doesn't already exist. Or maybe it does and we just don't know about it. I bet people would pay good money for that kind of experience. Especially people with terminal illnesses. To let go and explore when they've got nothing left to lose."

"The liability would be insane," David said.

"That's what waivers are for. We have everyone sign a waiver that says they won't sue, no matter what happens, and there goes your liability. It would be expensive to set up, but I bet if we thought it through and did some planning, we'd be the most popular project on Kickstarter." I responded to David's sideways smirk with an expression that said, *Don't look at me, I'm not even sure if I'm serious or not.* But what I was thinking was, *I am a goddamn genius.*

That night, we hosted friends of my in-laws, a family I'd come to know from my visits over the years. The patriarch of the family was in the midst of receiving experimental treatment for a terminal illness. While sipping my cocktail and doing my best to avoid saying anything relating to health as part of my perpetual effort to keep everyone around me smiling, I overheard one member of the family — a woman around my age — explaining to my father-in-law that the legalization of marijuana is going to be on the Massachusetts ballot this November.

"We could all get high together," said her mother.

I couldn't imagine my father-in-law getting any kind of high — he doesn't even drink — but I loved that I wasn't the one to throw this idea out there. If I'd said it, I'd likely get some kind of admonishing look from David. But since the suggestion came from an elder, everyone in the room smiled and nodded. "Seriously," my new hero continued. She gestured at her husband, "It would take away his pain and help with his appetite issues, and for us, well, we'd just have fun." She broke away from the group to explain to my mother-in-law how to go about cooking with the stuff, as if my mother-in-law would ever follow any recipe that called for the "other" oregano.

I don't smoke weed. Nor do I eat it, vaporize it, snort it, inject it, whatever. I'm just not into it. I tried it a few times (using the smoking and eating methods), but all it ever did was make me paranoid and nauseated. Still, despite my disinterest, I think Mary Jane, LSD, MDMA, hallucinogenic mushrooms, and every other happy-making recreational drug, should be legalized and regulated à la alcohol and tobacco. At least that way I could get a real business plan going for my special camp.

# Acknowledgments

*"Vocations which we wanted to pursue, but didn't,*
*bleed, like colors, on the whole of our existence."*
— Honore de Balzac

I would like to thank Jim Holman, publisher of the *San Diego Reader*, for giving me a chance to share my personal brand of crazy with the world via his publication. To give me a voice on his pages, even though he pretty much disagrees with everything I've put there, is a special kind of tolerance. And thank you Jane Belanger, my friend and editor, for making this happen. I'm still really sorry about puking all over your backyard that one time.

Thank you to my family, for being so very cool about me sharing your exploits. You have always supported me, even when you find my point of view to be upsetting. I have never doubted that each and every one of you has always had my back, whether or not you fantasized about stabbing it a little every now and then. Thank you to my sister Jane for buying me my first journal, to my sister Heather for helping me with grammar, and my sister Jenny for repeatedly checking in on me. Special thanks to my mother and father, who shaped me into the fun-loving neurotic I am. And to David's parents,

Ency and Robert, thank you for accepting someone as crazy as me into your normal family, and for whatever you did to make David so patient.

Thank you to my friends, for putting up with my time issues and talking me down from the occasional ledge. And my readers! Thank you, each and every one of you who has ever read my column. Thank you for every comment and every like on Facebook, thank you for every time one of you stops me (even in a grocery store) to tell me that you liked something I wrote. Seriously, that kind of thing makes my day.

Thank you to Terri Beth Mitchell for my cool book business cards, my logo, and for the cover design on this book. And for also being as neurotic as I am.

Most of all, thank you to DAVID. David, my love, my life. Detailing all of the reasons I have to thank you would fill an entire book. So here, I'll just say, thank you for loving me, and everything that means.

# About the Authors

 Barbarella Fokos has been writing ever since she could pick up a crayon. She's been blogging since 2000, and has been writing for the *San Diego Reader* since 2004. She makes frequent appearances as a guest on radio and television, and has won a regional Emmy Award for a television show she produced and hosted. But more often, she can be found drinking wine, watching videos of raccoons, and trying to convince her friends at the zoo to let her touch all the animals. So far, she's managed to touch a rhinoceros and a kangaroo. Barbarella lives in San Diego, California with her husband and partner-in-everything, David.

To keep up with her antics and subscribe to Barbarella's Inner Circle, please visit her hub, *DivaBarbarella.com*.

 David Fokos is a world-renowned fine art photographer. He's also a television director, a writer and editor, and *chef de maison*. If she didn't benefit so much from his many talents, Barbarella would be even more irritated than she already is with David's penchant for being really good at everything he does.

You can learn more about David and see his work at *DavidFokos.net*.

Made in the USA
San Bernardino, CA
31 July 2014